For Daddy –
Let's take some fun trips.
∴ Love,

CLAIRE

WEIRD WASHINGTON

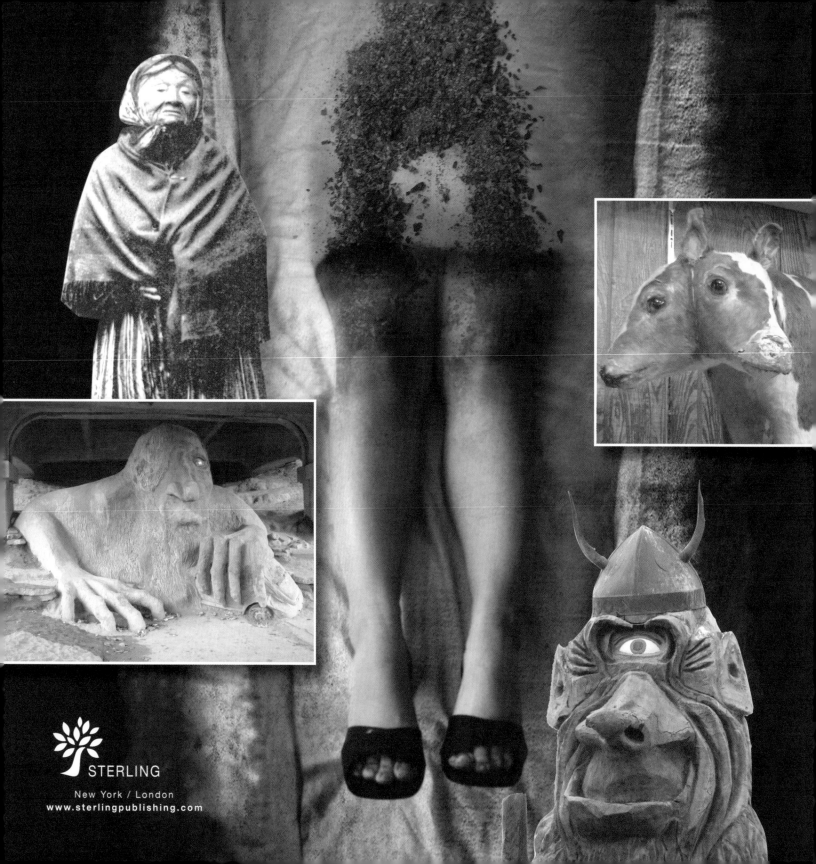

STERLING

New York / London

www.sterlingpublishing.com

WEiRD WASHiNGToN

Your Travel Guide to Washington's Local Legends and Best Kept Secrets

by JEFF DAVIS and AL EUFRASIO

Mark Sceurman and Mark Moran, Executive Editors

WEiRD WASHiNGTON

STERLING and the distinctive Sterling logo are registered
trademarks of Sterling Publishing Co., Inc.

Photography and illustration credits are found on page 253 and
constitute an extension of this copyright page.

Library of Congress Cataloging-in-Publication Data Available

10 9

Published by Sterling Publishing Co., Inc.
387 Park Avenue South, New York, NY 10016

© 2008 by Mark Sceurman and Mark Moran

Distributed in Canada by Sterling Publishing
c/o Canadian Manda Group, 165 Dufferin Street
Toronto, Ontario, Canada M6K 3H6

Distributed in the United Kingdom by GMC Distribution Services
Castle Place, 166 High Street, Lewes, East Sussex, England BN7 1XU

Distributed in Australia by Capricorn Link (Australia) Pty. Ltd.
P.O. Box 704, Windsor, NSW 2756, Australia

Manufactured in China. All rights reserved.

Sterling ISBN 13: 978-1-4027-4545-4
Sterling ISBN 10: 1-4027-4545-1

For information about custom editions, special sales, premium and
corporate purchases, please contact Sterling Special Sales
Department at 800-805-5489 or specialsales@sterlingpublishing.com.

Design: Richard J. Berenson
    Berenson Design & Books, LLC, New York, NY

CONTENTS

A Note from the Marks

Our weird journey began a long, long time ago in a far-off land called New Jersey. Once a year or so, we'd compile a homespun newsletter called *Weird N.J.,* then pass it on to our friends. The pamphlet was a collection of odd news clippings, bizarre facts, little-known historical anecdotes, and anomalous encounters from our home state. The newsletter also included the kinds of localized legends that were often whispered around a particular town but seldom heard outside the boundaries of the community where they originated.

We had started *Weird N.J.* on the simple theory that every town in the state had at least one good tale to tell. The publication soon became a full-fledged magazine, and we made the decision to actually do our own investigating to see if we could track down where all of these seemingly unbelievable stories were coming from. Was there, we wondered, any factual basis for the fantastic local legends people were telling us about? Armed with not much more than a camera and a notepad, we set off on a mystical journey of discovery. Much to our surprise and amazement, a lot of what we had initially presumed to be nothing more than urban legends turned out to be real—or at least to contain a grain of truth, which had sparked the lore to begin with.

After a dozen years of documenting the bizarre, we were asked to write a book about our adventures, and so *Weird N.J.: Your Travel Guide to New Jersey's Local Legends and Best Kept Secrets* was published in 2003. Soon people from all over the country began writing to us, telling us strange tales from their home state. As it turned out, what we had perceived to be something of very local interest was actually just a small part of a larger and more universal phenomenon.

After *Weird N.J.,* we wrote *Weird U.S.,* in which we documented the local legends and strangest stories from all over the country. We set out in search of weirdness wherever it might be found in the fifty states. And indeed, we found plenty of it!

After *Weird U.S.* was published, we came to the conclusion that this country had more great tales than could be contained in just one book. Everywhere we looked, we found unwritten folklore, creepy cemeteries, cursed locations, and outlandish roadside oddities. We wanted to document it all in a series of books, each focusing on the peculiarities of a particular state.

was three thousand miles away, that didn't stop him from contributing his unique brand of demented illustrations and stories to *Weird N.J.* magazine. Our friendship with Al grew over the years, and he was always one of our go-to guys whenever we needed artwork that was humorous, provocative, and insightful all at the same time. When it came time to find an author to point out the lighter side of Washington's myriad oddities, we knew our transplanted N.J. friend Al would be the perfect guy for the job.

Jeff and Al both possess what we refer to as the Weird Eye, which is what is needed to search out the sort of stories we were looking for. It requires one to see the world in a different way, with a renewed sense of wonder. And once you have it, there is no going back—you'll never see things the same way again. All of a sudden you begin to reexamine your own environs, noticing your everyday surroundings as if for the first time. And you begin to ask yourself questions like, "What the heck is that thing all about, anyway?" and "Doesn't anybody else think that's kind of weird?"

So come with us now and let Jeff and Al take you on a tour of the Evergreen State, with all of its haunted history, quirky character, strange sites, and enduring legends. It is a state of mind we like to call *Weird Washington*.

–Mark Sceurman and Mark Moran

The first person we looked to for help when it came to documenting all that is weird in the state of Washington was Jeff Davis. Jeff is without question one of the most knowledgeable people around when it comes to hauntings of the Pacific Northwest. He is the author of several books on the subject of ghosts and other mysterious creatures that lurk in the shadows of Washington and Oregon. Jeff also contributed some of his strange stories to our *Weird Hauntings* book in 2006, so we'd collaborated with him already and knew what a pleasure he was to work with.

The next person we invited to come on board for this *Weird Washington* project was Al Eufrasio. Al has lived in Washington for years now, but he actually grew up in our home state of New Jersey. Though he

Introduction

Washington was my birthplace and though I have been to many regions, I cannot imagine living anywhere else. In my travels, I have met a lot of people with odd, stereotypical views of Washingtonians. Most believe that all of us run around wearing flannel shirts and carrying axes. Or we walk around carrying cups of designer coffee and laptops. There are places where both views are true, but that is only scratching the surface.

Because Washington was settled so late, many Native American beliefs survived into modern times, shedding light on the many traditions surrounding the Evergreen State's natural wonders. Along with that, Washington has more than its share of flying saucers, Bigfoots, sea monsters, and other odd creatures. Then too, because we were so isolated from East Coast society, many quirky politicians, businessmen, religious groups, and others were free to develop their own unique characteristics. Sometimes with wonderful results, and other times with tragic endings.

I enjoy writing about what Washington is really like, so I submitted three stories for Mark Moran and Mark Sceurman's book *Weird Hauntings*. They contacted me and asked if I wanted to help write *Weird Washington* with their longtime associate Al Eufrasio. Al and I developed a rapport, and although he is a skilled researcher in his own right, it was fun to share with Al some of the lore I learned growing up. I enjoyed the chance to work on a great book like this, made great due to Al's collaboration with me, the support especially of Mark Moran, and the skilled staff at Sterling Publishing—that and everything that makes Washington so weird.

Although Washingtonians are sure to read this book, I am certain that people from across the country will also enjoy the many true, and truly weird, customs, places, and people that could have come only from Washington.–*Jeff Davis*

Contrary to what some people might think, being from New Jersey has its advantages. For example, after I moved to Washington in the mid-1990s, my Jersey connection led to my becoming aware of the innovative biannual magazine *Weird N.J.* A grassroots labor of love, it chronicled the folklore, hidden history, and quirky corners of the Garden State (and still does to this day). Thoroughly intrigued by its content, I contacted the guys who made it all happen: Mark Sceurman and Mark Moran. We forged a cross-country connection as they built up their publishing empire, eventu-

the Pacific Northwest: "Weird Scenery." As any Washingtonian worth their coffee knows, in the century-plus since this ad was first published, the scenery around here has only gotten weirder. We're a state of many and varied wonders, including a giant frying pan, a near-lethal hot sauce, haunted cemeteries, strange homes, and . . . Well, you'll see.

But before you get to the good stuff, realize that you

ally starting the *Weird U.S.* book series, thus expanding the *Weird N.J.* concept to other states.

All along I contributed illustrations and other material to their various literary endeavors. "Keep me in mind when you get around to *Weird Washington,*" I told them at one point, expecting—if anything—to be asked to whip up a couple of stories or cartoons. I was honored (to say the least) when I was instead offered the opportunity to co-author *Weird Washington* with Jeff Davis.

I had a blast researching and illuminating some of my adopted home's eccentric elements. As it turns out, Washington is rife with 'em. Even early settlers knew it. There it is, in a newspaper ad from the late 1800s, listed with other benefits of purchasing land in

have a responsibility beyond just reading this book. Washington has a strong feeling of community, and *Weird Washington* is intended in the same spirit: as a shared experience. If something in here strikes your fancy, research it further. Go exploring (but please respect private or off-limits property). Share it with friends and/or relatives. Finally, please note: The back of the book has a page with our contact information. Write in. Tell us about your own weird adventures across Washington (and elsewhere) or clue us in to something we've missed. You never know, some day you might see your story in print!

After all, it's a big, weird world out there. Let's make sure our little corner of it is thoroughly celebrated!–*Al Eufrasio*

Local Legends

HOTEL de HARO

Theodore Roosevelt

The *Evergreen State's legends* are not all about lumberjacks and Bigfoot. Many cities and small towns have old legends and strange tales known only to the locals. Some stories follow the settlement of the Pacific Northwest, like the tale of Princess Angeline, a Native American who lived past her own time and may still remain in Seattle. Evil spirits may still inhabit one of the buildings of Catholic Gonzaga University's Monaghan Hall, even after an exorcism. The town of Ellensburg remembers a mob lynching, which still reverberates on a quiet street late at night.

Not all the legends in Washington are tragic and dark. In the eastern desert and on the coast, there are rumors of buried treasure, guarded by tragedy, and perhaps spirits from another dimension. And in modern times, there is the story of escaped spy Christopher Boyce, captured because of his fondness for a special Washington State hamburger.

Which Wallula?

In 1859, gold was discovered in Idaho, and the town of Wallula was the jumping-off point for miners headed to the goldfields. From Wallula, they headed east on Dorsey Baker's Walla Walla and Columbia Line. It was also known as the Rawhide Railroad because, according to early travelers, the original rail lines were made of split wood, which Baker covered with rawhide to make the trains run smoother.

According to legend, two men once boarded the train's single express car and stole several pounds of gold bullion. They jumped off the train and went overland toward Wallula to catch a riverboat to Portland. Unfortunately for the bandits, a posse dogged their trail for many miles, and captured them just outside Wallula. Before the posse caught them, the robbers buried the gold. They were hanged as soon as the posse caught up with them, but the gold was never found.

Today some people confuse the sleepy town of Wallula, on the banks of the Columbia River, with the city of Walla Walla, thirty miles away. Treasure hunters are not confused. They know that somewhere near Wallula there is a treasure in buried gold. Their only problem is, which Wallula—since there were three of them.

In 1818, the Northwest Fur Company established a trading

post called Fort Walla Walla along the Columbia, just below a set of long rapids. They built it out of driftwood and called it the Gibraltar of the West. Unfortunately, "The Rock" was flammable and burned down in 1841. It was rebuilt out of mud bricks later that year. When the fur trade ended in the 1850s, the U.S. Army took over the post and occupied it from 1857 to 1860. When they left, the facility became the town of Wallula.

Some hopeful treasure hunters believe that the fur traders and/or the army left valuable stuff behind, like trade goods or an army payroll, though it seems unlikely the army would just misplace a payroll. And then there was the train robbery booty, also rumored to be buried nearby.

However, things are not that clear. After checking records, some of the more historically minded hunters believe that the robbery took place after 1883, when Wallula was a railway center. In that year, the entire town was moved about a quarter mile away from its old location to a huge freight yard with several railroad roundhouses. This Wallula had a permanent population of eight hundred people and a much larger transitory population. For decades, it resembled boomtowns like Deadwood, where people were robbed and murdered in back alleys, and their bodies simply dumped into the river. Other tales told of

site by moving certain buildings and other features, including the town cemetery. As the coffins were dug up and moved, several of them were found to be rotted, so the gravediggers put the bodies in new coffins before reburial. One grave in particular was memorable in a macabre sort of way. It contained the coffins of Mary, Mandy, and Florence Furgerson, who had all died in an epidemic.

All three coffins were in bad shape, and when the diggers opened Florence's, they found that her corpse was twisted, instead of laid out flat. And its hands were full of hair. Before embalming was popular, people buried their dead as quickly as possible, before the corpse rotted. This was very true in hot eastern Washington, especially to stop an epidemic from spreading. Doctors were overworked, and sometimes mistook patients in a coma for being dead. Some of these unfortunates were buried alive.

Poor Florence was probably in a coma, and her family mistakenly thought she was dead and buried her. When she awoke, she pulled out her hair in frustration and fear when she found she was entombed. She must have tried to fight her way out of her premature grave, but the coffins of her dead sisters held her down.

Treasure hunters still stop at present-day Wallula, looking for lost gold. Most of the time the locals tell the treasure hunters that the original two town sites are underwater. Sometimes, though, depending on the mood of the local and how gullible he thinks the treasure hunter is, he'll send people off to dig in the hills near present-day Wallula. Let's just hope they stay away from the cemetery.

miners' burying caches of gold before entering town and being murdered before recovering them.

By the 1920s, things had slowed down and Wallula became a sleepy town, with a reputation for ghosts and buried treasure. Treasure hunters poked around the remains of both Wallulas, looking for buried gold or anything else they could find. Then, in 1950, the Army Corps of Engineers condemned the town to make way for McNary Dam. In the weeks before both towns were flooded, construction workers, treasure hunters, and even geologists spent a lot of time digging for hidden buried gold. They were not successful, but other diggers found more than they bargained for.

As part of the agreement with the citizens of Wallula, the Corps of Engineers rebuilt the town on a different

Captain Johnson's Golden Slugs

The mouth of the Columbia River was named the Graveyard of Ships after storms and dangerous currents wrecked hundreds of sailing craft on the treacherous sandbars, within sight of land. Of course one man's tragedy can be another man's treasure, as Captain Johnson found—unless he also inherited a curse.

Captain Johnson—no one seems to recall his first name—was originally from Scotland but came to the Pacific Northwest on trading voyages several times in the 1800s. In 1848, he filed a settlement land claim on the north side of the Columbia River, along Baker's Bay. Atop a high hill overlooking the mouth of the river, Johnson built a mansion of white pine, which he imported from Maine. Behind the mansion, he built a cabin for his Chinook Indian wife and the two children they had together. His wife and her relatives were never allowed into the mansion, but the boys were admitted when other white guests came along with their children.

In addition to owning his own ship, Johnson was a salvage master, recovering cargo from several wrecks on the treacherous sandbars within sight of his home. One of these wrecks came from San Francisco and carried a cargo with many pounds of gold bullion in the form of golden slugs. Johnson salvaged a huge number of these slugs, each weighing between two and three ounces, with a value of between $40 and $60. At one point, he showed them to a friend, who estimated that Johnson had about $20,000 in slugs.

Captain Johnson was not a trusting man, and rather than keeping his gold in a strongbox or a bank, he hid it in many places on his property. Every day or so he walked along a trail to a hill known as the Devil's Slide, inspecting the hiding places of his gold. One day one of his children, George, who was three or four years old at the time, followed him and took some of the gold to play with. When Johnson saw his son, he scolded him sternly and told the boy that evil spirits guarded the gold. Terrible things would happen to any intruder who tried to handle it.

Johnson's scolding so frightened the child that he never followed his father on the treasure path again. It was a shame, because the captain drowned, sometime around 1857, without telling anyone where the gold was buried. The house and property, 640 acres of land, were sold to a man named Isaac Whealdon in 1858. Mrs. Johnson, who had no idea where the gold was buried, returned with her sons to her family in Chinook. None of the Johnsons, perhaps frightened by the old captain's tale of a curse, ever looked for the gold. Years later, as an adult, George Johnson refused to lead anyone along the path his father used to walk.

Over the years, Whealdon gave several people permission to dig for the treasure, under the agreement that they would share it with him and the Johnsons. None of them found anything. In one case, they might have succeeded if Whealdon's wife had not interfered.

In 1896, Mr. Whealdon invited several friends to his house to discuss the treasure. One of his guests was a Cree Indian woman named Mrs. Pierce, who had recently moved into the area. She had gained a reputation for "finding" missing objects, including the body of a drowned fisherman. The woman agreed to conduct a séance to contact Captain Johnson, and the night was perfect for a session. As they commenced, a storm began. In a few minutes, the Native American woman was apparently in a deep trance; suddenly she sat up and looked around and her manner underwent a strange alteration.

Her ordinary accent changed, and in a deep burr, she said that she was Captain Johnson. Whealdon and his wife were both Scots and claimed that the accent was

real. Someone else said that they recognized the voice as Johnson's. As the séance continued, the rainstorm outside became a fierce gale, rattling the windows and timbers of the house. Isaac Whealdon asked the spirit of the captain if he would lead them to the gold.

Captain Johnson agreed to take them to the hiding place of the gold if they would share with the Johnson family . . . and the medium. When they agreed, the woman stood up and led them all toward the door. The rain and wind were howling now, but they were determined to find the gold. Suddenly Mrs. Whealdon ran ahead of them and blocked the door. In a typically Scottish commonsense way, she told them that no one was going out on a night like that. She did not step away from the doorway until they all agreed to try another time.

Unfortunately, Mrs. Pierce refused to participate in another séance, and Mr. Whealdon never found the treasure. One man did find a gold piece on part of Captain Johnson's old homestead. He bought the land and continued searching in vain. He grew so frustrated with his failed treasure hunt that he committed suicide.

Captain Johnson's $20,000 hoard at today's prices would be worth . . . A LOT! All someone has to do is find it, though there are plenty of possible owners. Over the years, Captain Johnson's 640-acre land claim has been split up and sold to many buyers, and the town of Ilwaco sits in the middle of his land.

indian Princess at Pike Place Market

Every so often tourists approach the flower sellers at Pike Place Market in Seattle and ask a question that goes something like this: "I saw an old woman sitting on the floor other there. She looked like a Native American. At least she had a bunch of native-style woven baskets on a blanket, as if they were for sale. I wanted to buy some, so I walked over. By the time I got through the crowd, she was gone. Who was she?"

The flower sellers usually smile and say, "That was Princess Angeline." If the tourist is from the Puget Sound, they smile or get very pale. People from out of town just look puzzled, until the merchant explains that Princess Angeline died over a hundred years ago.

Princess Angeline was probably born in 1820 and was the first daughter of Chief Seattle. Her name then was Kikisoblu, and she was married at least once, to a man named Dokub Cud. After American settlers arrived in Seattle, she eventually met Catherine Maynard, wife of Doc Maynard, one of Seattle's founding fathers. Catherine Maynard told her, "You are too good-looking of a woman to carry around such a name as that, and I now christen you Angeline."

In the 1850s, when Angeline was in her mid-thirties, the U.S. government ordered the Suquamish Indians to a reservation far away from their homes in Seattle. But Angeline stayed on. People started calling her Princess Angeline, because of her father's standing as well as her own dignified bearing despite her situation.

Princess Angeline and a handful of other Native Americans found work in Seattle and lived in various places. She had a small cabin on Western Avenue, between Pike and Pine streets. To make a living, she did laundry for the settlers and sold various native handicrafts, like baskets she made in the evenings. As she grew older, Angeline developed arthritis but kept to her routines. For years, people watched her familiar figure walking along Seattle's streets. She always wore a red handkerchief over her head, as well as a shawl to keep out the cold. Her arthritis was so bad in the wet climate that she eventually needed a cane. She stopped frequently to rest, and as she did, people saw her "telling" her beads, because Angeline had converted to Catholicism in her youth.

Not that she knew it, but she also became world famous. Many newspapers published articles and books about her, as well as about her famous father. The two of them bridged the time between the end of the Native American lifestyle and the coming of the whites. Angeline died in 1896 and was given a magnificent funeral in Seattle's Church of Our Lady of Good Help. Her coffin, which was shaped like a canoe, was buried in Lake View Cemetery.

Over the years, Angeline's cabin was torn down and the area became part of the waterfront, until Pike Place Market was formed. The market quickly expanded, and the flower market was built on top of, or very near, the site of her cabin. No one knows when, but at some point people began seeing a little old Indian lady quietly sitting on the floor with several baskets at her feet. Some of the older people claimed they recognized her as Princess Angeline from popular photographs.

Over the years, people have told stories of many sightings of Angeline. Most of the time she is seen in Pike Place Market, near the flower stalls. Her apparition looks so natural that almost everyone who sees her thinks she is a living person, though oddly dressed. They discover she's not alive only when they go to talk to her or ask to take a picture. Then she vanishes.

The Seattle to Bainbridge Island ferry dock is not too far away from Pike Place Market. Some people have reported seeing an elderly Native American woman hobbling onto the ferry with the aid of a cane. Once aboard, the woman walks over to one of the benches overlooking the Puget Sound and sits down. People observing the strange old lady have reported that she vanishes before the ferry reaches Bainbridge Island—they never see her walk off the ferry when it docks.

Some people believe that Princess Angeline is looking for a new home. Some time ago, a group of shop owners brought in a shaman, who attempted to exorcise any spirits at Pike Place Market. Perhaps the shaman was not able to remove her completely, but she now feels unwelcome and is attempting to find a more receptive home.

Western State Mental Hospital in Steilacoom

It was pretty easy getting in; the ruins are located in Fort Steilacoom County Park, in Lakewood. I waited until dark to go in, after leaving my car outside of the park, which closes at night. At the end of the Park's parking lot, there is a path, which wound through heavy woods. Lucky I brought a flashlight. It was like walking through a wall of trees, and as I came out of the woods I saw the ruins of the hospital on a hill.

It was surrounded by a chain link fence and razor wire, but someone had cut the fence, and I got inside. The building looked like someone had tried burning it down, or maybe blowing it up. I walked inside, and each step echoed through the empty concrete shell, which was all that was left of the sanitarium. Someone told me that there were operating rooms, where they performed lobotomies, and electroshock therapy. One guy said that they even left behind an operating table, with leather straps to hold down the patient.

It was creepy. There was graffiti spray painted on the walls, most of which was profanity, but some of it had real weird designs. I heard that devil worshipers hung out there, and the designs looked it. Luckily for me they weren't around that night. I walked around, looking for a way into the basement and boiler room, which was haunted. When I came out of the woods, I heard the sound of frogs and crickets, and such. Then suddenly, the night noises stopped, and it was absolutely quiet.

I went down into the basement, and the boiler room. I walked across a heavy steel door, which clanged loud enough to raise the dead. I walked into a cold spot, so cold that I could almost see my breath. I took out my camera, hoping to get ghost pictures, but I took only two pictures before my batteries died. My flashlight started to go dim, even though these were new batteries too. I hotfooted it out of there before I was stuck in the dark. I banged into the walls, and fell down, and it felt like something was following me. It may have been my imagination, but I heard screams, from a distance, like echoes. I made it out and onto the path before my flashlight went out. By the time I made it back to the parking lot I convinced myself it was all in my imagination.—*Tom*

Although odd things happened to Tom and others at this particular ruined building, the horrible things like lobotomies never happened . . . there. They happened nearby.

In 1870, the territory of Washington bought the U.S. Army post of Fort Steilacoom from the federal government and converted the buildings into the Insane Asylum for Washington Territory. The first patients included fifteen men and eight women. The facility grew as new buildings were constructed. There was even a dairy farm that provided food and work for the patients. Over time, the asylum was renamed, eventually becoming simply Western State Hospital, which came to cover over 860 acres between Tacoma and Steilacoom.

In its time, the hospital was considered one of the best in the country, but that changed. By the 1940s, many of the buildings had deteriorated in the Pacific Northwest rains. Over 2,700 patients were crowded into crumbling buildings designed to house 2,200. They were cared for by fourteen doctors, assisted by thirty-eight graduate and student nurses. By national standards, there should have

been twenty doctors and a total of one hundred and seven nurses. Stories grew of patients being mistreated and even assaulted by orderlies. Some said these were only rumors—what was not rumors were the misguided medical treatments performed here.

One medical procedure that doctors thought could cure violent or schizophrenic behavior was the frontal lobotomy. In this operation, the surgeon inserted an instrument called a leucotome into the frontal lobes of the brain, where the surgeon severed nerves that were thought to control violent or antisocial behavior. That was true. At first, patients were much calmer and followed instructions. But over time, their higher reasoning facilities deteriorated. Western State Hospital in Steilacoom apparently became a pioneer in this procedure.

One of the more famous patients here was actress Francis Farmer. A beautiful woman, she was born in Seattle, acted on Broadway, and eventually made her way to Hollywood, where she was hailed as the next Greta Garbo. But Farmer became addicted to alcohol and amphetamines and, in 1942, following a series of

violent events, began an eight-year stretch in and out of various mental health facilities. In her biography, Farmer wrote about the traumatic time she spent at Western State, detailing electroshock and insulin shock therapy and other abuses. She denied having a frontal lobotomy, however, and the fact that she could talk about the events years later suggests she was telling the truth. Although all this did happen at Western State Hospital, the medical procedures themselves were not done in the ruined building in Fort Steilacoom Park, but in buildings still used by the hospital.

To keep the public from entering the abandoned hospital facility and perhaps hurting themselves, park officials have put a chain-link fence around it. But that hasn't done much to keep people out. In addition to ghost hunters, gangs hang around here, and in 2004 they assaulted and robbed at least twenty-three people, making a ghost seem like a small threat. There is still talk about demolishing the building as a nuisance.

Eeriness in Ellensburg

The sleepy town of Ellensburg has a few claims to fame. For one thing, it is world famous for the quality of the timothy hay grown there. In 1889, it was almost selected as the state capital. A mansion was even built there for the governor. Unfortunately, a catastrophic fire burned the downtown area, and the town of Olympia was chosen instead. Of course this vote could have been the work of certain law-and-order parties, who remembered that Ellensburg began as a trading post of dubious nature, called the Robber's Roost. The law-and-order folks believed that some elements of Ellensburg's population were prone to violent behavior—with some justification. Local people still remember one murder and its odd aftermath.

In the summer of 1895, two farmers, a father and son by the name of Vincent, came into town. They may have been tired from a long day of cutting down and baling some of that famous timothy hay. They may have come to town to sell it to brokers, stopping for a drink at the Ellensburg Saloon along the way. When having their drink, the men got into a disagreement with the bartender. The disagreement turned into an argument, which turned into a violent fight. In the end, the farmers killed the bartender and the saloon's owner.

The Vincents were arrested and put into jail to await trial. In the Ellensburg Saloon, several customers were outraged by the killings; no doubt the dead owner's heirs encouraged this with free liquor from the bar. After several hours of heavy drinking to get up their courage, the mob broke into the jail and took the two farmers out to hang them.

The liquor-fired vigilantes walked down Pine Street, looking for a suitable tree. They found one

on Sixth Avenue and Pine Street. The crowd paused on the corner to abuse the men, or perhaps they were having trouble finding a rope. Either way, they made a lot of noise for several minutes, which disturbed the owner of the house on the corner. He came out of his house and confronted the mob.

Instead of telling them to stop what they were doing, the man asked the mob not to hang the farmers in front of his house. He begged them to go somewhere else—not because what they were doing was wrong, but because his wife was sick,

and the noise was upsetting her. It is hard to imagine an angry, liquored-up mob changing its collective mind or direction, but this one did. They grabbed their prisoners and continued down the street, until they came to a large tree on the corner of Seventh Avenue and Pine Street, and there they hanged the farmers.

After the hanging, people avoided loitering on that street corner for several years. It seemed to have a dark aura around it, and some reported hearing echoes of the past violence. Do the farmers still haunt the location of their murders? Some people claim that they have heard the sound of a crowd yelling, as if they were wild animals who smelled blood. Others claim they feel the sorrow of the father and son whose crime was going into

the wrong saloon. Whether it's the thought of a ghost or the power of their own guilty consciences, people still avoid the street corner, sometimes for reasons they do not understand.

Other people are attracted to the place, but when they search for the hanging tree, as *Weird Washington* did, they have a problem. As in most legends, there is a lack of certain information. We found two houses that were probably there when the hanging happened, as well as several older trees. Were any of them used by the lynch mob? No one seems to know which of the intersection's four corners was the one at which the lynching took place.

Hanging Corner in Ellensburg

I can tell you from experience that something is definitely dark about that particular corner. I used to housesit for a friend who was a student at the university. She had an apartment on the corner of 7th and Pine. Usually, I would just go to the place to see if everything was as it should be, but I never stayed. I always felt like I was being watched, that something bad might happen if I stayed there too long. Even with all the lights on in the place, it was still creepy. Even now, I avoid going there if I can help it. Especially at night.

As I remember, it's an old wood house that was converted into apartments. Also, further down that particular block I used to baby-sit for a couple. It was the same as with the other place. There certainly was a menacing presence around that area.—*Sheila*

Exorcism at Gonzaga University

It's not just in movies that exorcisms happen; they happen in real life too. In fact, not one but several exorcisms were carried out in Spokane not all that long ago. In 1974 and 1975, Gonzaga University's Father Walter Leedale performed a series of exorcisms in the university's music department, at Monaghan Hall. Was he successful? Some people think so. However,

all the *Exorcist*-type movies end with some kind of foreshadowing that the evil is still lurking in the corners. How closely did the events at Monaghan Hall follow the script?

Gonzaga University was founded by the Catholic Jesuit order, which named it after Saint Aloysius Gonzaga, a Renaissance student who died of the plague while

helping the sick. Over time, the campus has grown, acquiring many of Spokane's historic buildings, including Monaghan Hall, built by James Monaghan around 1900. The university bought it in 1942, and in 1974 it was the music department building.

One November night that year a housekeeper went to the supposedly locked and empty building to pick up something she had left behind. She entered and froze upon hearing the sound of an organ playing. The music was slow, as if someone was picking out a melody with one finger. After a dozen or so notes, it stopped. She went to the organ-room door, which was locked. She used her key to open the door and turned on the lights. The room was empty. The only window was locked from the inside. She left quickly and did not mention the incident to anyone for some time.

Father Walter Leedale was a member of the music department, and his own experiences began around the same time. One day he watched the handle of a supposedly locked door turn and open, all on its own. Father Leedale walked through the open door and found the room empty. In January of 1975, he heard the sound of a flute playing outside his first-floor music studio. He searched in vain for the musician. In February, he was relaxing at the piano and surprised himself by playing the melody he had heard earlier. He played the eight-note song several times. The housekeeper was in the building and heard him. She finally told Father Leedale about her incident in November and finished by telling him he had played the same song she had heard.

At first Leedale looked for intruders, suspecting a prankster. He walked through the building with a student, searching for anything out of the ordinary. They heard a growling noise coming from the basement, which was locked. Leedale did not have the key with him, but after the student left, he returned with the key and opened the door. The room was empty except for an old bass viol leaning against the wall. He thought that a draft might have blown across the viol's strings, causing the growling noise . . . except that all the strings were broken!

On February 24, five people witnessed the same phenomena. That night a pair of campus security guards stopped at Monaghan Hall, when one of them thought he saw something on the third floor. He called Father Leedale and the music department chairman, Daniel Brenner. The four men saw a figure silhouetted in a second-story window. They went inside and found a man named Steve Armstrong, a live-in student, on the first floor. They agreed that Steve could not have gone from the second to the first floor before they entered. The five men searched the first and second floors before climbing the stairs leading to the third floor.

At the top of the stairs, they crept along a narrow hallway leading into an open practice room. The room was empty. They stopped as if by a silent command. Leedale felt a presence that made his skin crawl. It overcame Armstrong as well. Behind them, Brenner was paralyzed and could not walk into the room. According to Leedale, one of the guards reported feeling as if something was strangling him, though the guards later denied anything strange.

Leedale immediately conducted an exorcism, the first of several, because he sensed that whatever was in the building was both evil and determined to stay. In time, he thought he felt the evil presence fade away. But despite Father Leedale's assurances that the exorcism had succeeded, stories continued that Monaghan Hall was haunted.

In 1979, security guards patrolling the campus noticed light coming from windows that should have been dark. They went inside and eventually made their way to the attic, where four years earlier Leedale and the others had been overwhelmed.

One of the guards heard a noise behind him. He turned and saw a large portable blackboard wheeling slowly toward him. The guard backed away until he was standing against the wall. His partner rushed across the room to stop the moving blackboard, which by then was pressing against the first guard. The two of them had barely enough strength to move the blackboard aside. Once the guard was free, they were out of the building in seconds.

What happened here? There are several explanations. According to some, the original owner of the building, James Monaghan, was killed there. The legend goes on to say that Monaghan was musical and that the organ played by itself at his funeral. Perhaps this musical spirit was resurrected at Gonzaga. If so, why did Monaghan's spirit stay when ordered to leave by a priest, even though Monaghan was a devout Catholic? Or perhaps it is his killer who lingers.

The movie *The Exorcist* was released over the Christmas holiday in 1973. Every time a movie such as that has been released, there is a ripple effect of hysteria and paranoia among many devout people. Could it have taken a year for this effect to reach Gonzaga? Was it all a hoax? If so, it is too late to expose it. Even today visitors continue to call Gonzaga's music department to try to arrange a night's stay. Don't bother; they've turned down *Weird Washington* author Jeff Davis several times already.

Monaghan Hall is located at East 217 Boone Avenue, in Spokane.

Baby Graves of Tri-Cities

"OH MY GOD!"

Last night we went out to the Baby Graves cemetery and got the crap scared out of us. This cemetery is weird, it's over a hundred years old, and has nothing but babies buried there. They say that if you go there at night, and are really quiet, you can hear the babies crying. Maybe they call for their mommies? It wasn't easy to find the place, it's located in the hills outside of Kennewick, and the roads wind in and out of the hills, and there aren't any real landmarks. Anyway, we got there and walked around, and Tom started getting silly, yelling for the ghosts to come out. He even rapped on one of the headstones with his flashlight.

We didn't know that the babies have a guardian. There's an old man who lives in a shack not too far away, and he came running out of it, screaming at us. He was yelling that he was going to kill us, and he had a baseball bat in his hand. We ran to our cars, and got in them, but didn't have time to turn around. We actually backed down the dirt road, and almost went off the road into a ditch, and the man caught up with us. He swung the bat, and hit the windshield, and cracked it. Tom gunned the engine, and we left him behind, but he still followed us until we made it back to the main road. By the time we got back to Kennewick, everyone but Tom and me were laughing. I was still afraid and shaking, and Tom was [furious] about his broken windshield. —*Amy*

Weird Washington Visits the Baby Graves

In the spring of 2007, *Weird Washington* visited the Baby Graves Cemetery with Tri-Cities resident Eric C. (For those not familiar with Washington State shorthand, the Tri-Cities are Kennewick, Pasco, and Richland.) We discovered that like most legends, stories of the Baby Graves were partly true and partly false.

We found the cemetery near a crossing of several different roads, which probably dated to the years when all the homesteaders laid out their claims and put in roads around their property lines. The pioneers probably agreed to have a community cemetery in a central place, rather than having a separate family plot near each farmhouse. This sense of community helped the settlers bear the tragedies of frontier life.

A heavy iron gate and a barbed wire fence mark the cemetery entrance. It is difficult to determine how many people were actually buried here, since many of the old tombstones were probably wood and have rotted away over

the years. There are stone markers too, but money was always scarce in the old days, and some of these had to do double duty, particularly if the dead were children. Only the remaining families know for sure how many dead rest in the Baby Graves Cemetery.

The Travis family seemed to suffer the most. On May 20, 1893, their baby Norma died, age six months, seventeen days. The tragedy must have broken Mrs. Travis's heart. Six days after Norma died, on May 26, a set of twins were born into the Travis family. They lingered only a day before they too passed on. The three of them share a single stone.

Within the cemetery is a small picket fence. It was once white, but most of the paint has peeled off. Inside the little enclosure lie William and Mark Pearson, brothers who never knew each other. William was born on July 4, 1901, and died on July 10. Mark was born on June 30, 1902, and lived over a year before dying in November 1903.

It was obvious that people visit the cemetery every now and then. A survey a few years ago showed ten intact grave markers. In 2007, *Weird Washington* found

that the tops of two were missing; several of the remaining stones were scratched or broken. There were burned-out road flares, fireworks, and a few beer cans around the cemetery. Obviously, the place was a hangout for local parties, but there was also evidence that more

benign visitors have not completely abandoned the place. The iron fence was decorated with red ribbons, and someone left a toy rabbit for the Pearson boys.

Fortunately for us, there was no angry old man carrying a baseball bat living in a nearby shack. Perhaps he had left since Amy's visit. However, it is likely that some of the pioneer descendants live nearby. The closest house is about a mile away, and we might have been watched through binoculars as we tootled around the Baby Graves Cemetery.

Let Them Rest in Peace, Please
Dear *Weird Washington:*

It is a family gravesite. I know the family that owns the property and they will defend their own. They do ask that no one bother their family.–*Chris Z.*

Port Angeles Spyburger

Many of Washington's weird legends, like buried treasure and Native American princesses, revolve around our state's early days. Few people believe that modern spies and terrorists would hide in Washington. Even so, in the 1980s, convicted spy Christopher Boyce hid from a national manhunt in tiny Port Angeles for several months. The only reason he was caught was because of his fondness for the burgers cooked at a certain restaurant.

Depending on who tells Christopher Boyce's story, he was either an idealist or a traitor. Boyce was the son of an FBI agent who got his son a job working for defense contractor TRW in 1974. TRW was working on a top secret satellite spy system, and Boyce was one of the clerks on the project. He became outraged about the Vietnam War and sold some of the secret documents to the Soviets, through his childhood friend Andrew D. Lee. Boyce flew falcons as a hobby, and Lee was a part-time drug dealer, which led to their nicknames: the Falcon and the Snowman. After their arrests and convictions for espionage, their story was portrayed in a book and movie of that name.

Boyce was sentenced to life in prison but would have had a chance at parole. Rather than waiting for this opportunity, he escaped from the federal prison in Lompoc, California, on January 21, 1980. This led to an international manhunt that lasted for nineteen months. The FBI and U.S. marshals formed a joint task force that conducted hundreds of interviews and followed over one hundred leads, all of which were fruitless. That is, until one of the people who had sheltered Boyce was arrested and turned informer. The informant told his captors that Boyce was living near Port Angeles.

In early August 1981, a special task force of twenty-eight government agents descended on Port Angeles to quietly search for the escaped spy. Some of the agents posed as timber workers, others as fishermen, and some as tourists. Unfortunately, they did not realize that so many strangers moving into a small community like Port Angeles would be noticed. Several locals called the police, reporting strangers walking around their neighborhoods. The strangers turned out to be the agents, who were sometimes arrested by the local police. The task force had no choice but to take the county sheriff into their confidence. He and some of his deputies were on call to "spring" the agents if they were stopped by police not in on the hunt.

So, successfully eluding incarceration themselves, the agents could get to work. They learned that Boyce had obtained a Washington State driver's license under another name and that he often came to Port Angeles to eat at the Pit Stop Drive-in because he liked the hamburgers there. Federal agents Danny Behrend and Anne Miller, posing as husband and wife, rented a room in a motel just across the street from the burger joint. On the morning of August 21, they checked the Pit Stop Drive-in but saw nothing. Later that evening they got word that someone matching Boyce's description was at the restaurant.

The Pit Stop was a true drive-in, and when Behrend and Miller checked, they saw a man sitting in his car, eating. The two agents led the way, driving across the parking lot to the drive-in. Other agents

followed. Behrend pulled up next to Boyce's car and recognized him as the other agents surrounded the area. One of them yelled the now immortal warning, "Drop that hamburger!"

Within a few days, Boyce was back in a federal penitentiary, where he remained for over two decades before being paroled. However, his fame still remains in Port Angeles. For many years, people came from across the United States to eat at the Pit Stop Drive-in. The owners directed them to space number 10, where Boyce was arrested, and they ordered the special Spy Meal: a cheeseburger, onion rings, and a small Coke.

Unfortunately, all good things come to an end. In 1991, the Pit Stop's waitresses took their last orders and the restaurant closed its doors for the last time. Part of the building was demolished, and the parking lot was roofed over to make space for the offices of Carroll Realty. This included space number 10, which is now an office cubicle.

All is not forgotten though. People still come to Port Angeles looking for the Pit Stop and are directed to the real estate offices. *Weird Washington* interviewed owner Elisabeth Watkins, who said that occasionally old-time locals come into her office to talk business and reminisce. More than one of them still does imitations of a famous cartoon glutton as they remember the "Spyburger, with special spy sauce, uuuuhhhhhh. . . ."

Spokane Legends
I grew up in Washington State.

There are several topics that might be of interest to you. On the south hill in Spokane, around the area known as Edgecliff Park, there used to be a sanitarium called Edgecliff. When I was a child, it was all boarded up. But lots of kids would sneak in there and prowl around and there were tons and tons of stories of scary experiences. Now they've totally redone the sanitarium and it's a retirement center. Getting info on it is hard and a lot of people might try to deny that it was a sanitarium and all the stories. Maybe people just want to forget about it.

Another legend in Spokane is the Goatman up in the Nine Mile Falls area north of Spokane. There are stories about how people have heard him up there or how he would peep into people's homes. I don't know much more on that one.

Now if you want to go with characters, there is Dickie. A real life guy who is downtown a lot. He will walk a few feet and spin around and wave at people, walk a few more feet, spin around and wave. Walk a few more feet, spin around. He can't seem to stop. And if the emergency vehicles are coming through, he gets pretty excited. Now I know he is real because I have seen him plenty of times and have even talked with him. Rumor is he has shellshock from like WW II or something like that.–*Tony*

Teddy Roosevelt: The President Who Never Visited?

The guest book at the Hotel de Haro in Roche Harbor once contained two signatures from a man named Theodore Roosevelt. According to hotel staff, President Theodore Roosevelt stayed there twice. He used room 2A, which was renamed the Presidential Suite in honor of his stay. The first signature was made in pencil and undated. Later someone added a note beside it with the date of July 13, 1906. The second signature, from 1907, is no longer there. According to the staff, someone stole that page out of the register book in 1977.

Unfortunately, the dates of Roosevelt's supposed visits may not fit the facts.

Richard Walker, of *The Journal of the San Juan Islands,* investigated this story. Searching through local newspaper accounts of the time, he found no mention of a visit by President Roosevelt to Roche Harbor or to the San Juan Islands. This was strange, since an entourage of reporters would have surrounded Roosevelt wherever he went. Walker found local residents old enough to recall the early 1900s, but nobody remembered anything as important as a presidential visit in 1906.

Walker also contacted two historians who wrote books on Teddy Roosevelt. They said it was unlikely that Roosevelt stayed at the Hotel de Haro in 1906 or 1907.

In July 1906, Teddy Roosevelt was at Sagamore Hill, his home in Oyster Bay, New York, also known as the Summer White House. He was busy that year, keeping the Republicans in power and lobbying for natural conservation and political reform, and he accepted the Nobel Peace Prize for brokering a treaty that ended the Russo-Japanese War. He did travel, visiting the Panama Canal and Puerto Rico, but historians find it unlikely that Roosevelt could have stolen away to Washington State without being missed.

The simplest explanation is that Teddy Roosevelt was never at the Hotel de Haro and the signatures were practical jokes that became local legends.

On the other hand, someone could have gotten the dates wrong. Roosevelt visited the Pacific Northwest several times: May 1903, April 1911, September 1912, and July 1915. Could he have stopped in the San Juan Islands to visit John McMillin—a fellow Republican and acquaintance—before arriving in Seattle?

And what if the dates in the hotel register were correct? Though busy and completely in the public eye in 1906, Roosevelt had also spent long periods of his life traveling the countryside alone. Could he have engineered a country retreat to get away from the attention for a bit?

Or was there a darker reason?

Roosevelt was concerned about America's security in the Pacific Ocean, hence his Nobel Prize in 1906. He spent a lot of time traveling on international affairs. He also built up the United States Navy and, in 1907, sent the Great White Fleet on a cruise around the world to show the world that America would protect its global interests. Did Roosevelt stop in the San Juan Islands after finishing some secret meetings with other foreign powers? If so, there could have been a news blackout, keeping his visit secret. Except possibly for a signature or two in a hotel register.

Ancient Mysteries

When *settlers began arriving* in the Pacific Northwest in the 1850s, the Native Americans they met told them stories of catastrophic floods, violent eruptions, and massive rockslides, which shaped and reshaped the land. The settlers dismissed these stories as fantastic legends, but perhaps they shouldn't have brushed them off so quickly. Destructive floods and earthquakes did happen in the Pacific Northwest, and the people who lived through them told tales of the events and their consequences. Over time, perhaps thousands of years, the stories may have been enlarged or embellished, but a kernel of truth remained.

There are many ancient mysteries in Washington: There are the volcanic eruptions that created Mount Saint Helens and Beacon Rock, and lava flows where people have found handprints embedded in the once fiery rock. And there's the first tale we tell here, one still unfolding, of a man buried along the Columbia River, near Kennewick, over nine thousand years ago. We hope you dig it.

Who Is Kennewick Man?

Years ago, archaeologists and historians theorized that as the Ice Age ended, between ten and twelve thousand years ago, there was a land bridge between Asia and North America. People traveled across it, hunting large animals like the wooly mammoth and bison, making their way farther south along an ice-free corridor on the east side of the Canadian Rockies. They were called the Clovis People after a large spear point found in Clovis, New Mexico, once thought to be one of the oldest prehistoric sites in the Western Hemisphere. Most experts believed there was one long migration of peoples, and that modern Native Americans descended from them. This theory was put to the test with the discovery of Kennewick Man along the Columbia River.

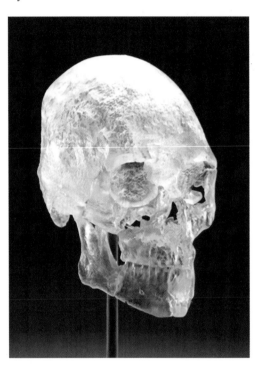

Over nine thousand years ago, a group of people gathered at the grave site of one of their friends and family members. The dead man had been a strong hunter and warrior in his youth, but had grown old. A few months before dying, he had survived being speared through the hip. The spear point was still embedded in his body, but it had healed over. Now, his friends and family paid their final respects, placed him on his back with his hands palms down on the ground, and buried him near the river. His body rested there, forgotten for thousands of years.

Eventually, his grave eroded out of the riverbank, dropping his bones into the water. Their discovery in the mud set off a series of events that inflamed relations between Native Americans, the government, and the scientific community. Each group wanted to do the "right thing," but what that meant varied for each.

The cities of Richland, Pasco, and Kennewick—known collectively as the Tri-Cities—are located near the junction where the Snake, Yakima, and Touchet rivers all flow into the Columbia. Each summer, the Tri-Cities host a weekend of hydroplane races called Water Follies.

In July 1996, Will Thomas and Dave Deacy were sneaking into the Water Follies via the western bank of the Columbia River when they discovered a skull in the water. They hid it along the riverbank and, after the races were finished, retrieved it and turned it over to the county sheriff.

When the sheriff and the coroner went to the site, they found a nearly complete skeleton. The sheriff then called in archaeologist James Chatters, who guessed the man had died sometime between 1820 and 1900. But when he sent a piece of finger bone for radiocarbon dating, he was shocked to learn it was more than nine thousand years old.

At that news, the sheriff ended the criminal investigation. He contacted the Army Corps of Engineers, because the bones came from federally controlled land. They in turn contacted local Native American tribes, wanting to turn the bones over to the appropriate group for reburial or study. But the mysterious remains were

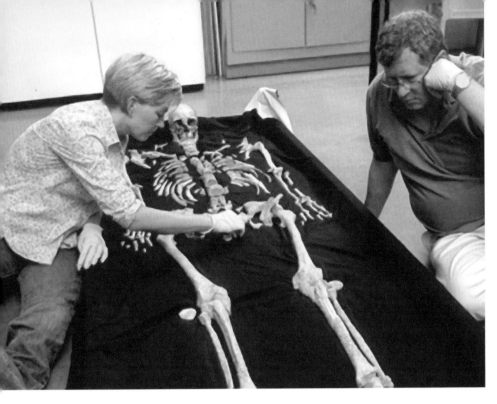

found in an area where many Native American tribes had passed through over the centuries. Five tribal governments laid claim to the skeleton, which they called the Ancient One.

Chatters released his preliminary report with his unexpected findings about the man the press had begun to call Kennewick Man. From the skull, he and an artist produced a reconstructed face that to some looked like the actor Patrick Stewart, probably because it was hairless. It was narrower than most Native American faces and had a large nose. Also, it lacked the rounded shape and other characteristics unique to Native American skulls.

It was possible that none of the local tribes—the Nez Percé, the Kakamas, the Wanapum, or the confederated tribes of the Colville or Umatilla Indian reservations—were related to Kennewick Man. Nevertheless, they filed suit against the Corps of Engineers, seeking to prevent any further study of the bones, which they considered disrespectful. Eventually, the federal government decided

that the five Indian tribes jointly owned the bones, but a federal judge ordered that a scientific study be carried out to find out which Native American groups were genetically tied to Kennewick Man.

In 2005, anthropologists began testing. Their preliminary analysis suggested that Kennewick Man died about 9,300 years ago. He might have been in his late forties or early fifties when he died, although he may have seemed older due to the hard life he lived. He had been healthy, standing about five feet nine inches tall, and was well muscled. The bone development of his right hand and arm suggested he was right-handed and had spent a lot of time using it to throw or thrust with a spear. As he aged, he suffered from arthritis in his lower back, knees, and right elbow. The bone analysis alone did not explain how he died.

Archaeologists compared his information with human bones of a similar age found around the world, as well as to modern human groups. The results suggested that Kennewick Man was related to an ancient people from Asia known as the Jomon, who were probably the ancestors of the Ainu, the aboriginal inhabitants of the Japanese islands, who today live in small communities on the northern island of Hokkaido. They are distinctly different from modern Asians, with facial and body hair, lighter skin, and little or no eyefold.

The Kennewick Man controversy did not end with the recent examinations of his bones. Scientists believe that other tests could be developed in the future, yielding even more information, which means the bones must be kept indefinitely. In the meantime, many Native American tribes wait to learn the identity of the Ancient One.

Handprints in Stone

Lemei Rock, located in the Indian Heaven Wilderness of the Gifford Pinchot National Forest, serves as the literal leaping-off point of one legend. An evil brave, the story goes, chased a beautiful woman to the peak of Lemei Rock. Trapped, the desperate woman looked down to see a lava flow far below. Rather than submit to the brave, she jumped to her death in the fiery lava. She landed feet first and then fell forward, burying her hands in the liquid rock. Her hand- and footprints were permanently left in the rock as a testament to her sacrifice.

Today evidence of the legend can be found in a unique display at the Trout Lake Ranger District visitors center. Mounted on the wall is a large plaster cast of a piece of rock that includes a set of hand- and footprints. The cast was made from an imprint in the basalt rock that makes up the floor of Goose Lake. The real prints are hidden under the waters of the lake, and their origin is still debated.

Some people believe that, as in the legend, the prints were formed several thousand years ago when the site of the lake was a large lava flow. Pioneers noted the prints in the late 1800s, and over the years, geologists and engineers have examined them. Some experts proclaimed the prints to be carvings. Others said they were real, insisting the handprints included fingerprints. Geologists say that if the prints were real, they could range from ten thousand to two thousand years old.

Like the Aztec and Inca, many Pacific Northwest natives studied the phases of the sun, moon, and seasons. There are several locations in the Northwest where the change of seasons was celebrated. Many years ago someone may have knelt at the edge of Goose Lake during the winter solstice, since Native Americans gathered there only in the summer and fall. Looking east, the person would be able to see the sun rise over a high mountain, signaling the change in seasons. Perhaps over time, that same individual returned to cut holes in the rock in the shape of handprints and footprints, showing others where to place themselves to experience the same phenomenon.

Goose Lake is a volcanic sinkhole, and in the '30s, the outlet at the bottom of the lake was dammed up. The imprints disappeared as the water level rose. In the 1990s, Larry King, of the American Rock Art Research Association, spent several days floating in a raft, scanning the floor of the lake through a metal tube with a glass bottom. He located the prints under several feet of water and then worked with Forest Service personnel to build a small coffer dam around them. After pumping out the water, they made a plaster cast of the prints. The dam was then removed, and the prints were left to themselves once again, hidden under water and a covering of mud and grass.

The plaster cast King made is the one that now hangs on the wall of the Trout Lake visitors center. In *Weird Washington*'s opinion, it is not a carving. The footprints resemble either soft-soled shoes or moccasins, and both the footprints and handprints are over an inch deep into the rock. We also didn't see any great detail like fingerprints. As with many legends, you'll have to go there and decide for yourself. Be sure to stop by Goose Lake too, as the ghost of a Native American woman sometimes appears on its shores, combing her long hair.

Ancient Mountain, Modern Eruption

Before 1980, Mount Saint Helens was the fifth largest mountain in Washington State. It was a strato-type volcano, built up of layers of volcanic lava and ash. It was probably forty thousand years old, but most of the cone was only two thousand years old, which was why it was so smooth.

Native Americans remembered Mount Saint Helens' many eruptions through their legends. One tells of the Great Spirit's two sons, Wyeast and Pahto. Wyeast lived on the south side of the Columbia River; Pahto lived on the north side. They both loved the maiden Loowit, and in their rivalry would throw fire and flame across the river at each other. At times, each brother crossed the Bridge of the Gods to fight the other for the love of this maiden. Their battles were so fierce that the earth shook and the bridge collapsed. The Great Spirit was angry at his sons for their foolishness and punished them by turning them into mountains. Wyeast became Mount Hood, and Pahto became Mount Adams. Loowit, whose only crime seems to be that she was too desirable, was turned into Mount Saint Helens, which the Indians called Loowit Latkla, or the Fire Mountain.

The mountain experienced an eruption about four thousand years ago that was so great, portions of the Lewis River were buried under several feet of volcanic ash. The next great eruptions happened in the Middle Ages; after that, the mountain more or less slept for centuries.

Then, on March 20, 1980, an earthquake with a magnitude of 5.1 struck the mountain. A week later, on March 27, steam vented out of the crater. Fortunately for Portland and the Puget Sound, seasonal winds carried most of this away to the northeast, toward eastern Washington.

At 8:32 a.m. on May 18, another magnitude 5.1 earthquake struck about a mile below the center of the volcano, causing the north face of Mount Saint Helens to break off and turn into a landslide. It fell northward at between 70 and 150 mph, covering twenty-three square miles. It buried Spirit Lake and crossed over the next ridgeline.

When the mountaintop slid away, it released an initial blast of hot gas and ash of around seven megatons of energy, which is about five hundred times more powerful than the blast over Hiroshima during World War II. In all, over one half a cubic mile of material slid down the face of the mountain or was blown off, dropping its height from 9,677 feet to 8,363 feet. The blast wave had a temperature of about 660 degrees and traveled at least 300 mph, knocking down trees over an area of two hundred and thirty square miles. The ash cloud circled the globe for fifteen days.

The earthquake and blast were followed by a pyroclastic flow, a gaseous cloud of superheated gases and molten rock. This flow moved down the mountainside at 50 to 80 mph. It was much hotter than

the rockslide, with a temperature of 1,300 degrees. It spread out and covered six square miles, leaving deposits of rock and ash up to thirty feet thick.

This was not the most powerful volcanic eruption in the twentieth century, but with a total estimated damage of over $1 billion it was the most expensive. In addition to the trees killed, 27 bridges, 200 homes, 15 miles of railway line, and 185 miles of roads were destroyed. Millions of fish and 7,000 large game animals, such as deer, elk, and bear, died.

At least fifty-seven people also died. The only thing that kept the human death toll so low was the fact that the eruption took place on a Sunday. If it had happened on a weekday, hundreds of timber workers might have been killed.

Since 1980, nature has recovered significantly in the lands around Mount Saint Helens. Deer, elk, and plants have returned to many areas within the blast zone. However, the land north of the crater still resembles the face of the moon. The U.S. Forest Service built two observation stations at the base of the mountain, perhaps too soon—after a relatively quiet decade, the mountain became active again, especially in 2005 and 2006.

The Cone of Silence

One interesting aspect of a volcanic eruption is the sound wave created by the blast. People heard the 1980 blast of Mount Saint Helens in Portland, Oregon, over fifty miles away. Strangely, there were closer places where the blast was not heard. *Weird Washington* author Jeff Davis was in one of those places that day.

I was in the Army Reserves and had drill on May 18. We went out to Camp Bonneville, east of Vancouver, Washington. Camp Bonneville was in a direct line between Mount Saint Helens and Portland. Some low hills and tall trees hid our view of the mountain. We arrived around 7:30 a.m., and left around 2:00 p.m. I was sitting in the back of an open truck, and as soon as we left the tree line, one of the other soldiers yelled and pointed to the mountain. We saw the column of ash, already 80,000 feet high. Even though the ash cloud was probably rolling and boiling around at high speed, it was so huge that it looked like it was moving in slow motion. But we never heard the blast.

Horsethief Canyon

Horsethief Lake and Canyon are now part of Columbia Hills State Park. The area received its name when workers helping to build the park in the 1950s thought that the narrow canyon would have been the perfect place for horse thieves to hide, and who knows, maybe they were right.

Several examples of Native American art are located in Horsethief Canyon. The artwork is a combination of petroglyphs—designs cut into rock—and pictographs—designs painted onto rock. The most impressive pictograph is Tsagigla'lal, or "She Who Watches." A longer translation of this name is "She who watches and sees all who are coming and going up and down the river."

There is no doubt that Tsagigla'lal was meant as a magical protection for the people who lived in her village for centuries or longer. According to some stories, there was once a matching pictograph on the south bank of the Columbia, opposite the one at Horsethief Lake. That pictograph watched over

Legend of She Who Watches

Pacific Northwest Native Americans believed that the earth had gone through several different ages. This legend dates to the beginning of the modern age, but long before the coming of the White Man. There are several versions of this memory; this is one of our favorites.

Long ago, in the before time, the Great Spirit wandered the world. He traveled along the Great River (the Columbia) and stopped at a village. He asked the people if they lived well or in poverty. They said that they were happy because of the guidance of their chief. He asked where their chief was, and they pointed to the hills above their village.

He went up to the hills and found a woman sitting in front of a hut, looking down at the village. She told him she was the chief, and she looked after her people, teaching them how to build and live well. He told her, "The world is changing, and women will no longer be chiefs. What will you do now?"

The woman asked the Great Spirit to turn her into stone, so that she could continue watching over her people. As a sign of mercy, he did just that, and her image was painted into the rockface overlooking her village. In the local dialect, she is named Tsagigla'lal, or "She Who Watches." She is still there today, looking out over a world that has changed very much since her time—and not always for the better.

the fisheries at the Dalles, which was a trade and meeting center of Native Americans for over ten thousand years. Perhaps Tsagigla'lal was a magical warning to the people there to behave themselves, with no fighting or cheating.

Worshippers still visit her at Horsethief Lake. Some people place offerings at the foot of She Who Watches, such as shells filled with flowers and wild plants. Some people have painted stars and sun/moon designs on the rockfaces. Though they probably felt they were expressing their religious beliefs, they were actually defacing the design made by the Native Americans. Some idiot also shot at some of the rock art, and the bullet holes are still there. To prevent further actions like these, Park Rangers conduct guided tours to the rock art site, by appointment only, on Fridays and Saturdays. Despite the damage, many people who visit She Who Watches still believe that they feel a strange power in the little canyon.

Mysterious Mima Mounds

Every year ten thousand people visit Washington's Mima Mounds Natural Area Preserve to marvel at the many rare plant and animal species living on its 625 acres. Dating back over seven thousand years ago, it is one of the last remaining wild grass prairies in the Puget Sound. In prehistoric times, Native Americans in the area harvested food plants like camas from the wet soils, but today's visitors are more likely to be interested in the origin of the mounds that cover most of the preserve.

These mounds are round or teardrop-shaped, and range from eight to seventy feet across, and from one to seven feet high. At one time, they covered twenty square miles. Even now, there are thousands of them. No one is sure how they came into being. Some people believe that they were Native American burial mounds. However, the local tribes have no known tradition of burying their dead there, and no one has ever found

any human remains or tools in any of the mounds.

Scientists have developed several theories about how they formed. Some think a mild, sustained earthquake caused the soils to form into mounds. One scientist put soil similar to that of the Mima Prairie on a plywood board and started shaking it, which caused the sample to form small mounds.

A favorite theory among the *Weird Washington* team is that pocket gophers created them. Mounds like this have been found only on land where gophers live or once lived. Scientists excavated several mounds and found evidence of extensive rodent tunnels inside the mounds themselves. Most of the soils in the mounds were fine enough to be moved by the little animals. They also found some larger rocks, but these were usually located at the bottom of or in the center of the mounds.

However, no one has found mounds like this made by modern gophers. And given the thousands of mounds, it would have taken a lot of gophers a long time to make them. There are at least a dozen more theories about the origin of the Mima Mounds. There is the ever-popular nuclear explanation, traceable to the testing at the Hanford Nuclear Reservation. And there's the outer space, asteroid storm theory. To develop your own view on the subject, take I-5 southbound and get off at exit 95. Go west on Highway 121 toward Littlerock. In Littlerock, continue west on 128 to the T junction. Turn right on Waddell Creek Road. The Mima Mounds entrance is about one mile ahead on the left.

The Pits and Rocks of Silver Star Mountain

Many people wandering the Olympic and Cascade mountains have come across mysterious pits or piles of rocks. Probably the best-known system is on the ridge south of Silver Star Mountain, in southern Washington. Archaeologists have mapped and counted at least twenty-six pits, trenches, and rock piles here.

Pioneers called the Silver Star Pits the "rifle pits" in memory of a group of soldiers traveling from the Vancouver Barracks to Fort Simcoe, in eastern Washington. Native Americans ambushed the soldiers as they crossed Silver Star Mountain, and, the story goes, the soldiers dug several pits and built low rock walls to protect themselves from the attacking Indians. After a day or two, the soldiers slipped away and returned to the Vancouver Barracks. However, a look at the pits makes it clear that it would have taken longer than one day for the soldiers to make them. This doesn't mean people didn't take cover in the holes and trenches, but they probably didn't build them.

Other pioneers told stories of Native Americans using the pits as hunting blinds. They would wait in the pits near the top of the ridge, while other members of their group went through the bottom of the deep valley, driving game uphill toward the hidden hunters.

When a Native American elder was shown a picture of one of the pits, he looked at the archaeologist with pity (at his ignorance) and said, "Oh, that's a refrigerator pit."

The elder explained that while hunting and gathering, the people had to store their food somewhere. They excavated holes in the loose rocks, lined them with leaves, put in the food to be stored, and covered the pits with more rocks. This insulated the food and kept out small scavengers.

However, this doesn't explain all of the pits at Silver Star and elsewhere. Perhaps the answer to the mystery lies in the fact that many people consider mountains and other high places sacred, perhaps because of their

isolation. It is likely that many of the pits were dug and rocks were piled as rituals for a vision quest: part of the spiritual life of Indian youths. Boys approaching manhood would go into the mountains or other sacred places where the spirits were close. Their aim was to see visions of the past or future, and find a spirit guide who would give them power for the rest of their lives.

The youths would not eat or drink, and stayed awake day and night without a blanket. The boys would engage in heavy physical work to weaken their bodies in order that the spirits would show themselves. They would gather rocks and pile them into walls or mounds, until exhaustion brought on the visions.

In 1992, *Weird Washington*'s Jeff Davis worked for the Gifford Pinchot National Forest. He hiked up to Silver Star Mountain several times and tells this story:

The pits are located about a half mile past the highest point on the ridge. On one visit, I was mapping out the pits, expecting my boss to arrive and help. It was a windy day, and I had trouble with my measuring tape. Several times I heard my boss's voice. It was only a few words, or a phrase, and then silence. But each time I looked up, no one was there.

I finished my work and left. I found out later that my boss was at the top of Silver Star Mountain, a half mile away, with a film crew. They spent several hours walking over the peak. The only explanation we had was that the wind carried my boss's voice a half mile across the peak to the pits.

Ozette, the Pompeii of the Pacific Northwest

There is a Native American legend whose theme is fairly common across the world, but has particular meaning for the Makah people.

Many years ago people who lived on the earth somehow angered the gods. There was a great storm, and most of the people stayed in their houses, except for an old man and an old woman who hid in a cave. After several days, they felt the earth tremble and heard a loud noise. When the rain ended, they left the cave and found that their village had disappeared, buried under the earth.

The old couple built a new house, had more children, and repopulated the earth.

The Makah Indian Tribe has lived at the tip of the Olympic Peninsula for a very long time. Archaeologists believe that some of their settlements, from Cape Alava to Neah Bay, were first occupied nearly four thousand years ago. Due to U.S. government regulations, the Makah left their village in Ozette in 1917, and the land around Ozette became part of the Olympic National Park. The Makah settlement there seemed destined to fade away, until a natural disaster brought back ancestral memories.

In the winter of 1969–1970, a riverbank began to erode away after a storm. The following spring a hiker noticed some wooden boards and Native American artifacts in the debris. He contacted the Makah Tribe, who notified Washington State University and the state of Washington. Within two months, they began a series of archaeological digs that would last the next eleven years and would confirm most of the Makah oral history.

Some time around A.D. 1500, a village of six large houses built of cedar planks stood at Ozette. It had been there for hundreds, perhaps thousands, of years. One night a massive landslide buried the village. It was so sudden that the archaeologists found the remains of several people still in their beds. The blessing of this tragedy was that the mudslide covered the village so completely there was little or no oxygen in the wet soil. This kept most of the bone, stone, and wooden artifacts in the houses from decaying.

During the dig, archaeologists found that the people of Ozette lived mostly by fishing and whale hunting in the Pacific. More significantly, the searchers found several large ocean-style fishing nets. For the modern Makah, this was a lucky find. Up until that point, U.S. policy had not allowed them to use nets for fishing. Government fishing rights allowed the tribe to use only the tools their ancestors had used before the coming of white settlers. No one knew that the ancient Makah had used nets. With this proof, the tribe was able to add net fishing to their rights.

Other unexpected finds included several unusual artifacts, such as wood planes with iron cutting blades. Where had the Makah gotten the metal? Perhaps from Asian ships that had made their way across the Pacific on the currents. But what happened to the people in the boats? Did the Makah find some people alive and allow them into their tribe? Or did they find only dead bodies? So far, there are no answers.

In total, archaeologists found over fifty-five thousand artifacts, all of which were turned over to the Makah. There was whaling, sealing, and fishing gear, wooden boxes, cloth, and clothing made of animal hair and bark. They also found baskets, jewelry, and many other tools and household items.

The Ozette dig project revitalized the Makah tribe. Many took up traditional crafts such as wood and bone carving, and basket weaving. Tribal elders began teaching children their native tongue and recording traditional stories for future generations. Some began practicing the old-style hunting, including a gray whale hunt in May 1999 (the gray whale was not on the endangered species list, and the Makah are the only tribe in the contiguous United States whose treaty guarantees them the right to hunt whales). Nothing of the whale they caught was wasted: The meat and blubber were eaten or turned into oil for later use, and the bones were given to Makah artists for traditional handicrafts.

For more about this ancient tribe, visit the Makah Cultural and Research Center located in Neah Bay. They have a replica of one of the houses at Ozette, as well as displays of artifacts and lifestyles. Guided tours of the site are available for a fee.

Fabled People and Places

Washington State has a reputation for being rustic and out-of-the-way. Some visitors expect to see locals dressed in flannel shirts, carrying axes, and cutting down trees all day. In fact, that's how things were for many years, and Washington developed a reputation as a place where strange people and places hid in its mountains and forests.

And maybe we deserve it. There's reason to believe that ancient Chinese sailors visited Washington centuries before Columbus, naming it the land of Fu-Sang. Author Jonathan Swift left his hero Gulliver marooned in the land of the giants, which he set in Washington. Did Swift know that some Native Americans believed that giants live in the Cascade Mountains?

Or how about a seemingly bottomless hole that sucks down garbage like a giant trash disposal but can't be precisely located? Is it real or just the product of one man's imagination?

These and other mysterious people and places are the ones we call fabled — their existence is questionable, but their effect on our imaginations is not. True weirdness comes in many forms, so don't forget to look for it in that space between fact and fiction.

Mel's Hole

Art Bell hosted a nightly
AM radio talk show, which eventually became
Coast to Coast AM, syndicated on hundreds of
radio stations across the United States. On February
21, 1997, he had a guest who identified himself as Mel
Waters. Mel told Art Bell and several million listeners
that he lived near Ellensburg and that there was a
bottomless hole on his property.

Mel said that before he bought the property,
many people had used this hole as a dumping
ground for garbage, old appliances, dead
animals, and even an occasional car. Some
locals reported seeing a black beam
of light shine out of the hole
(although he failed to

explain how a black light could shine). He also said that a hunter had thrown his dead dog into the hole, only to see it alive in the woods a few days later. Living animals and birds, however, stayed away from the hole.

According to Mel, the hole was nine and a half feet wide and had a rock retaining wall around it and a metal cover. When he removed the cover, he noted that the hole was smooth-sided down as far as he could see. The hole was so deep he could not see the bottom when he shined a flashlight down it. When Mel dropped things into the hole, he never heard any of them hit the bottom.

Trying to ascertain the hole's depth, Mel lowered a weight (a roll of Life Savers) on a fishing line and saw that it was deeper than the spool on his fishing pole. So he got more wire—a full eighty thousand feet more, or over fifteen miles. He claimed to have unfurled it all (weighted, of course) into the hole without ever hitting bottom.

In the dirt around the hole, Mel found an old World War II–era German handgun. The gun, however, did not make any sound when fired, and when it was put near a radio, the radio began receiving broadcasts from the past (so said Mel). He also found a red paper envelope near the hole; in it he found several Roosevelt dimes with a date of 1943 and a B mintmark.

A few days after the initial broadcast, Mel called Art Bell again. He said that after the interview aired, he had been away from home, but when he returned, he found a roadblock across his driveway. Soldiers guarded the barricade and turned him away with warnings of a plane crash in the hills above. Mel told Bell he was leasing his property and moving to Australia, where he was going to grow medicinal plants and start a wombat preserve.

Early in April of 2000, Mel reappeared on *Coast to Coast AM*. He reported that after 1997, he had leased

his property to an unnamed party for $3 million a year, in perpetuity. Part of this deal included Mel's agreeing to stay in Australia. Mel broke the agreement when he visited the United States in 1999. This turned out to be more than just a trip home—it was a trip to who-knows-where: According to Mel, he was lured off a bus near Olympia and taken into custody, and he woke up twelve days later in San Francisco.

There he found an IV scar and surgical tape residue on his arm, suggesting he had been drugged. His rear molar teeth had been taken, as were his wallet and his belt buckle. Someone suggested that the government had embedded a device in his other teeth that allowed them to track him when he returned to the United States.

The missing belt buckle was made with three of the 1943 dimes he had found in the red envelope. Some listeners pointed out that the Roosevelt dime was not cast until 1946 and that there is no mint in the United States with a B mintmark. Looking for an explanation, some suggested that the dimes and German pistol from the hole came from an alternate reality in which the Nazis won World War II, Roosevelt died before 1943, and a mint opened in Berlin to create the

In the dirt around the hole, Mel found an old World War II–era German handgun. The gun, however, did not make any sound when fired, and when it was put near a radio, the radio began receiving broadcasts from the past.

new dime. Of course, why would the Nazis make a coin celebrating their enemy? Mel said one of the other dimes turned up later, but somehow it was invisible to cameras closer than fifteen feet away.

Several groups of people have tried to find Mel's Hole, narrowing the search area down to Manastash Ridge, near Ellensburg. There are several mine shafts and natural lava tubes in the area, and some are quite deep, though none go down fifteen miles. Recently an expedition including Philip Lipson and Charlette LaFevre of Seattle's Museum of the Mysteries searched for the fabled hole. Their guide was Native American shaman Red Elk. In their words:

Hole Still Holds Its Secrets

We'd heard that individuals had looked for Mel's Hole but after brief attempts gave up. We ourselves didn't start looking for the hole until 2001, when Red Elk related to us that his father had shown him the hole over 40 years ago and he could take us to the general location. He took us to a yellow gate on Manastash Ridge and said this was the area that had been blocked off soon after Mel Waters related his story on the radio.

Since then, we have heard reports from dirt bikers of a hole on the ridge in the same general area, but they consider a hole a nuisance and a spot to be avoided. We've searched the ridge half a dozen times over the past years, visiting the nearby Manastash Ridge Observatory, finding empty shacks, rescuing owls, and even locating a mining shaft that we believe many may have mistaken for Mel's Hole. We've heard stories of a "Goat Man," of Civil War slaves hiding out in the canyon, even of recent "moon-shining" and people still panning for gold. Indeed, geologically, Ellensburg is on the edge of an ancient oceanic plate and a rare agate called "Ellensburg blue" is only found along a 25-mile stretch in Ellensburg. With the gold digging, agate mining, "moonshining," and other activities in the area, it's no wonder locals do not give out their secrets. It's likely the handful of locals who do know of the hole know it as a dump site and are not likely to divulge its location.

The ridge has property owned by the Department of Natural Resources and the lumber industry, so private property is dispersed among the acres in a very unmarked territory. With the exception of the houses near Manastash Road, there is no electricity in the area, making it very much a survivalist area and indeed harder to locate the area of the hole.

We can't, of course, verify the paranormal qualities attributed to Mel's Hole, but we do think it exists and may very well be a volcanic vent hole. Indeed, two cave systems and four fault lines have since been found on the ridge.—*Charlette LaFevre and Philip Lipson of Seattle's Museum of the Mysteries*

In the years since Mel's return, the subject has generated thousands of e-mails on many blogs. Some people claim to have met Mel and seen the hole. Although Mel does not answer too many e-mails, someone identifying himself as his nephew keeps up the correspondence. Mel and his nephew have been able to show that they know the Manastash Ridge area and its people quite well and have provided many tantalizing clues in the search for the hole.

Still, no one has supplied proof of Mel's story to reporters or law-enforcement officials. There are no dimes or pictures of the dimes, and no one can seem to find the German pistol. Investigators have never found any record of a Mel Waters owning property in Ellensburg. If this was a hoax, perhaps it got too hot for Mel, because he has apparently now found another hole to hide out in.

Tacoma's Tire-Gobbling Mystery Hole

In 1973, James Johnson watched his dog sniff around a small hole in the backyard of his newly purchased home. Johnson looked at the hole, which he suspected was a mole or gopher tunnel. He ran a plumber's snake down it, but never reached the bottom. Intrigued, he called the city of Tacoma, which investigated. By that time, the opening had widened to about four feet. Johnson and the engineers found that the top several feet were lined with brick. The engineers said that it was an old community well and was about thirty feet deep. They recommended that Johnson fill it with gravel, which he would have to do at his own expense.

This was in the days before many environmental laws existed in the United States. Rather than spending a lot of money on gravel, Johnson bought over one hundred and sixty tires, and threw them into the opening. He covered the hole with a board and tried to forget the incident, until about a year and a half later, when he wanted to build a porch that would cover the old hole.

Johnson removed the board and found that the tires, which had been at the top, had sunk down, almost out of sight. Puzzled, he started asking neighbors about the hole. According to some, it had existed at least as far back as 1920, at which time the homeowners had tried to fill it in like Johnson did. Instead of tires, they had used rocks and household garbage. Perhaps there was a buildup of methane gas from the decaying garbage, or some other force in the hole was displeased. For whatever reason, there was an explosion, and much of the fill was spit out of the abyss.

There were many theories about the origins of the hole. One person suggested that it was a tunnel dug to help transport illegal Chinese workers from the Port of Tacoma into the city. Because of its age, a few people speculated that it had been dug by local Native American tribes. Some thought that there was treasure at the bottom or (our favorite explanation) that Bigfoot dug the hole.

Local cavers heard about the tire-gobbling hole and asked Johnson's permission to investigate. They set up a pulley-and-hook mechanism and fished out all the tires, as well as a concrete block about eighteen inches square, then lowered one of their members down into the hole. Some of the longtime locals had suggested that there was some unseen being or force within the hole that had grabbed people or things lowered into it in the past, but after several minutes the cavers pulled their volunteer out safely.

He reported that the hole widened to nearly ten feet across below the brickwork and was over thirty feet deep. There were several inches of water down at the bottom, which supported the belief that in the past the hole had been a well. The cavers took a pole and pushed it into the bottom hoping to hit solid bedrock, but it went through several feet of mud without stopping.

The city engineers suggested that the tires had settled into the sandy bottom of the hole. Something that the engineers did not explain was the presence of several egg-shaped rocks the caver found at the bottom of the hole. Eventually, Johnson grew tired of the media attention. He filled in the hole with gravel and sand, capped it, and built a deck over the entire thing.

Ramtha, Warrior for Enlightenment

JZ (the Z stands for Zebra) Knight was born Judith Darlene Hampton, in Roswell, New Mexico, which might have fitted her for a strange and mysterious life. According to Knight, in 1977 a powerful spirit appeared to her as she stood in her kitchen wearing a paper pyramid on her head (something she did because she ascribed psychic power to the Egyptian pyramids). He told her his name was Ramtha and that he lived 35,000 years earlier. He was from the ancient land of Lemuria, though he had lived in Atlantis. Ramtha was a warrior, conquering most of the world before he reached self-enlightenment and went on to shed his mortal body, becoming spiritual energy. He returned to earth and had chosen Knight to be his vessel, speaking these words to her: "Beloved woman, I am Ramtha the Enlightened One, and I have come to help you over the ditch of limitation. . . . And I am here, and we are going to do a grand work together."

Ramtha educated Knight about spiritual enlightenment, which she passed on to her followers at Ramtha's School of Enlightenment, in Yelm. Among the principles of Ramtha's dogma is the view that humans are God.

Ramtha's students have received seminars on telepathy; remote viewing of the past, present, and future; psychic healing; and many other things. Of course not all of Ramtha's students can afford to pay up to $1,000 to attend these seminars, so Knight heads a commercial company that publishes books, audio, and television productions of Ramtha's teachings.

There are several levels of study at the Ramtha institute, and the exercises grow more difficult as students advance. Some disciples believe that they can stop the process of human aging, and even that they can create objects such as flowers or feathers with the power of their minds. Of course, to do this they have to meditate regularly and attend at least one retreat in Yelm every year. Enlightenment comes at a price!

Worldwide, several thousand people believe in the teachings of Ramtha. One recent guest speaker was Robert Kennedy Jr., who spoke on the environment. Another famous devotee is actress Linda Evans, the star of *Dynasty*.

Since she first appeared, Knight has been surrounded by controversy. Some firmly believe that she is indeed gifted, while others believe she is the head of a cult. In 1992, a psychic in Berlin, Germany, claimed that she had begun channeling Ramtha as well. Knight sued, and after three years an international court agreed that the German psychic had infringed on Knight's copyright over her communication with the ancient warrior (which she had obtained in the 1970s). They awarded Knight $800 in damages.

Over several years, Knight has donated over $1 million to students as scholarships, and the school hosts at least one open house a year with local officials. Ramtha and Knight continue to live on in weird Washington. Here's to the next 35,000 years!

Was Fu-Sang Washington State?

In A.D. 499 a man named Hui-Shen arrived at the court of the Chinese emperor Ching-Chou. Hui-Shen was a Buddhist missionary, originally from Kabul, Afghanistan. He told the emperor that he had just spent fifty years in a strange country he called Fu-Sang, located 20,000 li (Chinese miles) east of China. Some scholars believe that the land of Fu-Sang was the West Coast of North America. Was Fu-Sang in what is now Washington State?

Voyages from China to North America were certainly possible. During the Han dynasty, a few hundred years before Hui-Shen's journey, the Chinese built four-masted sailing ships, which carried up to seven hundred passengers and hundreds of tons of cargo. In the fourth century, Chinese explorers made voyages from China to Southeast Asia and India.

Hui-Shen described many odd things about the people of Fu-Sang, some of which could have referred to the Native Americans living in North America. But some stories of Fu-Sang did not fit North America or anywhere else.

The land of Fu-Sang was rich in some minerals like copper, and had smaller amounts of gold and silver, but the people did not use iron. The Fu-Sang people gathered purplish red fruit from a tree that Hui-Shen called a mulberry tree. They also gathered the bark of the tree and made paper and fabric. They lived in communities of large houses made out of the mulberry wood, but did not fortify their towns. The people were generally peaceful and were ruled by a chief with the help of several advisers. When a man wanted to marry a woman, he built a smaller house alongside her family home until she accepted him as a husband.

With the exception of the presence of fruit, the trees and their uses could be the western red cedar. The Fu-Sang houses and towns were reminiscent of the villages of Native Americans along the Washington coast. There families lived in huge houses built of red cedar planks. In general, a chieftain headed each house, and the chief of each house selected one of their members to be the village chieftain. In many Pacific Northwest villages, when a couple was to wed, it was not unusual for the man to move in with his wife's family, which would have seemed strange to the Chinese. According to Hui-Shen,

the people of Fu-Sang kept domestic deer, which they raised for meat, milk, and cheese. They trained these deer, and also horses and buffalo, to pull carts and sledges.

Farther away were other lands, where women were white but covered with heavy hair. Children drank milk from the hair of their mothers. These people certainly did not live in prehistoric Washington State. Some historians speculate that Hui-Shen landed far south of Washington among the civilizations of Central America. However, not much has been mentioned in the Mexican annals of history about hairy women there nursing children from their hair!

In the past, Pacific trade currents carried many derelict ships toward North America. These currents began near Japan and headed northeast, off the coast of the Aleutian Islands, paralleling the coast of North America for several hundred miles. Maritime records from the sixteenth through nineteenth centuries record at least sixty Asian ships adrift in these currents. Six of these vessels landed between Alaska and the mouth of the Columbia River. In the past, beachcombers in Washington and Oregon collected glass balls on the shoreline—floats from Japanese fishing nets— which prove the possibility of a wreck of an intentional expedition across the Pacific.

People are said to have found Chinese coins, weapons, and even a skeleton wearing Chinese armor along the Washington coast. In addition, there are stories among some of the native peoples that mention mythological beings (perhaps the visitors from China), their ships, and technology. Unfortunately, no one has found solid evidence that any of these sailors from Asia came to Washington or that they ever returned to China.

Finding Fu-Sang by Figuring the Li of the Land

Part of the controversy surrounding where Fu-Sang was depends on the length of a li, the Chinese mile, which changed over time. During the Han dynasty, about two hundred years before Hui-Shen's journey, a li was about 1,365 feet long. Twenty thousand li, at 1,365 feet in length, would be 7,000 miles, roughly the distance from China to North America. Tales of Hui-Shen's journey were not written down until A.D. 635, over one hundred years after he supposedly traveled. Hui-Shen began his epic voyage from a place called Ta-Han. We do not know for sure where that is, but it seems likely it was a trading port city in the Sea of Okhotsk, at the far limits of China's influence. It is recorded that he traveled 20,000 li, or about 7,000 miles. From there he traveled northeast and then southeast, on a strong ocean current to the western edge of North America, which is about 7,000 miles from China.

Native American traditions and historic records of several oddities at Crescent Lake lead some people to believe that there is something dark and mystical about the deep waters.

Soap People of Crescent Lake

Many years ago the Clallam and Quillieute tribes fought for many days on the shores of a long lake in the Olympic Mountains. Eventually, the Mountain Storm King grew so angry with both groups that he broke off the top of his head and threw it at the warriors. It landed in the lake—the rock and water killed all of the combatants, and none of their bodies were found. The rock that was his head remained, splitting the lake in two, creating Crescent Lake and Lake Sutherland. Or so the story goes.

Geologists say that thousands of years ago, glaciers carved one long lake through the Olympic Mountains. Years later a massive landslide did indeed divide the lake in half. Crescent Lake is about eight and a half miles long and over six hundred feet deep. It is very cold, with a temperature that hovers around forty-four degrees. The hot mineral springs that empty into the lake fail to raise the water temperature, even in summer.

That seems straightforward enough. But Native American traditions and historic records of several oddities at Crescent Lake lead some people to believe that there is something dark and mystical about the deep waters. The case of Hallie Illingworth is an example of the strange conditions that might make you wonder if Crescent Lake has yet to give up its secrets.

In the summer of 1940, two fishermen noticed a large object floating on the surface of the lake. They investigated and found that it was a bundle of blankets tied together with ragged rope. The blankets had either ripped or decayed, and through the holes the men saw that they had been wrapped around a human body. When the blankets were removed, the police were amazed at the condition of the body inside. Instead of being bloated and rotted, the body, that of a woman, had undergone a remarkable transformation.

When alive, the woman had weighed over one hundred pounds; her corpse weighed about fifty pounds. Her flesh was hard to the touch, and the skin was white, so white that it resembled a mannequin's. The coroner determined that the deceased had been murdered and that her killer had tied weights to the dead body, which then sank six hundred feet to the bottom of the lake. The water there was very cold and had a high alkaline content. This killed the bacteria that would have rotted the woman's flesh. The coroner also found calcium in samples from the lake floor. He theorized that over a period of years, the calcium and alkaline water had leached some of the organic deposits out of her body and replaced them with minerals. This actually turned her body fat into soap through a process he called saponification. When the ropes securing the weights that held the body on the floor of the lake rotted away, the body floated to the surface like a bar of soap.

It took two years to bring the soap woman's killer to justice. Eventually, a dentist identified the body using dental plates. It turned out that the dead woman was Hallie Illingworth, a waitress at the Lake Crescent Tavern, now known as Lake Crescent Lodge. She had been reported missing in 1937, three years before her body floated to the surface of the lake. An investigation turned up evidence that she and her husband had had a rocky relationship; he was eventually tried and convicted of her murder.

The coroner also found an underwater current and shelf at the bottom of the lake. He believed that many more bodies could be lodged under this shelf, preserved in the form of soap, as was Hallie. Several other people are believed to have drowned in Crescent Lake, but their bodies have never been recovered.

In 2002, investigators solved another missing persons report. On July 3, 1929, Russell Warren drove from Forks to Port Angeles, where he picked up his wife, Blanch, who had been in the hospital. He also paid their grocery bill and bought a new washing machine. After they left Port Angeles, the Warrens vanished. Russell Warren had promised to be back to celebrate the Fourth of July with the couple's two sons, but the boys never saw either Russell or Blanch again. They died thinking that their parents had abandoned them.

The Warrens' route took them on a country road that followed Crescent Lake, and some thought the two had somehow gone into the lake with their car and drowned. In 2002, volunteers took up the cause of their disappearance. They believed that Russell Warren, who had been in a hurry to get home, had fallen asleep at the wheel and driven his car into the lake. Eventually, divers found the wreckage of the Warrens' 1927 Chevrolet along with remnants of the washing machine. Some time later, they found a man's remains tangled in the roots of a submerged cedar tree. Tests confirmed that these belonged to Russell Warren, ending part of the mystery.

Is the bottom of Crescent Lake filled with piles of soap bodies that will continue to slowly rise to the surface over time? It's anyone's guess. But travelers would be wise to drive slowly around the edge of the lake if they don't want to end up lathering the end of someone's fishing line.

Washington State, Land of Giants?

Jonathan Swift's book *Gulliver's Travels* may be one of the most famous works of English literature. Since it was published in the early 1700s, it has never been out of print. It's been made into various animated and live-action movies and was even a miniseries in the 1990s. In the book, the hero, Lemuel Gulliver, makes several sea voyages, during which he meets various races of people, including the six-inch-tall Lilliputians, the Laputas, who lived in cities on clouds, and a race of giants from the land of Brobdingnag. Although most people consider *Gulliver's Travels* a child's fantasy tale, to adults of the time it satirized both the genre of popular travelogue books as well as European society.

In the second part of *Gulliver's Travels,* after a long voyage, Gulliver's ship had anchored in a bay in a strange land, and he came ashore with other sailors to find fresh water. A human being about sixty-six feet tall appeared and captured him. The others in his party escaped to the ship and set sail. The giant put Gulliver on display as a curiosity, until the Queen of the giants bought him and kept him at court.

In the beginning of the tale, Swift describes the voyage that took Gulliver to Brobdingnag. This story was written in the early 1700s, long before most European explorers sailed as far north as the Puget Sound. Despite this, the currents Swift described really existed. A few curious people have plotted this voyage, and some editions of *Gulliver's Travels* have maps showing Brobdingnag in Washington State.

Some Native Americans believed that the Northwest really did have a race of giants living there.

Many of the native peoples who lived on or near the Cascade Mountains thought they shared the land with giants who were about forty feet tall and spent most of the summers in the high peaks, above the snow line.

Perhaps they were so big that it was hard to regulate their temperature and keep cool. The giants appeared after the snows fell, when the Native Americans were living in their winter lodges. The giants were a curious folk. Sometimes people reported seeing a giant's eyeball looking down through the lodge's chimney. In the mornings, the people sometimes found giant footprints in the snow as proof of the visit.

Of all the creatures left behind from an elder age of magic and gods, the giants were probably the most solitary and peaceful. Except during storms, that is. In extreme weather, or if their peace was disturbed, the giants would lash out, ripping trees out by their roots, and tumbling rocks down the mountains, creating avalanches.

Some people believe that the giants are still there today.

The Ghost Ship *Equator*

Most visitors to the Tenth Street Jetty at the Port of Everett probably don't even notice the dilapidated old wooden ship sitting there under a roofed dry dock. Many of the planks have pulled away from the wooden pegs that fastened them to the ship's ribs, and there is a lot of rot on the remaining woodwork. But it was while traveling on this very ship that world-renowned author Robert Louis Stevenson got his inspiration for his stories about the South Seas. Stevenson is best remembered for his classic, *Treasure Island.* But he wrote many other, darker works, including the South Seas stories, which were full of villains, murder, and the unforgiving nature of life at sea.

The *Equator* was built in Binicia, California, in 1888 by the Turner shipyards. She was an original schooner design, named after Mathew Schooner, called the greatest ship designer of his time. Many Turner ships set speed records in their class. Schooners were so well designed that many of them were able to transition from sailing ships to propeller-driven travel. The *Equator* is one of a handful of Turner ships left in the world. And it was a lucky vessel.

The *Equator* sailed for the South Seas trading network soon after she was built. Early in 1889, a hurricane swept through the South Pacific, with winds estimated at over two hundred miles an hour. Six warships were destroyed by the hurricane, and hundreds of people were killed. The only ships that survived in the eye of the storm were the British warship *Calliope* and the *Equator.* After the storm, the *Equator* continued on her course, eventually picking up Robert Louis Stevenson.

Stevenson suffered from weak lungs (probably tuberculosis) and nearly died several times. He traveled the world looking for a place with the right climate for his health. Earlier that year he had arrived in Hawaii aboard the luxury yacht *Casco.* He stayed in the islands for several months with his wife, mother, and stepchildren. During his stay, Stevenson became friends with Hawaii's King David Kalakaua. When he decided to move on, he gained passage on the *Equator,* which was leaving for Samoa in June 1889. King Kalakaua came on board the schooner to see the Stevensons off and wish the party fair winds and a safe voyage.

Stevenson mixed freely with the crew as the ship went from port to port. He wrote several ballads and novels based on the stories and characters he encountered on the voyage. One sailor's tale inspired him to co-write *The Wrecker* with his stepson, Lloyd Osbourne. *The Wrecker* is a tale of insurance fraud, murder, and danger on the high seas, with many elements of intrigue that would apply today. The time on the *Equator* seems to have been memorable for the author, and he references the ship several times in other works and letters.

Stevenson eventually settled in Samoa, where he continued to write and lobby on behalf of the native people. He died there of a cerebral hemorrhage on December 3, 1894, while opening a bottle of wine. People have reported seeing his ghost on the Stevenson estate as late as the 1970s, and his ghost may haunt the *Equator.*

Over time, the *Equator* was outfitted with engines and a propeller and changed routes, spending years sailing between California and Washington State. In 1956, she was stripped and beached in Everett as a breakwater. In 1962, local historians and volunteers freed the ship from the breakwater, and for several years it floated quietly at a dock at the Port of Everett. Or did it?

Several people have reported seeing balls of light floating over the decks of the ship. Others saw strangers on board who disappeared as suddenly as they appeared.

Workers reported that some of their tools disappeared, only to reappear in odd places. Skeptics suggested that people were seeing things, that the workers simply misplaced their tools, and that the globes of light were just Saint Elmo's fire, a natural effect of static electricity in storms. Too bad the reports of orbs did not coincide with storms; they were seen in clear weather too.

In an effort to find out what was happening, two psychics came aboard and held a séance, during which observers reported two glowing lights appearing over the stern of the ship, finally hovering near the psychics. The psychics said that the glowing lights were the spirits of Stevenson and King Kalakaua. Stevenson represented an industrialized and cultured Europe that King Kalakaua tried to bring to Hawaii in his reign. Both men believed in an afterlife, and the psychics said the two of them met again in a friendship that outlasted their deaths.

Although work was done on the *Equator* to stop the effects of earlier rot, it was too late for the craft to ever be seaworthy again. Eventually, the port moved it to a dry dock. When we spoke with an officer at the Port of Everett, he told us that officials were flexible and were looking for proposals from preservationists. We can only hope that someone will step forward with a plan to save the scuttled *Equator,* a ship with a storied past that is still inspiring weird stories today.

Who Was the Real Butch Cassidy?

I've heard that there is evidence to support the fact that Butch Cassidy never died in the shootout in Bolivia, but that that was some other gunfighter and Butch used that opportunity to get out of the criminal world and relocate to Spokane under a

different name, William T. Phillips, and live out the remainder of his life.—*Tony*

The theory that famed Wild Bunch gang leader and Sundance Kid partner Robert LeRoy Parker, alias Butch Cassidy, actually spent his retirement years in Washington is offered in a book called *In Search of Butch Cassidy* by William Pointer. Pointer believes that a manuscript called "The Bandit Invincible," ostensibly a biography of Cassidy written by an elderly man named William T. Phillips, is in fact an autobiography written by Cassidy himself. Pointer claims that the details Phillips knew of Cassidy's life and his apologetic tone suggest that Phillips and Cassidy were really one and the same. In addition, Cassidy's sister Lula maintained that her brother died in Spokane in 1937, although many historians have discounted her story as unreliable.

D. B. Cooper's Dive into Oblivion

Northwest Airlines flight 305 from Portland to Seattle was a routine trip that normally took less than an hour. Flo Schaffner, flight attendant, was no doubt alarmed by the situation that developed on the afternoon of November 24, 1971—the day before Thanksgiving. The flight turned surreal when the clean-cut passenger in seat 15D, who wore a business suit and sunglasses, passed her a note and calmly told her, "Miss, I have a bomb." His briefcase contained alleged sticks of dynamite and a tangle of wires, appearing to bear out the claim. Whether the thirty-six passengers and flight crew of five would live to see the holiday was literally up in the air.

In an era when many planes were hijacked for political purposes, this passenger's goal was classic extortion: He simply wanted to collect a $200,000 ransom. A bit more worrisome was his demand for four parachutes: two backpacks and two backup chest packs. He insisted that everything be delivered to Sea-Tac Airport before the plane landed. The crew relayed the information to Seattle air-traffic control, which contacted Seattle police, who in turn contacted the FBI. The hijacker was named Dan Cooper, not that it meant much. In those days of lax airport security, it wasn't hard to buy a plane ticket under a false name.

Scrutiny of Cooper's demands reveals some shrewd forethought. Insisting that the money and chutes be at the airport when the plane landed gave the authorities roughly thirty minutes to get them there. Any long delays were unadvised, as the short flight had limited fuel to use in a holding pattern. This reduced the authorities' chances to mark the money. Cooper had specified that it be paid in $20 bills, which he'd calculated would weigh a manageable twenty-one pounds. In addition, the smaller denomination wouldn't arouse suspicion, as higher bill denominations might. The demand for parachutes obviously indicated Cooper's intended method of escape and suggested he'd force at least one other person to jump with him. The lawmen dared not endanger innocent lives by providing faulty or booby-trapped chutes!

Thus, it was decided to play Cooper's game for the time being. At five forty p.m., the Boeing 727 was cleared for landing. The money was provided by Northwest Airlines, and despite the time constraints, the FBI managed to acquire some distinctive $20 bills. The vast majority were dated 1969, with serial numbers beginning with L.

They were frantically photographed onto microfilm. The parachutes were acquired from an area skydiving school.

Cooper ordered the pilot, Captain William Scott, to taxi to an isolated section of the tarmac, away from the gathered law enforcement. There he ordered the interior lights turned off to discourage any police snipers. A lone Northwest employee approached the plane, delivering the money and parachutes. Cooper then allowed all the passengers and Flo Schaffner to disembark, leaving only himself and four crew members. At Cooper's insistence, they plotted a course to Mexico with a refueling stop in Reno. Then he laid out some new rules.

He Chutes, He Scores

Cooper insisted that for phase 2 of his caper, the plane be flown at a maximum height of 10,000 feet at a speed of 150 knots (approximately 200 miles an hour). That's about the reasonable limit for skydiving. Cooper warned that he was wearing a wrist altimeter to monitor the crew's compliance. In addition, he insisted that the cabin not be pressurized. At 10,000 feet, they could still breathe normally, and the air pressure inside and out would be equalized, avoiding a big rush of air when he dived.

With the crew forced into the cockpit, the plane took off at seven forty-six p.m. Military jets were scrambled to follow the 727 from a distance, but they proved ineffective: They were simply too fast to follow the relatively slow-moving 727. Conversely, a helicopter carrying lead FBI investigator Ralph Himmelsbach couldn't keep up with it!

Fifteen minutes later an indicator light in the cockpit showed that the 727's rear door had been opened. Via intercom, Captain Scott asked Cooper if he needed any help. "No!" the crew heard Cooper yell. At eight twenty-four, they felt a bump and noted a change in the plane's angle. They knew it must have been due to Cooper's lowering the stairs at the rear door, forgoing Mexico, and jumping then and there. This was a little surprising, as the weather outside was particularly unfriendly. The temperature was below zero, and a minor storm was afoot, with gusting winds and freezing rain. Acting on the side of caution, the crew stayed in the cockpit. However, Captain Scott noted their location over the Cascade Mountains of southern Washington.

Soon after landing in Reno at ten fifteen p.m., the crew finally ventured out. The cabin was empty; they found no sign of Dan Cooper, who had apparently made the jump into the inhospitable sky in his business suit and raincoat. Left behind were two parachutes and Cooper's necktie.

Obviously, the immediate question was, Did he survive? And, if so, where was he? Despite over thirty years of investigation and conjecture, we're no closer to knowing the answers. Dan Cooper was never known to be seen again, alive or otherwise. For all practical purposes, he simply vanished.

A Legend Is Born and a Clue Is Found

Of course, the authorities weren't about to write him off so easily. The FBI immediately began following the most obvious lead. They interviewed several men named Dan Cooper on the off-chance that the culprit had used his real name when buying his plane ticket.

A reporter got wind of one such interview with a Cooper, first initials D. B. He wrote an article making it seem as if the authorities were searching for someone with those specific initials. The name stuck, and the hijacker went down in history as D. B. Cooper.

By the rebellious standards of early 1970s America, Cooper's caper was almost an admirable exploit. With one daring scheme, someone managed to stick it to both a corporation and the law. D. B. Cooper became a folk hero, often compared to the western outlaw Jesse James. Popular songs and books were written about him, and a feature film, *The Pursuit of D. B. Cooper,* starring Treat Williams and Robert Duval, was made. In Ariel, a small town near the location where Cooper is believed to have jumped, a tavern began holding an annual D. B. Cooper Day party.

In February 1980, eight-year-old Brian Ingram, on a hike with his family, found $5,800 in partially decomposed $20 bills buried in the sand on the banks of the Columbia River. The FBI cross-referenced the serial numbers, and the match was positive. This was part of the ransom paid to D. B. Cooper. The find temporarily revitalized the investigation, which had been languishing for a few years. The nearby wilderness was searched extensively, but nothing more was found. The eruption of Mount Saint Helens likely wiped out any additional evidence that may have been there, including Cooper's remains, if he didn't survive.

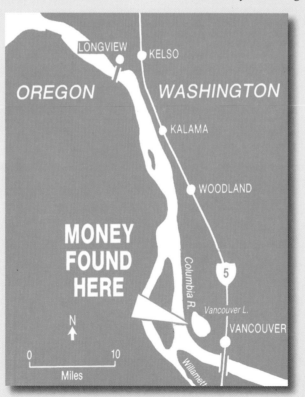

In the end, the only certainty about D. B. Cooper's dive into oblivion is that it remains America's only unsolved hijacking.

A BULLETIN FROM THE F.B.I.

Following is an artist's conception of the hijacker who extorted $200,000 from Northwest Airlines on November 24, 1971.

THIS MAN IS DESCRIBED AS FOLLOWS:

Race	White
Sex	Male
Age	Mid 40's
Height	5' 10" to 6'
Weight	170 to 180 pounds
Build	Average to well built
Complexion	Olive, Latin appearance, medium smooth
Hair	Dark brown or black, normal style, parted on left, combed back; sideburns, low ear level
Eyes	Possibly brown. During latter part of flight put on dark, wrap-around sunglasses with dark rims
Voice	Low, spoke intelligently; no particular accent, possibly from Midwest section of U.S.
Characteristics	Heavy smoker of Raleigh filter tip cigarettes
Wearing Apparel	Black suit; white shirt; narrow black tie; black dress suit; black rain-type overcoat or dark top coat; dark briefcase or attache case; carried paper bag 4" x 12" x 14"; brown shoes

If you have any information which might lead to the identity of this individual, please contact the nearest FBI Office which would be found in the front of your telephone directory.

Since then, there's been speculation that the wrong area was searched. In any case, none of the rest of the money has ever turned up.

Likely (and Unlikely) Suspects

Over the years, the FBI has amassed a list of roughly ten thousand suspects who may or may not be Cooper, always coming up short of anything definitive. One prime suspect was Richard McCoy Jr., who pulled a nearly identical hijacking, successfully making off with half a million dollars. He later died in a shootout with the FBI. Evidence that McCoy was D. B. Cooper was largely circumstantial, but compelling.

Some people have even playfully implicated certain celebrities, including daredevil Evel Knievel—for obvious reasons—and oddball director David Lynch (a native Washingtonian who ostensibly needed the money to fund his film *Eraserhead*, and who later named a character in *Twin Peaks*—an FBI agent, no less—after D. B. Cooper).

Currently, the FBI considers the most likely suspect to be the late Duane Weber, a former burglar and forger turned Florida antiques dealer. His widow, Jo, has described many comments he made over the years that, in hindsight, raise suspicions. The clincher came when he was on his deathbed in 1996. Weber, who had always been secretive about his past, flat out told Jo, "I'm Dan Cooper."

In 2003, DNA tests were conducted in an attempt to put the mystery to rest once and for all. Hair and residue on Weber's personal items were compared to DNA found on cigarette butts left on the 727 by D. B. Cooper (back in the days when smoking was still allowed on planes). True to form of all things involving D. B. Cooper, the results were inconclusive.

In the end, the only certainty about D. B. Cooper's dive into oblivion is that it remains America's only unsolved hijacking.

Unexplained Phenomena

ot many places can outdo the state of Washington when it comes to strange and inexplicable events. In fact, the term "flying saucers" was first coined after a UFO sighting in the blue skies of our home state. The "men in black" also appeared first in Washington, after a UFO sighting in Maury Island.

In addition to spectacular phenomena like flying saucers, Washingtonians have reported a number of other weird happenings, such as rocks raining from the heavens, people bursting spontaneously into flame, and mysterious flying men. Some of these incidents turned out to be hoaxes. Others, we're not so sure.

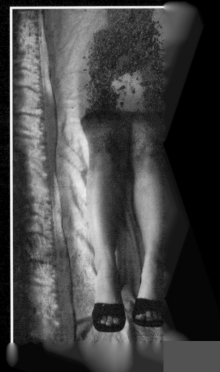

The Great Windshield-Pitting Crisis

In March of 1954, several people called the police in the town of Bellingham, reporting that small holes had mysteriously appeared in their car windshields. The police investigated and decided that vandals had caused the damage with BB guns or buckshot. A few days later people in Mount Vernon, twenty-five miles south, had similar damage to their cars. Slowly, the phenomena seemed to move even farther south, when drivers in Anacortes reported pockmarked windshields.

The authorities in Anacortes took immediate action. On April 13, the police set up roadblocks south of town, looking for a group of window-gouging culprits. Meanwhile, motorists continued to call the police, reporting pits and small holes in over two thousand car windshields. A few people even claimed that they watched the window glass bubble and pit in front of their eyes. It was obvious that this could not have been the work of a handful of vandals.

There were a number of explanations for the cause of the strange holes. The sheriff at Whidbey Island suggested that radioactive dust from recent H-bomb tests in the Pacific had somehow damaged the glass. Another person believed that a new navy radio transmitter had caused the windshields to vibrate and crack. Some people also felt that tiny insect eggs, such as those of sand fleas, had been laid inside the glass, and the hatching young caused the pitting.

But one by one the theories fell. Geiger counters detected no radiation on any of the cars. As for radio waves, physicists found that a car windshield would have had to have been at least one mile wide for radio waves to crack or pit it. And no sand fleas were found in any of the windshield glass.

On April 15, 1954, the pitting phenomena reached Seattle. Local police recorded nearly three thousand mysterious instances of car windshields being damaged, with a strange fine dust and some small pellets appearing on some of the cars. Fearing a dangerous mass panic, the governor, Allan Pomeroy, called the University of Washington and had its science departments investigate. They found that the strange dust and pellets were simple coal dust, which had been drifting around Seattle's air for years. They noted that in most cases, only the front windshields were pitted, not the back. Finally, only older cars had significant windshield pits; new cars had little or no damage.

Officials released a statement the next day. They said that during normal driving on roads with rocks and debris, all cars develop pits and cracks in their windshields. The older the car, the more the damage. Normally, drivers look through or around the holes, rather than at them—that is, until a newspaper report of mysterious windshield pitting causes people to look at their windshields and see the damage. This, the official explanation said, is what had been happening. A report from the police crime lab backed up the scientists, saying that five percent of the damage was caused by hoodlums and ninety-five percent by mass hysteria.

The reports virtually stopped on April 17. In the weeks during the incident, though, there were some extra fender benders, as people spent more time looking at the sky or their windshields than at the road. Fortunately, there were no fatalities.

Maury Island Incident

The 1947 Maury Island incident is one of the lesser known UFO occurrences, but it should be better known for several reasons. It is probably the first time a witness claimed that a "man in black" intimidated him into silence, and although it took place before the famed UFO crash in Roswell, New Mexico, there were many similarities between the two. Moreover, both of the military intelligence officers investigating the sighting died in a tragic air crash before they could complete their investigation. Unfortunately, the two principal witnesses, Harold Dahl and Fred Crisman, became objects of suspicion and controversy as the investigation continued.

In 1947, logs floating on the water's surface were a common hazard in the Puget Sound. They escaped from "jams" waiting to be turned into lumber at nearby mills on the shore. Several men worked as an informal harbor patrol, snagging these logs and taking them to the mills for a salvage fee. Harold Dahl worked on one of the patrol boats, and his supervisor on shore was Fred Crisman.

Dahl reported that on June 21, he was on his boat with two men, his son, and their dog. Around two in the afternoon, Dahl's boat approached the east shore of Maury Island, about six miles west of Des Moines.

Dahl looked in the sky and

saw six objects floating about two thousand feet above his ship. The objects were made of reflective metal, doughnut-shaped, and about one hundred feet in diameter. The center holes were about twenty-five feet in diameter. Dahl said he also saw round portholes and what he thought was an observation window. Five of the craft circled over the sixth, which dropped slowly. It stopped and hovered about five hundred feet above the water.

Dahl put to shore because he was afraid the center

Federal Bureau of Investigation
United States Department of Justice
407 U. S. Court House
Seattle 4, Washington
August 18, 1947

DIRECTOR, FBI   RE: FLYING DISCS SIGHTED BY
                                     TACOMA, WASHINGTON
                                     SI - X

Dear Sir:

The following, in general, are the facts regarding the
flying disc story that started by the Tacoma Times, the Boise Statesman, which
subsequently resulted in news stories that a B-25 carrying Army Intelligence was shot
and the Chicago Times that a B-25 carrying Army Intelligence was shot
down or sabotaged over Kelso, Washington on August 1, 1947 because it was carrying some flying disc fragments.

The original story, as related by   in his boat near Maury
was to the effect that   while patrolling in his boat near Maury
Island, Washington, sighted six flying discs, one of which fluttered to the
earth and disintegrated, showering his boat with fragments which caused some
damage to the boat and killed his dog.   wrote a letter to
of Ziff-Davis Company which publishes fantastic adventure magazines in
Chicago, sending him fragments of the flying disk and relating the above story,
by   telegraphed   Boise, Idaho, who was the first to report
requested Trans-Radio News in Chicago to verify the story as related
by   then engaged and whom   had previously made a contract for
sighting the flying disc and whom   had previously made a contract for
a story regarding the flying disc, to come to Tacoma and check the story,
related by   came to Tacoma, Washington July 30, 1947 and
arranged for a meeting the following day, July 31, with   who also
in his room 502, Winthrop Hotel, Tacoma, Washington,   United Airlines Pilot who
called to attend the meeting   flying disc fragments, and Army Intelligence to attend
had also reported seeing flying disc fragments, and Army Intelligence to attend

                                     RECORDED   162-83944
                    EX-64   &   34 SEP 30 1947
                                     INDEXED
                                     14

aircraft was going to crash into his boat. Once on land, he took several pictures with his camera. The lower ship stayed in position for about five minutes, with the others still circling above. Then one of the ships left the formation and moved down, touching the lower ship. The two kept contact for several minutes, until Dahl said he heard a thud. Suddenly thousands of pieces of what he thought were newspapers dropped from inside the center ship.

Most of the debris landed in the bay, though some hit the beach. Dahl recovered a few pieces, finding it was a lightweight white metal. Along with that metal, the ship dropped about twenty tons of a dark metal, which he said looked like lava rock. When this material hit the water, it was so hot that steam erupted. He and the other men took cover after several pieces landed on his boat, damaging it. Some debris hit his son on the arm, burning him, and another piece killed his dog.

After the rain of metal, the craft rose into the air and, together with the other ships, headed west out to sea. Dahl went to his boat and tried to call for help, but the radio did not work. He sailed back toward his dock, dropping the dog over the side in a burial at sea. Dahl took his son to the hospital for treatment and then told his boss, Fred Crisman, what had happened.

When the prints from Dahl's camera were developed, they showed the strange airships. However, the negatives had spots on them, which Dahl said might have been caused by exposure to radiation. Crisman did not believe Dahl's story, but he nevertheless went back to Maury Island, where he gathered some samples of the rocks that had been dropped. He said that while he was gathering the rocks, one of the airships appeared overhead, as if it was watching him.

Dahl told investigators that the next morning, a man wearing a black suit visited him and suggested they go to breakfast together. Dahl drove his own car, following the stranger's new black Buick to a restaurant. While they ate, the stranger asked no questions; instead he gave a detailed account of what had happened to Dahl the day before. The man in black warned Dahl that bad things would happen to him and his family if he told anyone about the incident.

Disregarding this ominous advice, Dahl and Crisman contacted publisher Ray Palmer (a year or two later Palmer founded *FATE* magazine) in Chicago and sent him a package containing a box of metal fragments and statements about the strange happenings on July 21 and 22. Palmer got in touch with Kenneth Arnold (see the following story: "Coming of the Saucers, Mount Rainier"), who had begun investigating UFOs.

Arnold arrived in Tacoma in late July with airline pilot E. Smith, examined Dahl's boat, and interviewed both Dahl and Crisman. At this point, however, their story began to get a little vague. They didn't produce the pictures Dahl had supposedly taken of the event, and Dahl told Arnold that his son had disappeared. (He said later that his son was found waiting tables in Montana, but couldn't remember how he got there.) Then, on the afternoon of July 31, Captain Lee Davidson and First Lieutenant Frank Brown of the U.S. Army Air Force flew up to Tacoma from Hamilton Field, California.

In addition to being pilots, the two men were intelligence specialists. They met with Arnold, Smith, and Crisman for several hours. One of the officers said that he thought there might have been something to the story, but they couldn't stay to investigate further. They had to leave around midnight, in a hurry to be at Hamilton Field on August 1, the day when the air force was to split from the army.

The two officers flew out of McChord Air Field around two o'clock in the morning on a B-25 bomber, with a crew of two enlisted men. About twenty minutes later the airplane crashed near Centralia. The two crew members managed to parachute to safety, but Davidson and Brown were killed, making them the air force's first casualties.

Dahl and Crisman said that the air force officers had taken with them some of the strange metal the airship had dropped. Local newspapers and the FBI received anonymous phone calls stating that the plane was shot down to cover up the information Brown and Davidson had found. Because of the loss of life, the air force broadened its investigation and the FBI launched its own.

The air force investigators determined that the crash had been a terrible accident, caused by one of the engines catching fire. When another air force investigator visited Dahl's boat, he said that the damage he saw did not match the damage described. There were no piles of metal on Maury Island, and the existing samples looked like slag from a metal smelter. His conclusion matched that of the FBI investigator: that Dahl and Crisman had faked the incident to gain publicity for a magazine article.

The FBI warned the men that their hoax had not succeeded but said that if they dropped the matter, the government would not prosecute them for fraud, which had resulted in the deaths of the two officers. A very generous offer, considering the damage that had been done.

At first, Dahl and Crisman went along. They recanted the story, said it was a fake, and refused to give any further interviews on the matter. But a few years later, in the January 1950 issue of *FATE* magazine, Crisman stated that the incident HAD happened, and Kenneth Arnold included Maury Island in his 1952 book *The Coming of the Saucers.*

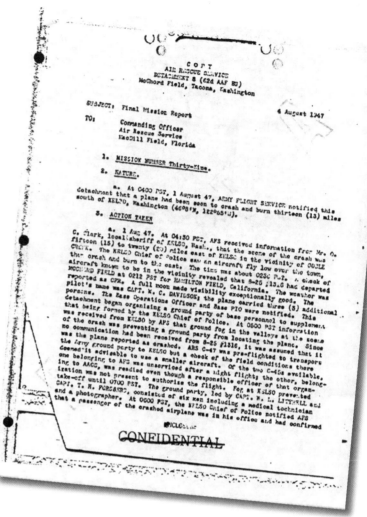

Today most people believe that Crisman and Dahl faked the incident, perpetuating a hoax that got out of control. Other people believe that the U.S. government was behind a conspiracy that may have involved anything from UFOs to dumping nuclear waste in the Puget Sound. They believe a shadow government agency sabotaged the B-25 bomber in order to eliminate the investigators and to label Dahl and Crisman as frauds.

Even sixty years after the incident, some other investigators visited the crash site, hoping to find some of the strange rocks to prove things one way or another, but so far, no final answers have been found.

Coming of the Saucers, Mount Rainier

In late November 1896, a couple named Mr. and Mrs. St. John told the *Tacoma Daily Ledger* about a strange nighttime sighting. They said they were lying in bed around midnight, looking out the window. Mrs. St. John saw a strange light in the sky east of Mount Rainier. She woke her husband, and he saw it too. They said it was as bright as a lighthouse beacon. It flashed several times, and each time it flashed, various colored lights shot out from the center of the object like spokes of a wheel.

Did this strange object reappear over fifty years later? Certainly something like it was seen again in 1947, and this sighting led to the popular use of the term "flying saucer." The phrase owes its existence to a newspaperman's misquote of a pilot named Kenneth Arnold regarding a strange experience he had on June 24, 1947, one similar to the St. Johns's experience in 1896.

Kenneth Arnold lived in Boise, Idaho, where he owned a business that made and installed fire control systems. Business must have been slow in the summer of 1947, because Arnold spent June 24 in his

airplane, flying over the Washington Cascades. He was looking for a missing marine airplane, hoping for a $10,000 reward. At two fifty p.m. he was traveling east over the mountains toward Mount Adams, when he saw nine large metallic flying objects.

These craft were about twenty-five miles away, at an elevation of ten thousand feet, traveling very, very fast.

He noticed that they did not fly in straight lines like ordinary airplanes or make wide turns. Instead, they dipped and swerved, seeming to follow the mountain peaks from Mount Rainier to Mount Adams. Arnold started the stopwatch on his airplane control panel. Based on the distance between the two mountains (forty-five miles) and the time it took the objects to travel it, he estimated they were flying at twelve hundred miles an hour. At first, Arnold thought they were jet aircraft, even though their speed was far faster than that of the jets of that era.

Once the strange craft vanished in the distance, Arnold continued his search, until he landed in Yakima. He reported the incident to the Civil Aeronautics Administration and the next day flew to Pendleton, Oregon, where the press mobbed him. Before Arnold's sighting, there had been earlier reports of similar objects, and the press and U.S. government always referred to these objects as flying disks, as did Arnold.

He told the reporters that the nine craft were about a hundred feet across, thin, and disk- or crescent-shaped. Although the front was round, the rear looked chopped off and came to a point. He said that he was amazed that there was no tail, as on a normal aircraft, and that the craft did not make any noise. When one of the reporters asked him how the objects maneuvered, Arnold replied that they moved kind of like a saucer would move if someone skipped it across a lake. The reporter wrote down that Arnold said the aircraft looked like flying saucers, and the misquote stuck.

Although this was not the first unidentified flying object ever reported, the publicity set off a rash of new sightings. After a radio interview, a number of people from the Seattle area and the Midwest contacted the media and reported seeing multiple flying objects on the same day. On July 4, a United Airlines flight crew reported seeing flying objects over Idaho. A few days after that, on July 8, another flying saucer was reported to have crashed in Roswell, New Mexico, and the alien aircraft craze really took off. Newspapers contacted military officials, who denied that they were testing experimental jet aircraft in the Washington Cascades.

Skeptics believed that Arnold could have been fooled by mirages created by air inversions or even by reflections of his own airplane off the atmosphere. Later, someone suggested that he'd seen a swarm of meteors that flashed and burned out quickly. Despite these suggestions, no one could prove that Arnold was mistaken, including the air force, which had launched its own investigation. Their findings led them to form a team that eventually turned into Project Blue Book, a formalized government investigation of UFOs undertaken from 1952 to 1970.

The issue of whether UFOs are really flying craft from outer space is full of controversy, and much of this, including its central term, had its beginnings in our home state. It is interesting to note that although skeptics do not believe that Kenneth Arnold saw flying machines from other worlds, none of them accuse him of deliberate fraud. Arnold's clear honesty and candor led the way to open discussion of the phenomena.

Spontaneous Human Combustion

The question of whether or not spontaneous human combustion, a living human being suddenly bursting into flames, really happens is a very old one. Hollywood has shown people in flames as a consequence of God's wrath on sinners. Victorian author Charles Dickens killed off one of his villains in this mystical way, and many scholars have witnessed or described dramatic, though perhaps less supernatural, examples of the phenomenon.

Well, wouldn't you know it: Washington has had at least one instance of what might have been spontaneous human combustion—with a twist: The victim was already dead.

On the night of December 6, 1973, Betty and Sam Satlow were closing up the tavern they owned in Hoquiam. Sam told Betty she could go home, perhaps because she had been drinking heavily and was not much help. Around five a.m. the next morning, Sam went home, where he found Betty unconscious at the wheel of her car, which was parked in the garage. He called paramedics, who tried unsuccessfully to revive her. An autopsy showed that she died of carbon monoxide poisoning, with a fifty-three percent saturation in her blood.

The logical assumption was that Mrs. Satlow had committed suicide, but there was no evidence that she had hooked a hose from her exhaust to the inside of her car. The autopsy also showed that she had a blood alcohol level of .26 percent, which is very high, so police suggested that she might have just fallen asleep in her car and simply did not wake up. The coroner decreed the question of suicide was indeterminate and left it at that.

After the autopsy, Betty's body was taken to the Coleman Mortuary, where she was embalmed and placed in a metal casket. The family gathered for a service on the night of December 9, and then the casket was closed and the funeral parlor locked up for the night. The next day, in the early morning hours, a tenant living in an apartment above the mortuary's chapel woke up smelling smoke and called the fire department.

When the firemen arrived, they found that Betty's coffin was at the center of a tremendously hot fire. Once they put out the flames, they examined the metal coffin, which seemed to have acted like an oven. They found that Mrs. Satlow's upper body was reduced to ashes and a few bone fragments. Below the hips, her body was more or less intact, perhaps because there was less oxygen inside the sealed lower coffin lid.

At first, police thought the fire was a bizarre case of vandalism. However, the fire department could find no evidence of arson, no lighter fluid or accelerant, and no sign of a break-in. Ruling out vandalism, they had no rational explanation as to how the fire started. The police turned over portions of the coffin to the U.S. Treasury Department laboratory, which examined the materials. The lab technicians could not explain how the fire started either.

Spontaneous human combustion is a hard-to-prove phenomenon. Most of the time, there are no witnesses. Friends or family members simply find a handful of burned bones and ashes that was once their loved one. The victim is usually at rest, either sleeping or sitting in a chair, though some have been engaged in vigorous exercise when they caught fire. The blaze usually leaves the flesh, blood, and most of the bone from the victim's body completely burned. This would happen only if the temperature was very, very hot—thousands of degrees—yet nearby furniture is often unburned or barely singed. Autopsies usually reveal that the victim's body seems to have burned from the inside out. Various rational explanations for the phenomenon have been put forth: electrical wiring shorts, static electricity, and sometimes something as simple as a dropped match. Yet there are some cases that just don't lend themselves to the rational.

Fifteen-Dollar Fire Ball

Ordinarily, lightning is caused by a buildup of electricity in the air, which seeks a ground on the earth. This ground is usually the tallest object around, like a tree or a building. Knowing the way lightning works, most people also know the precautions they can take to avoid being struck: don't stand under a tall tree in a thunderstorm, stay away from metal, and so on. But these precautions don't work in the case of ball lightning, as Robert Burch found out.

In 1951, Burch was staying on the fifth floor of the YMCA in Bremerton. Like many men of that time, he'd come to the Seattle-Tacoma area to get a job in its booming economy. On November 6, he was standing in front of a mirror in his room when something caught his eye. He had his back to an open window, and he watched as a reddish orange ball of fire headed straight for him. When it was only inches away, the fireball exploded with a blinding flash of light and a loud bang.

Burch felt a sharp pain in his arm and was knocked down by the force of the explosion. It took him a while to stand again and look around his room. He found that the windowsill where the ball of energy had entered was blackened and still hot. The paper in his wastebasket had caught fire, and the two radio cabinets were also damaged by the heat and electrical energy.

Once the fire was put out, Robert Burch left for the hospital, with the help of a local

policeman. As it turned out, the officer had been standing outside the YMCA building, and according to some sources, watched the ball of energy seemingly fall out of the sky and enter the YMCA window. At the hospital, doctors treated Burch for shock and second-degree electrical burns on his arm. He recovered and was back to work soon after his encounter with what some people think was ball lightning.

The fire department disagreed with that assessment. According to them, Burch was running two radios as well as a lamp out of the same electrical socket. This overloaded the wiring, causing the electrical discharge. Maybe they felt Burch invented the report to avoid paying the YMCA a $15 charge for the damage the explosion did to the room and furnishings. Whatever the case, the firemen couldn't explain the testimony of the policeman who witnessed the event while standing outside the building.

Reports of ball lightning usually occur after a thunder and lightning storm, but the phenomenon has been seen in clear and sunny weather. The ball is usually said to be anywhere from eight to sixteen inches in size. Witnesses have reported perfectly round balls, teardrop shapes, and even rod-shaped masses of energy, which they described as being reddish yellow or bluish white in color. Sometimes the lightning appears, hovers in the air for a few seconds, and quickly dissipates. In other cases, it moves with a bouncing motion, striking an object as if on purpose. The most frightening reports come when the lightning enters a room through open doors or windows, terrorizing the people inside. In World War II, air force pilots noticed balls of light following them and called them "foo fighters."

Despite all the sightings, scientists doubted that ball lightning could exist. Electricity needs some kind of ground to manifest itself, and ball lightning apparently does not. There have been various attempts to explain it over the years. One suggestion is that sometimes when lightning strikes the earth a small portion of whatever it hits is vaporized. This gas is infused with electromagnetic energy, which keeps the gas compressed for a few seconds before it dissipates. If it strikes an object, it releases the energized gas in the form of an explosion.

In one experiment, scientists vaporized pure silicon with an electrical arc and did indeed produce luminous orbs the size of Ping-Pong balls. So perhaps Robert Burch wasn't just trying to dodge a $15 fine after all.

He watched as a reddish orange ball of fire headed straight for him. When it was only inches away, the fireball exploded with a blinding flash of light and a loud bang.

Flying Men of Chehalis and Longview

Human beings have always dreamed of flying like birds on the wing. There are reports dating back to the early twentieth-century about jet packs and secretive inventors with weird flying suits. Naturally, Washington has had two reported sightings of strange flying men.

On January 6, 1948, Mrs. Bernice Zaikowski was standing outside her farmhouse on the outskirts of Chehalis when something in the air attracted her attention. She looked up, she said, to see a man flying about twenty feet above her barn. He was in a vertical position, kept aloft by a set of silver wings that were fastened to a kind of harness, and she heard a whizzing or whirring sound that came from the wings or harness. As she watched, Mrs. Zaikowski saw the man reach up to his chest to adjust what she thought were controls on the harness. Some children approached and watched the man with her. A few minutes later, he flew away.

This event took place shortly after several UFO sightings in Washington State. The air force officers investigating the Maury Island sighting had crashed only a few miles away from Mrs. Zaikowski's home. Was there a connection?

A similar story was told by Mrs. Viola Johnson, in Longview. On April 8 of the same year, while on break from her job, she reported seeing not just one flying man, but three. Around three p.m., she saw what she thought was a small flock of seagulls flying toward her. As they got closer, she saw that the gulls were really three men wearing what she described as gray, minuteman-style uniforms. They began circling overhead, at an altitude of about two hundred and fifty feet. She rushed inside the store and alerted her co-workers to the strange sight outside.

Only the janitor, James Pittman, made it out in time to see the fliers. Pittman told reporters that he too saw three men in the air, wearing some kind of strapped-on motor. He had only a quick glimpse, but said that he did not see any wings on the men, just a harness, as they flew away northward at "medium" speed. Johnson and Pittman said that a boy standing outside also saw the flying men.

It is interesting that although the two stories were similar, they had some very different details. Mrs. Zaikowski saw one man and did not mention a uniform. Mrs. Johnson saw three men dressed in distinctive uniforms. But the big difference is how the men flew. Although the men in both sightings wore some kind of harness that made mechanical sounds, Mrs. Zaikowski's flier had wings, while Mr. Pittman said that he did not see any wings on the men.

The Chehalis sighting has been described on several Web sites and in magazines such as *FATE*; however, there are a few unresolved issues with this incident. The local Chehalis newspaper did not carry any stories of flying men, which would have been front-page news in Chehalis and in Tacoma and Portland.

Mrs. Johnson's story made the front page of the *Longview Daily News,* but the newspaper archive reveals one interesting story that might provide a clue to the sightings. On April 7, the paper had a front-page story declaring that it was National Laugh Week. The writer suggested that, "In these days of stress, having a laugh at anyone's expense is worth enjoying." There was some kind of competition to send in the funniest story. Did Mrs. Johnson and Mr. Pittman stage their sighting to fool their co-workers?

Or were the men in black active in Washington State, hiding all evidence of high-tech flying suits from the general public? The air force did not admit the existence of a manned jet pack until the late 1950s. Perhaps Longview and Chehalis were the fliers' first testing sites.

Raining Rocks

Strange objects that seemingly fall from the sky have been reported for centuries, both in America and around the world. These things range from animals such as fish to grain and even blood. But perhaps the most common objects that people report raining down from the sky have been rocks of various sizes. Explanations for the source of these missiles run the gamut from charged psychic energies, to pranksters, tornadoes, or poltergeists. One follower of the weird, Charles Fort, jokingly suggested that a civilization of people live in the clouds, and from time to time, they throw garbage down to the earth below.

Yet, none of these explanations seems applicable to the fall of rocks that landed on one house in Spokane during the summer of 1977.

On August 30, Mrs. Billy Tipton phoned police and

More rocks zoom in

By DALE GOODWIN
Spokesman-Review staff writer

About 20 more rocks hammered a South Side Spokane home Friday, bringing the total to about 150 hits since the bombardment began Tuesday afternoon.

Police said they remained mystified by the rock-throwing caper and said no new leads had been turned up.

Rocks, some lobbed and others hurled at high speed, continued sporadically to pelt the home, S2403 Manito Blvd., Friday, beginning about 11:30 a.m., Mrs. Billy Tipton, wife of the owner, said.

Two more windows were riddled by speeding rocks Friday, bringing the total number of broken windows in excess of a dozen, Mrs. Tipton said.

She said there is no pattern for the bombardment. Tuesday the first hit was at 3:30 p.m., Wednesday at 9:30 a.m., Thursday and Friday about 11:30 a.m.

Police have interviewed persons who live as far away as five or six blocks but have turned up no leads, Mrs. Tipton said.

"There is just no rhyme nor reason for this," she said. "I am sure it is not a vendetta."

She praised the police department for its efforts. "Policemen are working long hours here, then coming back on their off time to help out.

"This whole ... I'm mad," she ...

The rocks a ... direction, Mrs ...

"They fire s ... direction to ge ... and then hit ... tion."

A rock pier ... window in the ... noon and shat ...

Rocks hittin, ... have a horizo ... said. A 15-foo ... the porch and ... tall line the bo ... ing such shots ... police said.

Tentative pl ... and fire depar ... get a better ... hood were not ... although the ... them, along w ... were still bein ...

Police Sgt. ... "Everyone ha ... who is doing t ... tigating them ...

The east, w ... the house hav ... from the rocks ...

Bombarding of Home With Rocks Is Mystery

Spokane police this afternoon were seeking whoever has been bombarding a South Side residence since late yesterday afternoon.

Police Capt. Charles H Crabtree said that at least eight windows have been broken out of the home of Billy Tipton, S2403 Manito Blvd. Crabtree said the rocks had also struck other portions of the house, inflicting mino damage.

"We don't know wher they're coming from, but most of the projectiles ar rocks about an inch in diamter," Crabtree said.

Police motorcycle office Roger L. Gehrig said he wa struck in his motorcyc boot by one of the rocks whe he was about a block wa from the Tipton home abo noon today.

Officer A. W. Schaber sa

New Windows Due for Home

Glass installers took measurements today to begin replacing more than a dozen windows smashed out in a bizarre rock attack on a ...

... ten and her three sons, one 7-year-old and two teen-agers.

The home has been pelted by more than 150 rocks since Tuesday afternoon.

... one barrage, P ... harles Crabtree ... it when he climb ... of the home at ... lvd. to see whe ... re coming fron ...

... hough the hom ... d with police, r ... able to expla ... or catch the ... culprit.

... 20 golf-bal

Barrage continues at South Hill home

By DALE GOODWIN
Spokesman-Review staff writer

Rocks continued to pelt a South Side Spokane home Thursday although the frequency of the bombardments had decreased since they began Tuesday afternoon, Police Lt Jerald E. Oien said.

Rocks hitting the front side of the house apparently have had a straight trajectory he ...

Thursday night, Oien said. At least half a dozen windows on the front and north side of the house have been broken.

Police said some of the rocks have been lobbed at the house while others have been hurled at high speed.

... dge, there ha ... ttacks," police ... an Leuven said ...

... uce Campbell ... ad been turned ... hope to have ... en windows in

Rock Projectiles Baffling Officers

"It's scary — it's like living in something out of 'Twilight Zone' — it's unbelievable."

That was the reaction of Mrs. Billy Tipton, S2403 Manito Blvd., to the bombardment of her home by golf-ball ... which resumed at ...

... searched the neighborhood, the rocks propelled with considerable velocity, continued to smack into the Tipton home.

Crabtree climbed atop the roof of the home yesterday afternoon and ... most immediately two rocks were ... ... nding near him ...

Rock bombardment halts

Spokane police detectives said Saturday no additional rocks had pelted a South Side house since Friday night.

But the investigation is continu... ... o the mysterious ... h perhaps 150 ... d windows in the ... rs. Billy Tipton, ... Blvd., since

... the house have been broken since the attacks began Tuesday afternoon.

The east, west and north sides of the house have sustained damage from the rocks.

Rocks hitting the front of the house had a horizonal trajectory, police said. A 15-foot overhang protects the porch, and trees more than 50 feet tall line the boulevard in front, making such shots "nearly impossible," police said.

Mrs. Tipton and her three sons have installed plastic covering over the windows to protect the home from the elements.

In addition, glass installers Saturday took measurements to begin replacing the smashed windows.

From the end of August to September 6, one hundred to one hundred and fifty stones fell on the Tiptons' home.

complained that someone was throwing rocks at her house. When the police arrived, they learned that the case was more than simple vandalism. A window was broken on the front porch, which was protected by a covered roof. In order to break the window, a vandal would have needed to stand out on the street and throw a rock like a baseball. This was not possible, because the front of the house was shielded from the street by a high wall. Other broken windows were hidden from the road by trees.

In addition to the stones that broke the windows, Mrs. Tipton complained that several rocks had hit the roof of the house; these rocks seemed to have fallen vertically, from high above. Captain Charles Crabtree climbed onto the roof to get a view of the neighborhood. While he stood there, two rocks landed next to him. The captain could not tell where they came from. If a human vandal was behind this scheme, he was obviously not afraid of the police.

With that in mind, the police set up stakeouts in the neighborhood, but the rocks still fell, day and night. From the end of August to September 6, one hundred to one hundred and fifty stones fell on the Tiptons' home. The hail seemed to stop after that, and the police ceased their surveillance. They never caught a suspect but theorized that someone in the neighborhood was throwing the stones with some kind of rocket launcher.

Others believe that people who are frustrated or angry are capable of causing psychic reactions like remotely moving objects, or causing rocks to fly around and pounding noises to be heard. The Tiptons had three adopted sons who ranged in age from late childhood to adolescence. Could their energies have caused the falling rocks? And what about Billy Tipton, the man of the house?

Billy Tipton was a Spokane celebrity who, in the 1930s, began a career as a jazz musician and singer. He had released several successful albums and founded the Billy Tripton Trio, which became a popular house band at the Tin Pan Alley Club. However, by the time of the rock throwing, Tipton was retiring from music and his marriage was in trouble. The children were unruly, and the couple argued frequently about how to raise them.

Could Mr. Tipton have unconsciously caused some kind of poltergeist activity? He certainly had enough stress—because he was keeping an incredible secret. (Here's where the story gets very weird!) Billy Tipton was a woman.

Billy Tipton was born as Dorothy Lucille Tipton in 1914. She had always been interested in playing music, but at that time, women couldn't play in professional jazz bands. In 1933, Tipton began dressing as a man and appearing in small clubs. As Dorothy became more famous, she adopted a male persona all the time, using her father's nickname of Billy. The general public did not know this until Tipton died in 1989, and the coroner's examination revealed the truth.

Tipton had several wives, and according to at least one of them, Billy said that "he" had been involved in a car accident, which injured his back and ribs so badly that he had to wear a body brace. This same accident, according to Billy, also limited his sex life. This claim led to the adoption of the three boys, who remembered seeing their father wearing a body brace at all times.

So: Frustrated musician with a very taboo secret? Teenage angst? Local pranksters? What was behind the rain of rocks? All we'll ever know is that this one is truly weird—and truly unexplained.

Bizarre Beasts

Maybe *it's the climate* or maybe it's the coffee, but throughout Washington State there is a colossal catalogue of cryptids—strange, sometimes scary critters unknown to mainstream science. Imagine, for example, you are hiking in the Olympic Mountains when you hear the sound of thunder overhead. Could it be the powerful Thunderbird, which has darkened the skies over Mount Saint Helens and Mount Olympus for centuries? Or take another hike near Mount Saint Helens. Suddenly there's a really BAD smell, and you realize that you're being watched by something not . . . quite . . . human. You've come across the most sought-after forest creature in the world: Bigfoot. Want to avoid higher primate encounters? Try the rain forests near the Puget Sound, where one look up into a pine tree might reveal the elusive and endangered Tree Octopus.

Come to think of it, maybe you should just stay in and vicariously enjoy these experiences through this book; it's safer that way. So sit back, sip the joe, and read on.

The Thunderbird

Virtually every Native American culture has stories of a giant magical bird, which most call the Thunderbird. The name comes from the sound the bird's wings make when in full flight, like thunderclaps. The Thunderbird's wings, it was said, were larger than two canoes, and the feathers the size of canoe paddles. Its eyes glowed red, and lightning shot out of its claws. At least two Thunderbirds flew in Washington: one in the Cascade Mountains, and the other in the Olympic Mountains of the Puget Sound.

The first bird lived part of the time inside Mount Saint Helens. It created earthquakes and volcanic eruptions when it rolled over in its sleep. When awake, it lived at the bottom of Spirit Lake, at the foot of the mountain. The native people saw the water bubble and froth when the Thunderbird was angry. According to one legend, this bird attacked many other creatures, until Raven killed it, after which the Thunderbird's body fell into the Columbia River, where it formed several islands. Other people believe it is still alive and is responsible for the recent eruptions at the mountain.

The second Thunderbird was friendlier to humanity. Many generations ago, the Quillayute people of the Olympic Peninsula were starving, in part because a giant killer whale was eating all the fish. Their chieftain appealed to the Great Spirit for help, and it summoned the Thunderbird. The Thunderbird appeared to the people with the body of the whale in its claws and gave it to them to eat, then flew to Mount Olympus, where it made its home. Though this bird was helpful to humans, it valued its privacy. Hunters climbing the mountain were frightened away by the ice- and rockfalls it created when it smelled them nearby.

In addition to explaining natural phenomena such as earthquakes and volcanic eruptions, the Thunderbird

legends have some basis in fact. Some people think they were (and are) eagles, which are not common in the area but are known to the native people there. And the largest living bird in North America, the California condor, makes its home in the Sierra Madre. A long way to travel to Washington State. Or is it?

Even the Lewis and Clark expedition had an experience with a giant bird. On November 18, 1805, Captain Clark led a party of eleven men to Cape Disappointment, where they saw the Pacific Ocean for the first time. On that trip, one of the men killed a bird they had never seen before, one with a wingspan of over nine feet. Based on their description, it was a California condor. A small population of these birds probably had survived in the mountains of the Pacific Northwest until the arrival of Europeans, when they were hunted into extinction.

There are other possible explanations for the mighty Thunderbird. In 2005, a group from the Oregon Archaeological Society was excavating a site near

to pick up and swallow small prey whole. These birds probably thrived at the end of the last Ice Age. Paleontologists think they died out as the glaciers melted.

In the late 1960s and early 1970s, several people living in southeast Washington reported seeing a large bird with a wingspan the size of a Piper Cub airplane. And passengers on an airplane once sighted one of these birds flying next to them. A cryptozoologist, a researcher who studies such unknown animals, noted that most of these sightings happened when people were at the edge of large storm fronts. He suggested that birds this size needed the high winds to generate enough lift for them to fly, which earned them the name of Thunderbirds.

Some wildlife biologists are discussing plans to introduce California condors to the Columbia River gorge. The birds are not afraid of humans or human activities, and many of those raised in captivity and released into the wild have been killed when interacting with people or structures such as power lines. The human population in the Columbia River gorge scenic area is much lower than in southern California, and the birds may have a better chance of surviving here.

Woodburn, Oregon. They found what they thought was an elk bone, but upon further analysis it was discovered that the bone and several others on-site belonged to an ancient bird known as the Teratorn. Teratorn bones have recently been found in Argentina and all across North America—in Oregon, California, Florida, and New York. The largest example found had a wingspan of over twenty-four feet and weighed over 170 pounds. It was probably a carnivore, as it had a beak and jaw designed

The native people have many stories about Sasquatch. They said
it resembled human beings, but did not speak human languages.
Almost all legends also say it was gigantic and smelled bad.

On the Trail of Bigfoot

Forgetting the tabloid newspaper stories about Bigfoot coming from outer space to mate with humans, tales of Bigfoot (also known as Sasquatch) in the Pacific Northwest go back hundreds—possibly thousands—of years. Recent archaeological investigations have shown that across the world many creatures thought to have been extinct survived into our modern age. Some believe that Bigfoot was the first great ape to inhabit the Pacific Northwest, with man following second.

The native people have many stories about Sasquatch. They said it resembled human beings, but did not speak human languages. Almost all legends also say it was gigantic and smelled bad. The feet of these creatures were shaped like a bear's, but were over eighteen inches long. They lived in holes in the ground in the mountains or deep in the woods, and emerged in the spring and fall to fish by the river, mostly avoiding people. Some were friendly, while others were thieves and very dangerous.

The Lummi Indians of the Puget Sound frequently saw two kinds of Sasquatch. There was a big, peaceful timber giant and a small, meaner one. The second creature carried a magic stick, with which it could hit any tree trunk three times and knock the tree down. Other stories about the Sasquatch say that they chattered like animals or owls and charmed people. They entered human camps and stole things, and sometimes kidnapped or killed children.

Scientists have discovered fossils in Asia of a great ape they called *Gigantopithecus*. Based on fossil evidence, the *Gigantopithecus* was a vegetarian creature that stood over six feet high. People looking for an explanation for Bigfoot believe that the *Gigantopithecus* spread to North America, and while the Asian *Gigantopithecus* died out, its North American relatives survived.

Sasquatch in Love

Many cryptozoologists believe that as vegetarians, the Sasquatch are not normally aggressive. An exception to this is when a male detects the presence of a fertile female, whether Sasquatch or human. Their need to mate might drive them to kidnap the female, as the following stories seem to indicate.

Puget Sound

On the Fraser River, along the Canadian–Washington border, a Salishan woman was captured by a Sasquatch, who took her for a mate. She came back to her people with hair growing over her body and unable to speak her tribal language. It took several powerful shamans to return her to normal. Later she was with some hunters who saw some Sasquatch. She asked the hunters not to shoot them, because they could be members of her family.

Fort Vancouver

In the 1830s, the Indian wife of a Hudson Bay Company employee was kidnapped by a Sasquatch while walking outside the Fort Vancouver stockade. It carried her into the woods, but by screaming and fighting, she escaped after a few minutes. She encountered some hunters who pursued the creature. They may have shot at it and tracked it for a while, but it escaped them.

Patrick, the Sasquatch Boy

The Colville Indians encountered several of the small, stick-wielding Sasquatch, which they called the Skanicum. In the 1890s, a group of Colville camped near Keller, along the Sanpoil River. A new bride left camp and went to the river to fetch water, where a Skanicum kidnapped her and made her his wife. The next year the Indians rescued the woman, who was pregnant. She carried the baby to term and named him Patrick.

According to Dr. Edward Fusch, in *Scweneyti and the Stick Indians of the Colvilles*, the Indians said Patrick was short—about five feet four inches tall—but his arms hung down to his knees. He had large and strong hands, a sloping forehead, a large lower jaw with teeth that stuck out, and pointed ears. Despite his odd appearance, he was very smart and successful. Although he died around the age of thirty, he had three daughters and two sons. All of his children had some Skanicum features.

The Burgoyne Brothers

In the mid-1800s, many men abandoned their farms in the lowlands of the Pacific Northwest to look for precious metals in the Cascade Mountains. Three brothers, the Burgoynes, lived and farmed in Kelso but had a small cabin at Grizzly Lake, near Mount Saint Helens. After harvest and before the winter snows blocked the mountain passes, the brothers mined copper there. One winter, one of the brothers decided to stay at the cabin, while the other two took their ore and returned to Kelso.

When summer came, the two brothers returned to the mountains with fresh supplies. The cabin was in shambles, with signs of a struggle everywhere, and their brother had disappeared. His diary was still there, however, and in it the surviving brothers found descriptions of strange, hairy men hanging around the cabin. One of the remaining brothers, seemingly not disturbed by the tales told by his mysteriously missing kin, decided to stay over the next winter. When the third brother returned the following summer, the second

brother was missing as well. Taking the hint, the last Burgoyne brother never returned to the cabin.

Attack at Ape Canyon

In the early twentieth century, Fred Beck and four other men operated a mining claim, called the Vander White, in a narrow valley east of Mount Saint Helens. Today the area is known as Ape Canyon, named after their experiences there.

The men had built a sturdy log cabin at the bottom of the valley, near their claim, which they had worked at for six years. In the last year, 1924, they noticed several large footprints near their workings. They also heard a weird whistling noise every night around their cabin. One day they saw a large hairy creature watching them from behind a tree. Beck and one of the miners shot at it. They may have hit the beast, but it still ran away.

That night the apes struck back. From the top of the canyon, they dropped rocks onto the cabin. Later they surrounded it, pounding on the walls and roof and tearing off large pieces of framing as they tried to break through the door. At one point, a hairy arm reached through a gap in the log walls and attempted to take an axe leaning against the wall. Beck managed to turn the axe head sideways, blocking its removal, as another man shot at the creature. This did not drive off the attackers, who stayed until dawn.

The next day the miners abandoned their claim. Before they left, Beck saw one of the strange beasts standing at the rim of the canyon. He shot it, and watched it fall to the canyon floor. The miners came back later with curious friends and saw several sets of large footprints, but no trace of living creatures.

Bigfoot Sightings, Real or Not?

Most Bigfoot sightings last only a few seconds. A confused mind could easily interpret the rush of a large bear, an elk, or a horse running in front of a car's headlights as a Sasquatch. There are also cases where the Bigfoot legend has been promoted by people deliberately faking footprints and sightings. But not all the sightings can be explained away as fakes or the result of confused witnesses. Can there have been thousands of stories about the Sasquatch for hundreds of years without there being some truth to the matter? The real question is, How much truth?

Bigfoot at Camp Bonneville

I remember my father telling a story about something that happened to a friend of his. In the 1960s he was in the National Guard. On one of his drill weekends, he and his unit were at Camp Bonneville, in southwest Washington. One of the soldiers left in search of a "green latrine" in the woods. The isolated spot he chose was near one of the camp garbage dumps. Shortly after he got there, he heard heavy bodies moving through the garbage. He turned around and saw four or five tall, furry creatures rooting through the piles of garbage. They turned and looked at him. There was a stand-off for several seconds until he remembered to run away. The creatures headed in the opposite direction. By the time the soldier gathered some friends to investigate, there was no trace of a Bigfoot or any other creatures near the dump. Everyone was convinced it was a family of bears, but he denied that theory.–*JD*

Bigfoot Saved My Life

Back in the '80s I would go into town every so often and check my post office box. Sometimes when I walked by Main Street, a voice would shout out "Bigfoot saved my life." I would turn around and see no one there. This went on for a couple of years, around once every two weeks or so.

Then, I finally saw the man who yelled it. I went over and talked to him. He told me that someday when he got up enough courage he would tell me the story of how Bigfoot saved his life.

A full year had passed, then I heard it again. "Bigfoot saved my life." The man motioned for me to come over, told me his name was Mike, then shared the following story:

"It took me a long time to decide I'd tell this story because I don't know who would believe it. It is a short story and a true story about how Bigfoot saved my life. It happened four years ago. I was hunting deer with three friends back in some log hills above the town of Duvall. I turned around in a partially logged area and saw my three friends lagging way behind. So I kept on going and was way ahead of them. I pulled out some candy and started chewing on it. Well, I tripped on a root and fell and the candy caught. I was choking. I couldn't breathe and it seemed like the end for me. Just as I was breathing my last, I looked up and saw Bigfoot. The shock of it forced the candy to dislodge. It was good knowing I was going to live. I looked up again and Bigfoot was gone. Bigfoot saved my life."–Cliff Crook

Sasquatch on the Rocks

There were three Bigfoot sightings near Orting, in the vicinity of Mount Rainier, in one year. In one case, on September 26, two bow hunters confronted a Bigfoot from a distance of about three hundred yards. They had no desire to get any closer to the strange beast and watched it through binoculars for several minutes. The critter stood facing them, standing upright on the edge of a rock outcrop on a cliff face. It was covered with shiny black fur and had a simianlike body, wide shoulders, and a broad chest. They described its face as being apelike. When it left, they investigated the place where it had been standing but did not find any footprints or other signs. If they had been watching this creature with only their naked eyes, we might think it was just a bear, but since they used binoculars, that explanation is unlikely.

Bigfoot on Film

One of the most recognizable pieces of motion picture film in the world is a 1967 movie taken by Roger Patterson and Bob Grimlin that shows what seems to be a Sasquatch walking through a logging clear-cut and gradually fading into the woods. Almost from the moment that Patterson and Grimlin showed their film, supporters and critics surrounded them.

In December 1998, the Fox network aired *World's Greatest Hoaxes: Secrets Finally Revealed*, which claimed that the 1967 film was a fake. And in fact, in the next few years two men came forward claiming they were parties to the hoax. One, named Philip Morris, made gorilla suits for show business. He claimed he sold Roger Patterson a gorilla suit, which Patterson modified for the film. The second man, a retired Pepsi company worker from Yakima named Bob Heironimus, said that he wore the suit for Patterson and Grimlin's film.

Eventually, Seattle author Greg Long took up the story. Long spent several years interviewing witnesses and finally wrote a book entitled *The Making of Bigfoot:*

The Inside Story, debunking the whole affair. Strangely enough, the book, which was released in 2004, did not change anyone's mind. To those who thought the film was a fake, the witnesses' statements of how it was done reaffirmed their belief. To those who believed the film was real, many of those statements were inconsistent, or had holes, which proved the book was wrong and reinforced their belief that the Patterson film was real. Debate still rages today.

Dr. Grover Krantz, physical anthropologist at Washington State University, displays casts of footprints he believes were made by a Sasquatch in a logging area of southwestern Washington.

The Skookum Cast

In the Chinook jargon, the word Skookum has different meanings. It can mean strong or powerful, and it can mean demon or evil spirit. It is also used interchangeably with Sasquatch and Bigfoot to describe the strange ape-man.

Skookum Meadows, north of Carson, has long been believed to be Bigfoot habitat. It is high in the Cascade Mountains and inaccessible once the winter snows fall. Before one winter, a team from the Bigfoot Research Organization (BFRO) conducted several experiments at the wet meadow. They camped nearby, thinking the Bigfoots were inside the meadow itself. They set up a loudspeaker system and broadcast what they believed were Bigfoot calls in the hopes of getting a response. They also placed several hidden cameras with trip wires along trails and put cameras near several traps baited with apples, presumably a Bigfoot favorite.

The researchers played the Bigfoot calls and checked the cameras many times. They thought they had gotten some responses, but weren't sure. One day an early check on one of the bait traps out in the meadow showed the apples settled in a few inches of water. Upon checking the same trap later, they were surprised to see that the apples had vanished, but something else was left behind. In the soft and muddy soil at the edge of the meadow they saw the imprint of a large body.

The researchers collected several hair samples and managed to make a cast of the imprint, which was later examined. Some wildlife biologists thought the cast showed part of the thigh, rib cage, and arm of a large manlike creature lying in the mud, reaching out to pluck

the apples from the water. They believed that some of the hair came from a kind of hominid, or great ape; other, unidentifiable animal hair was found in and near the imprint. Skeptics believe that another large animal, like an elk or bear, left this behind as it lay down. Unfortunately, since there was no other evidence, such as a body, the controversy continues.

Preservation Efforts

Skamania County has done something to help preserve North America's elusive Man of the Forest. On April 1, 1969, it passed Ordinance No. 69-01, which reads in part:

> WHEREAS there is evidence to indicate the possible existence in Skamania County of a nocturnal primate . . . commonly known as "Sasquatch," "Yeti," . . . or "Giant Hairy Ape" . . . THEREFORE BE IT RESOLVED, that any premeditated, willful and wanton slaying of any such creature shall be deemed a felony punishable by a fine not to exceed Ten Thousand Dollars and/or imprisonment in the county jail for a period not to exceed five (5) years.

There are various theories as to why this ordinance was passed. Was it an April Fool's joke that got out of hand? Or an attempt to gain publicity and improve tourism? Regardless of the cause, the effect is still the same. If there are *Gigantopithecus* in Skamania County, they are a protected species.

Flying Jellyfish

Charles Fort, author and investigator of the odd, speculated that there was a species of nearly transparent jellyfish that float in the upper atmosphere. Over the years, pilots have reported seeing odd-shaped objects in the sky that they thought resembled jellyfish. And other people have found large numbers of dead birds with burn marks on them, which they believed could be caused by jellyfish stings.

This raises the question, If these creatures exist, then why aren't there more sightings? People who believe in sky jellyfish suggest they might have the ability to change color and blend in with the background, like an octopus. For those who want more proof, consider the little town of Oakville.

Oakville is located along U.S. Highway 12, between Elma and Rochester. Today about one thousand people live there, and it is known as being the site of both an annual zucchini festival and the last horseback bank robbery in Washington State. But it was a strange rain that made Oakville famous for a few weeks in August 1994.

That month bizarre happenings occurred twice. On August 7, Sunny Barcklift looked out through the rain at the black asphalt roof of a small shed on her property. She noticed it was covered with globules about the size of grains of rice. When she and others picked up some of the globs, they saw they were clear and had a jellylike texture. Shortly after handling the material, however, Barcklift and two other people went to the hospital, suffering from fatigue and nausea. A few days later a kitten that had lived outside Barcklift's home died of a strange intestinal problem.

On August 16, another rainstorm brought more of the gelatinous globs to Oakville. The National Weather Service received a phone call from an unidentified man, who claimed something had rained down from the sky and burned a hole through his children's outside trampoline. Fortunately, no one became ill.

A local doctor doubted the strange material caused any human illness and suggested the kitten drank some antifreeze, which killed it. Nonetheless, he had a lab examine samples of the blobs. The initial analysis suggested that they contained many different substances, including human white blood cells. The doctor thought they could have come from the waste fluid of an airplane toilet, which could explain the human cells as well as the antifreeze. However, airplane waste fluid is blue; the blobs were clear or white.

Health authorities had a second analysis done, and this time the lab reversed the initial finding of human white blood cells. Although there were living cells in the blobs, they had no nuclei as human cells do. That left investigators with an unidentified living material falling out of the sky.

Someone suggested a different theory. In early August, the U.S. Air Force had conducted a series of live bombing exercises off the coast of Washington. Someone, no one seems to know who, suggested that bombs had exploded in the middle of schools of jellyfish, blowing them into bits and launching the fragments into the atmosphere. The pieces were small enough to float along in the clouds until they came down in rainstorms.

Maybe the air force was to blame for the exploded jellyfish—but what about the crabs?

It was also around this time that large numbers of dead crabs were found along the Washington coast, surrounded by small globs of jellyfish-like material. The couple who reported the dead crabs became ill after handling the material. But for this incident to be related to the Oakville globs, the material would have had to float for nearly two weeks, over a distance of seventy

miles, from the bombing range to Oakville.

Conspiracy theorists suggest some form of germ warfare was the cause. In 1997, the show *Unsolved Mysteries* featured the Oakville rain and interviewed several residents who had experienced the weird phenomenon three years earlier. They reported that the strange rain fell six times (not just two), and that scientists found two different kinds of bacteria in the blobs. Several people mentioned seeing black helicopters flying over the area at the time. The show's host, Robert Stack, stopped short of suggesting the United States government deliberately sent helicopters to leave trails of toxic jelly blobs on Oakville.

Later in 1997, the city of Everett also had a mysterious rain of gelatinous blobs. Were these the same kinds of blobs that fell on Oakville, and could they be explained away as bomb testing or germ warfare conspiracies? We at *Weird Washington* personally like the idea of flying jellyfish going through some kind of spawning ritual high up in the earth's atmosphere.

Northwest Tree Octopus

The existence of the Pacific Northwest Tree Octopus is still being hotly debated on the Internet. It just seems so plausible. These creatures supposedly begin their lives like any other octopus, as an egg in the water. In this case, the eggs are in Hood Canal, off the Puget Sound. Shortly after hatching, the young octopuses leave the waters of the canal and make their way to the forests of the Olympic Peninsula. Due to a combination of the moistness of the mountain air and a special adaptation of their skin, these many-limbed beasts can survive without being in the water. They use their arms and suckers to climb from tree to tree, seeking prey such as insects, frogs, rodents, and other small animals. Because of their ability to change color, Tree Octopuses are hard to detect by forest visitors. The octopuses return to the Puget Sound only to breed.

The skeptical reader may want more facts. If so, visit the Web site of Save the Pacific Northwest Tree Octopus (zapatopi.net/treeoctopus), which includes several articles about cephalopods and links to bona fide Web sites on marine life. In the end, you may decide that the story just does not work. The woods are not wet enough, and an octopus actually does need to be in water to move. However, the Tree Octopus is an interesting urban legend, and you can declare your desire to save at least the concept of them through the purchase of T-shirts, coffee cups, and bumper stickers.

Monsters Behind the Dam?

The sturgeon is a common living fossil inhabiting Washington's freshwater lakes and rivers. It resembles and feeds like a catfish, sucking up small plants and animals as it glides along the river bottom. A mature sturgeon normally grows to ten feet long and weighs about five hundred pounds, but fishermen have caught some specimens that are over twenty feet long and weigh two thousand pounds!

A longtime dam worker told *Weird Washington* that giant sturgeon have been trapped behind the many hydroelectric dams in the Pacific Northwest, including the Bonneville Dam, near Stevenson. At Bonneville, the turbines that generate electricity are powered by water that flows through a series of intake vents constructed along the dam. Sometimes the water flow through the vents slows down or is cut off entirely, stopping the turbines. The worker blamed this on sturgeon, which get sucked up against the intake valves and block them with their huge bodies. The suction never sucks the sturgeon into the shaft, and they manage to swim away after a few minutes.

Officials at the Bonneville Dam told us no blockage has happened recently, and the water intakes at the dam are not located at the bottom of the dam, but somewhat higher up. They believe it is unlikely the bottom-feeding sturgeon would be sucked against these intakes. Leave it to a government official to throw cold water on a good monster story.

The Gush Gush Monster of Lacamas Lake

There is a lot of high-value housing surrounding Lacamas Lake these days. But do the new homeowners know of the strange monster that may be wandering their shores at night?

Some Camas old-timers like to tell stories about the Gush Gush monster of the lake. One lifelong resident said he and his friends used to go down to the lakeshore to park with their girlfriends. He remembered hearing a noise like something large walking through thick mud. It made a gush-squelch, gush-squelch sound. When they were not otherwise hormonally occupied, the friends would make a game of trying to follow the sound to its source.

The noise of the Gush Gush monster is probably nothing stranger than sounds from an old dam built on the lake in the late nineteenth century. To increase water pressure to power the early turbines, laborers dug a long flume through solid rock. The vacuum from the water as it flows through the flume probably creates this gurgling noise. But then . . . why investigate too deeply? Let's leave some mystery for the couples who park at Lacamas Lake at night, looking for the monster.

Cadborosaurus

In recent times, people exploring remote locations have found traces of living animals once thought to be extinct. The *Cadborosaurus* may be one of the hardy survivors they have found. This sea animal, seen many times along the Northwest coast, made several appearances at Cadboro Bay, British Columbia, which led to its name. Many people there described it as having a long neck and a head like a horse, with a body that could be over twenty feet long. Some say it has a series of humps on its back when it swims. It is sometimes described as having fur, other times with a smooth coat. Its color has varied from green to brown, but the physical proportions are remarkably similar.

There is a long list of sightings along the Washington coast. In the 1930s, a twenty-foot-long animal with a curved neck and horselike head was seen at Neah Bay, at the tip of the Olympic Peninsula. In 1934, near Waldron Island in the San Juan Islands, a sea critter swallowed a duck that had been shot by hunters. Several local people saw the animal in the area a few days later.

In March 1953, two women from Klamath Falls sighted a Caddy while vacationing near Port Townsend on the Strait of Juan de Fuca. One of them was a trained biologist, and she gave a detailed description of the animal. She first saw what looked like a tree limb about a quarter mile offshore, she said. It submerged, only to reappear again a few minutes later, even closer. The exposed portions of the animal were over ten feet long, with three humps, a partially submerged body, and a long, curved neck. The neck was about six feet long, and the head was about two feet long. The animal was a dark brown color, with orange reticulations in a giraffelike pattern. The creature's head was flat, and behind it was either a lowered fin or mane on the neck. The sighting lasted about eight minutes before the creature submerged and disappeared.

From time to time strange carcasses have washed up on Northwest shores. In 1936, a twelve-foot-long critter with a goatlike head washed ashore at Aberdeen. Attempts were made to study the supposed Caddy remains, but when an animal dies and rots at sea, it loses more than its flesh. Most fish bodies are a mix of true bone and cartilage, and if allowed to rot for long, the cartilage falls off, leaving only the bone and a skeleton that does not look like that of the original animal. So for the moment, *Cadborosaurus* remains one of the many unknown creatures spotted in the waters of our state.

A Radioactive Heron?

In the mid-1990s, many Tri-Cities residents and people passing through the Hanford Government Reservation were surprised to see a large, pinkish red bird in the Hanford Hills. Except for the coloring, many people thought that the bird, which was four or five feet long, was some kind of a heron. Herons are bluish black, while this bird was rosy-white, with scarlet feathers on its shoulders. Many people called the Hanford Reservation, asking if it was a heron suffering from radiation poisoning.

Local wildlife biologists began looking for the bird, and when they eventually found it, they identified it as a pink flamingo. The locals' mistaken identification was understandable, since biologists once considered flamingos to be part of the heron family. Having solved the identification problem, the biologists were faced with another issue. How did the flamingo arrive in Washington State? Flamingo remains, dating to about twelve thousand years ago, have been found in the Pacific Northwest, but today the climate is too cold for them. Modern flamingos live on the Atlantic and Gulf coasts in subtropical and tropical America. Maybe the Hanford flamingo was just visiting its ancestral home.

Or perhaps it arrived via a sky fall. All over the world, there have been accounts of sky falls, or rains, of things such as fish, frogs, alligators, nuts, straw, stones, raw meat, and even blood. There are several theories about these incidents, which Charles Fort made a career of recording and reporting. He suggested (jokingly) that there were floating continents in the sky and that when there was a storm on the floating continent, it dumped garbage on the earth below.

Another theory is that tornados can pick up objects and act like centrifuges, spinning things around and separating them. The heaviest objects drop off first, the lighter objects later. Could some kind of freak storm have picked up the flamingo and transported it to Washington State?

The displaced bird was seen several times over the summer but disappeared in early fall when the weather began to turn cold. Was it just gathering strength for its long trip home? *Weird Washington* would like to think so.

Monsters of Lake Washington

Unseen monsters in Lake Washington have been said to suck swimmers to their deaths, and at least one huge horned serpent is reported to live in the lake and cause terrible landslides and earthquakes there. Even the lake itself has been known to act up: One legend speaks of it swallowing Mercer Island one night and spitting it out the next morning.

Lake Washington is the second-largest natural lake in the state. The cities of Bellevue, Seattle, Renton, and Kirkland all border it, and its shores are home to the very wealthy, including Bill Gates. Even so, there are many acres of green space parks, paths, and wetlands.

According to Native American lore, there were once eighteen villages along the shores of Lake Washington. The people living there fished from the shore, as well as from canoes. They encountered many strange animals or beings on the lake, and like many legends, these have a basis in fact.

Recent engineering projects have exposed past lake levels, some of which included the remains of old-growth trees. Scientists studying the evidence suggest that there were several earthquakes, some as large as 7.0 on the Richter scale, as recently as a thousand years ago. These caused landslides and tidal waves, which altered the shoreline and certainly killed or displaced many people. One landslide may have caused an immense portion of Mercer Island to fall into the lake, resulting in a huge wave that struck where modern Bellevue was built.

As mentioned earlier, the source of many lake monster legends may be real, though rare, creatures like sturgeon or seals. Or they may be animals abandoned by people.

In February and March 2006, at least two people reported seeing some kind of strange animal swimming on the east bank of the lake, near Medina. One witness told police he saw what looked like a small alligator. Another person reported a creature that had a head shaped like an alligator.

Wildlife experts thought the animals were caiman, a smaller relative of the alligator, which grows to a length of about seven feet. Caimans are indigenous to Central and South America. Outside their native habitat, experts recommend that they be kept in pens or enclosures heated to over eighty degrees. A caiman abandoned in Lake Washington in February would survive twenty minutes or so in the forty-seven-degree lake water.

Over the last two decades, several caimans were seen or captured in the Puget Sound, all in the summer. In the 1960s, many people reported seeing an alligator-like animal killing and eating ducks in Lake Washington. Over a thirty-day period in 1986, there were many alligator sightings in Green Lake, which once emptied into Lake Washington. It could be that owners who can't handle the aggressive reptiles dump them along the shoreline to fend for themselves. The animals die off in the winter, but every summer or two someone drops off another one, which in turn terrifies lake dwellers until the next winter.

Local Heroes and Villains

As *politicians have been known to say,* when questioned about their motives for seeking public office: "It's all about the people." Oftentimes, they're less than sincere in voicing that sentiment. But we at *Weird Washington* assure you that this explanation accurately answers the question, "What defines an area's local flavor?"

For good or ill, many notable folks have contributed, and still contribute, to Washington's collective ambience. Many of them have danced to a decidedly different beat than the usual, literally as well as figuratively. What follows is a sampling of just a few such personalities. Whether prominent or obscure, good or evil, or even conflicted as to whether they're human or simian, our local heroes and villains illustrate the variety of characters that comprise Washington's diverse population. Through their stories we can perhaps ponder our own, and consider how *we* might help shape the "Washington experience."

Your Hostess, Lou Graham

In its evolution from rowdy boomtown to major metropolis, Seattle has had many visionaries leave their mark on the local scene. Lou Graham—not a man, but a woman of exceptional business savvy—was one such outsize personality. Graham was born Dorothea Georgine Emile Ohbene in Germany, in 1861. She appeared in Seattle in 1888: five feet two, plump, blue-eyed, with hair parted into two curly masses on either side of her head. She was considered quite attractive by the standards of her day, and her good looks complemented her persuasiveness and her no-nonsense will to succeed.

In those days, there was a tug-of-war going on over the city's politics of morality. Some of Seattle's leaders saw card rooms, bars, and brothels as scandalous, unwholesome enterprises that should be shuttered for good. Others felt that too much propriety was bad for Seattle's bottom line, as most of the city's income came from "sin taxes" imposed on such establishments. Many wondered how a semi-graceful balance could be struck.

Enter Lou Graham, with a new take on the world's oldest profession. Meeting with city leaders shortly after her arrival, she made them an irresistible proposition—a bordello of the utmost refinement. This would not be a common brothel, but a Shangri-la for the world-weary businessman: a club of high standards and expensive furnishings, where refined men-about-town could meet and mingle over drinks, fine music, and encounters with classy, intelligent ladies. Furthermore—to clinch the deal—all services would be free to lawmakers!

Lou imposed one small condition. She'd be happy to contribute her

share to Seattle's coffers, she said, but only if it could be done discreetly. No police were to come to her establishment to collect her "dues," as was customary with run-of-the-mill brothels. She would pay her "fines" at city hall, either in person or via messenger, so as to protect the high-end reputation of her business as well as the privacy of her patrons. The politicians were sold on the idea of free sex and booze; agreeing to the payment arrangement was a no-brainer!

The bordello was set up at 221 South Washington Street, and it was every bit as resplendent as Lou had promised. It was an immediate hit with her target demographic. An entourage of Lou's finest beauties would often accompany the madam on carriage rides through the city, a living advertisement for the sensual delights to be had at the Washington Street pleasure palace. The locals weren't considered street-smart Seattle businessmen if they couldn't speak knowledgeably about the finer points of Lou's fine bordello.

Lou became known as the Queen of the Lava Beds and one of Washington's wealthiest landowners. Her establishment weathered the economic depression of 1893 surprisingly well, and she was even able to extend loans to prestigious Seattle families who would otherwise have gone bankrupt. Unfortunately, she died of syphilis in 1903 during a visit to San Francisco. (Call it an occupational hazard.) These days, you can still see her legendary bordello, but it's now known as the Washington Court Building, mostly housing attorneys' offices, ironically enough.

Prolific Killings of the Serial Kind

Unfortunately, Washington is also known for its serial killers. Over three dozen of them have plied their deadly trade here in recent decades, and the *Seattle Post-Intelligencer* has conveniently listed them all in a frightening "Who's who" you can read through on the paper's Web site.

While it's staggering to see such a large group of like-minded mass murderers in one vicinity, it's actually not a record-breaking number when compared to other states. But the ghastly goings-on in the Evergreen State are legendary. Here are tales of three of the most prolific Washington-based evildoers, two of whom are well known and of relatively recent vintage, and one whose murderous actions occurred quite some time ago.

The Green River Killer

In the late 1990s, we asked a colleague, an avid fly-fisherman, if he knew of any good fishing spots along the Green River. "No, I don't fish the Green River," he replied. "It's had a certain stigma ever since the murders."

He was referring to the Green River serial murders, so-called because the bodies of five young women were found within a one-mile stretch of the river in Kent between July and August of 1982. This was just the beginning of a long, real-life nightmare that would see at least forty-eight prostitutes—most ranging in age from their teens to their early twenties—strangled to death throughout the 1980s and beyond. The remains of most victims, often clustered together, were found in wooded or isolated parts of south King County. A few others were found elsewhere in the county and in Oregon. There's a very good chance that yet more victims remain undiscovered.

All had disappeared from the "SeaTac strip" along Highway 99 south of Seattle. Prostitution boomed here in the 1970s and '80s, when the Seattle-Tacoma International Airport began buying up properties in adjacent neighborhoods to demolish for an expansion. Whole blocks of vacant homes awaiting demolition attracted even

more prostitution, drug dealing, and general unruliness to an already seedy area.

The King County Sheriff's Office formed a Green River Task Force to investigate the case. Led by Detective Dave Reichert, various incarnations of the task force doggedly hunted the unknown killer over the years. They often faced setbacks both in the investigation and on the public relations front. Media hype, "assistance" from publicity-hungry locals, and accusations of indifference plagued the task force. On his side, the culprit had dumb luck and a prostitution subculture reluctant to cooperate with police. Scrutiny of two likely suspects went nowhere, wasting valuable resources. As the years wore on, some evidence was lost and many leads went cold.

Anyone who has lived in the area will understand our friend's apprehension about the Green River. The unassuming suburbs of south King County seemed to be cursed with a dark and morbid undercurrent. With the Green River killer still at large, many residents felt a subtle, "watch your back" uneasiness.

Everything changed on November 30, 2001, when Gary Leon Ridgway—who had gradually become the prime suspect—was arrested as he left his job in Renton. He'd provided a saliva sample to police in 1987, and a new technique in DNA forensics had shown a match between the sample and DNA evidence taken from

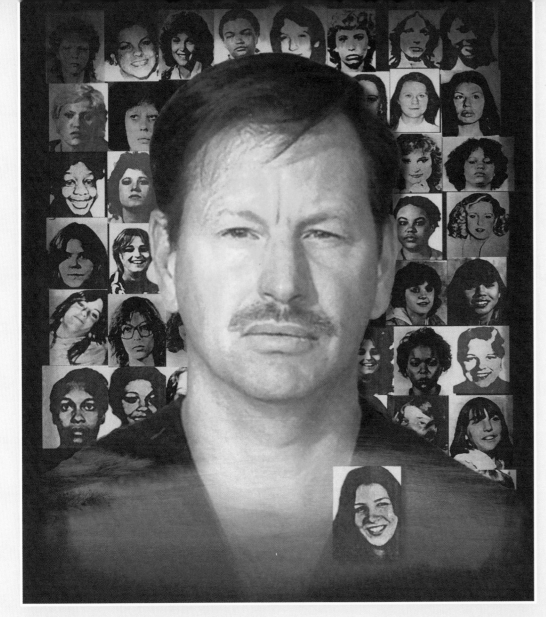

and domineering, prone to yelling at her husband and two sons at the slightest provocation. She tended to dress suggestively and wear lots of makeup, according to Gary's second wife.

Sometime in Ridgway's teens, he began feeling the urge to kill. He mutilated small animals and, in his mid-teens, stabbed a six-year-old neighborhood boy to see, as he put it, "what it felt like to kill somebody." The boy survived, and for some reason, Gary was never brought up on charges in connection with the stabbing. He graduated from SeaTac's Tyee High School in 1969 and had two unsuccessful marriages, with his second wife divorcing him after he developed an interest in bondage. (He'd get his wife into choke holds or scare her from behind, then claim that he was "only playing around.") He'd also come home progressively later and later, sometimes dirty or wet, offering no explanation as to why.

Within a few months of his second divorce—even after joining a dating group and developing relationships with several women—he embarked on the longest and deadliest serial-killing spree in modern-day America. As he would later describe it in court in a prepared statement:

three victims. As Ridgway awaited his day in court, police interviewed his friends and relatives, piecing together his background.

He was fifty-two by then and had lived in Washington since he was eleven. Before that, his family was constantly relocating because of his father's job as a truck driver. This may partially account for his consistently poor performance in school. His young mother, Mary, is said to have been very temperamental

In most cases, when I murdered these women, I did not know their names. Most of the time, I killed them the first time I met them and I do not have a good memory for their faces. I killed so many women I have a hard time keeping them straight. . . . I killed most of them in my house near Military Road, and I killed a lot of them in my truck, not far from where I picked them up. I killed some of them outside. . . . The plan was: I wanted to kill as many women I thought were prostitutes as I possibly could.

I picked prostitutes as my victims because I hate most prostitutes and I did not want to pay them for sex. I also picked prostitutes as victims because they were easy to pick up without being noticed. I knew they would not be reported missing right away, and might never be reported missing. I picked prostitutes because I thought I could kill as many of them as I wanted without getting caught.

As for disposal of the bodies:

I placed most of the bodies in groups, which I call "clusters." I did this because I wanted to keep track of all the women I killed. I liked to drive by the "clusters" around the county and think about the women I placed there. I usually used a landmark to remember a "cluster" and the women I placed there.

Ridgway loved the media attention his sinister exploits attracted. He was a fan of fellow south King County resident and true crime author Ann Rule. He attended a few of her book signings and secretly hoped she would someday write an account of his crimes. She eventually did, but 2004's *Green River, Running Red* probably wasn't the ego-bolstering narrative he was hoping for. The book includes extensive biographical profiles of Ridgway's victims, putting human faces on them and refuting the killer's belief that nobody cared about prostitutes.

In a controversial deal, Ridgway was spared execution for his crimes in exchange for revealing the locations of remains of previously unrecovered victims. Critics argued that the deal would be used by future killers as a strategy to avoid the death penalty. Authorities contended that it was necessary to bring closure to the families of the victims. The upshot: On December 18, 2003, Gary Ridgway was sentenced to forty-eight consecutive life terms in prison, one for each victim on the official record. Raw emotion punctuated the sentencing hearing as Judge Richard Jones allotted three hours for the victims' families to address Ridgway directly. Some of them called Ridgway evil, cowardly, garbage, and worse. He listened intently, but cried only when a few offered him forgiveness. It was the last contact he had with the outside world before he was taken to permanent solitary confinement.

Since then, the SeaTac strip has undergone some beautification projects, and prostitution in the area has diminished significantly. Detective Dave Reichert, the lead investigator on the task force, went on to become King County sheriff and was later elected to the U.S. House of Representatives. Though permanently affected, both the victims' families and Ridgway's have accepted the outcome and prefer to look forward, rather than back. In short, life continues flowing, much like the Green River.

Ted Bundy: A Stranger in Need

Washington's reputation as a spawning ground for serial killers has a lot to do with one mass murderer in particular—Ted Bundy, one of the most notorious villains ever to blight America.

Fourteen years before his execution in Florida for the murder of twelve-year-old Kimberley Leach—after two clever escapes from custody and an interstate murder spree—Bundy began his savage "career" by bludgeoning to death eleven young women in Washington, where he'd lived since the age of four. He preferred college girls: Most were kidnapped from around the campus of the University of Washington, while two were last seen at Evergreen State College and Central Washington State College. His Northwest victims also include a female student from Oregon State University, a woman he'd met at a Burien bar, and two women he kidnapped in broad daylight from Lake Sammamish State Park in Issaquah.

Bundy was a self-taught master of manipulation, who often preyed on his victims' sympathies by posing as a stranger in need of some kind of assistance. He would pretend to have a hard time loading or unloading his VW Beetle, often wearing an arm or leg cast, faking an injury as the reason for his difficulty. When a kindhearted young woman fell for his act and tried to help him, he had her right where he wanted her. He would make sure the coast was clear and knock her unconscious with a crowbar or some other blunt object. He would then load the woman into his car and drive off, finishing his despicable work elsewhere in a more private setting.

Bundy had a penchant for overachievement, sparked by a girlfriend who dumped him because she thought he lacked ambition. Wounded by the breakup, he embarked on a zealous crusade for self-improvement. Impressed by his initiative, his ex-girlfriend agreed to resume their

courtship. Bundy eventually proposed to her, but when she accepted his offer of marriage, he broke off all contact with her. It seems that his appetite for success was just a means to get revenge on his one-time sweetheart for breaking up with him.

Still, the dependable, clean-cut reputation he'd earned in the late '60s and early '70s worked to his advantage. Initially, nobody connected Bundy to the murders he committed. He was a budding law student and a member of the Washington State Republican Party, for which he'd volunteered on a gubernatorial campaign. He also worked the late shift at a suicide crisis center.

It wasn't until he'd moved to Utah and gotten arrested for suspicion of burglary that the full extent of his murderous activity became clear.

In late 1984, Bundy wrote to King County homicide detective Bob Keppel, who had come into his own while investigating Bundy's murders in Issaquah a decade earlier. Now on Florida's death row, Bundy was offering his "expert" insight into the mind-set of serial killers to help solve the Green River murders. The irony of this was not lost on observers: For all his supposed expertise on the serial-killer mentality, Bundy was still denying—against overwhelming evidence—that he had killed anybody.

Keppel and lead Green River Task Force investigator Dave Reichert traveled to Florida and interviewed Bundy, a process detailed extensively in Keppel's memoir, *The Riverman: Ted Bundy and I Hunt for the Green River Killer.* Though the two detectives had sincere hopes that Bundy could contribute something of value to the investigation, their ulterior motive was to play to his ego and see if they could get him to confess to his own crimes. Ultimately, Bundy didn't offer any major insights into the Green River murders, much less confess anything. Still, Keppel was impressed at one mass

Coincidentally, Ted Bundy's co-worker at the suicide crisis center was future true-crime author Ann Rule. The two had an amicable relationship and kept in touch all the way through Bundy's stint on death row. In 1980 Rule launched her writing career with *The Stranger Beside Me,* an account of Bundy's crimes set against the backdrop of their friendship.

murderer's ability to develop what turned out to be a reasonably accurate profile of another—Green River Killer Gary Ridgway—based solely on newspaper articles written long before Ridgway was apprehended.

In the end, it struck many people as ironic that Ted Bundy spent his final weeks legally twisting in the wind, trying to get his own death sentence commuted or delayed. It seems that he was not at all enamored of the fate he so viciously imposed on his victims. In his final hours, he finally confessed the majority of his crimes to Bob Keppel. Audiotapes of this four-hour conversation are used to this day in training FBI criminal psychologists. He died in Florida's electric chair at seven a.m. on January 24, 1989, to the cheers of a jubilant crowd in attendance.

A Murderous Gohl

It's hard to name another town of twelve thousand with a tough streak to match Aberdeen's a hundred years ago, during its heyday as one of America's major lumber ports. Its high concentration of sailors and lumberjacks ensured a certain level of rugged aggressiveness that manifested itself in drinking, brawling, and debauchery. Lumber was Aberdeen's lifeblood, and testosterone seemed to be its chief by-product.

Into this raucous atmosphere entered Billy Gohl, a laborer and all-around thug who would plunge Aberdeen's reputation to drastic new lows. He came to town in 1902, age somewhere in his thirties or forties. Not much is known about his background, except that it was criminal. His stocky frame and barrel chest lent him an intimidating air. Some accounts describe him as clean-shaven, with hair parted down the middle. In a set of mug shots taken years later, he scowls menacingly, sporting a shaved head and a mustache. It's said that he was eminently persuasive, a master at getting his own way.

A member of the Sailors' Union of the Pacific in San Francisco, he elbowed his way into the position of delegate at the Aberdeen branch in 1903, a perfect place to pursue some serious wrongdoing. The union office served as the sailors' bank, work agency, mail drop, and more. Arriving sailors would stash their valuables with him while they went out on the town. Some depended on him as an interpreter, since he was fluent in several languages. Most of them thought he did a good job handling their grievances against local lumber mills or ships' captains.

Gohl presented a relatively trustworthy veneer to migrant sailors, but that image couldn't have been more misleading. He bombed an Aberdeen hotel because he had a long-term dispute with Lee Williams, the proprietor of the hotel's bar (or tobacco shop—accounts differ). When he learned that one of the two people killed in the explosion was another old enemy, Gohl reportedly snickered, "I never dreamed there'd be a bonus in it!" He once stranded four nonunion sailors on a small island at low tide, knowing they would drown when the tide came in. He shot and killed another from his office window. Had more sailors gotten wind of his vicious exploits, Gohl's true magnum opus might not have been so devastating. But he was known to have allies in the local police department who looked the other way when it came to many of his unsavory activities, including murder.

Floater Fleet

Within a few years of Gohl's arrival in Aberdeen, it became common to find the bodies of migrant sailors floating in Gray's Harbor, all killed in one way or another while they were drunk. They were all devoid of money and valuables, a likely, if not definitive, sign of robbery. Authorities often consulted with Gohl to establish a positive identification, since chances were good that the victims had checked in at the union office before their demise. The locals famously—and morbidly—referred to the bodies as the Floater Fleet.

Few seemed to connect Gohl's violent inclinations with the Floater Fleet, but, without a doubt, those murders and thefts were his doing. His methods were quite simple. The union office was on the Wishkah River and had a chute that dropped from a trapdoor into the water. Billy made sure to man the office at slightly odd hours when there was no activity at surrounding businesses, or when ships' whistles sounded loudly. When unsuspecting lone sailors dropped by to conduct business, Gohl would bump them off and take their valuables. When the coast was clear, he would drop them down the chute, and the bodies would float down the river as it emptied into Gray's Harbor.

As the body count in Aberdeen mounted, sailors, fearing for their safety, began avoiding the port in droves. The town's economy slumped as sailors spent their free time in nearby Cosmopolis, Hoquiam, and Montesano. At one point, the pace of the murders picked up substantially, with forty-three bodies found within an eight-month period. Gohl, ever deceitfully playing the sailor's friend, faked outrage as the body count rose. He criticized the police for "not doing enough" to catch the killer. This deadly game went on for a few years.

Billy Slips Up

In 1909, the old guard in Aberdeen City Hall was voted out of office, and Gohl's murderous actions began to catch up with him. In a burst of his usual bravado, he hinted about some of his crimes to an undercover detective who'd gained his confidence. The detective relayed the information to the new constable in town, George Dean. Without his powerful friends, Gohl at last came under

serious police scrutiny. On February 2, 1910, he was arrested for the murder of Charley Hatberg, one of his former lackeys, and the Ghoul of Gray Harbor, as he would become known, was at last behind bars.

On May 12, 1910, a jury (made up entirely of out-of-towners) rendered a guilty verdict in the murder of Charley Hatberg, and Gohl was sentenced to life imprisonment. He escaped execution only because the state death penalty had recently been abolished. However, it was reinstated soon after, as the magnitude of Gohl's crimes became clear. Gohl did not escape the ultimate punishment, however. He died of complications from syphilis in 1927, at Eastern State Hospital in Medical Lake, Washington.

The historical record on Billy Gohl is rife with inconsistencies and contradictions. This account offers an overview of his rise and fall, but should not be considered definitive. Gohl was most uncooperative in accounting for all the men he murdered, but if the accepted body count of 124 is accurate (to say nothing of suspicions that many more bodies remained underwater or were washed out to sea), he was likely the most prolific serial killer in American history.

The Dancing Wild Man of Factoria

Factoria, the southernmost neighborhood of Bellevue, is known mainly as a tightly packed retail center where parking is as hard to find as a reasonably priced cup of coffee. But to one wild-maned, hyper-energetic maverick, Factoria is the ultimate dance floor! Along the strip of office parks lining Southeast 38th Street, Kenny Nagamatsu gets his groove on daily, with a wild abandon that constantly turns heads and slows traffic.

For about a decade, Kenny has publicly hopped, bopped, shimmied, and shaken to the tunes on his portable CD player. His enthusiasm has inspired countless smiles and just as many double takes among the throngs of white-collar workers who drive by. During his dance moves, he'll often wave at passing cars, getting friendly honks in return. When he really gets going, he yells an emphatic "OWWW!" and performs an odd, hopping pirouette. This, coupled with his somewhat feral appearance, has earned him the moniker the Dancing Wild Man.

For all his boisterousness, Kenny is remarkably soft-spoken. When approached by your friendly *Weird Washington* representative, he seemed taken aback that anyone at all would be interested in his background. With a vaguely British accent and a surprisingly shy demeanor, he spelled out his basic motivations: "I don't care what people think of me, and I don't care what I look like." As he explains it, he simply loves his tunes and doesn't care who knows it, volunteering that the Beatles and the Monkees really get him going. He also holds down two jobs. That is, two different eateries pay him to perform his unique dance routines while holding up advertising signs.

So, in short, he's got the look, the moves, the recognition, and steady work doing what he loves best. By any standard, he's good to go! Rock on, Kenny!

For about a decade, Kenny has publicly hopped, bopped, shimmied, and shaken to the tunes on his portable CD player.

It's Good to Be Kring

Long before blogging and YouTube made it easy for folks to share their thoughts and opinions with the masses, there was public access television. It was this medium that propelled the notoriety of one of Seattle's most (in)famous daughters: Shannon Kringen. Her TV show, *Goddess Kring*, has aired regularly on Seattle's SCAN-TV, Channel 29, since 1995, developing a considerable cult following.

It's a low-tech, no-budget, one-woman affair, produced almost entirely in Kring's small apartment in Seattle. It's taped and edited with an old camcorder and VCR, and these days it's transferred to DVD with a simple DVD recorder.

As Goddess Kring, Shannon offers viewers a largely experimental mix of freeform poetry, dance, video diary, show-and-tell, and editorializing. On any given week she will bare her soul—and, often, her Rubenesque body—to public access viewers. Her nudity and her occasional sexually charged monologues, though not the focus of every episode, have shaped her public persona. It probably says more about society's addiction to sensationalism than it does about Shannon that people tend to identify her with these exhibitionistic riffs, rather than other elements of the show. On the other hand, it is hard to forget a chubby, naked, body-painted woman, romping around on TV and reciting abstract poetry with an echoey voice filter, even if she presents less controversial entertainment the following week.

Shannon's predilection for televised self-expression began innocently enough. An outgoing, free-spirited sort, thanks to parents with a bohemian lifestyle, she grew up in California and later attended Seattle Central Community College to study art. While there, she befriended a group of public access TV enthusiasts, who thought her offbeat personality and hippie-chick aura warranted a show of her own.

At first, Shannon balked at the idea. Eventually, though, a bad breakup with a boyfriend inspired her to pursue this unorthodox type of performance art. "I got upset," she says, "and I ended up just talking, pouring my heart out on videotape." The experience was strangely comforting. Coincidentally, her monologue lasted about twenty-nine minutes—the perfect length for a TV show. She was hooked. Her spur-of-the-moment expression of angst became the first episode of her show.

Goddess Kring (both the show and the persona) is just one of Shannon's many exercises in stream-of-consciousness self-expression. She also does photography, paints, dabbles in music, writes, maintains her Web site, www.shannonkringen.com, and makes a living as a figure-drawing model. Another cherished vocation is shoe painting: She spruces up footwear with abstract, fluorescent, and glittery coats of creativity. In fact, Shannon's often recognized in public by the decorated shoes she wears. She's especially proud of the pair of painted shoes she gave to singer Tori Amos. The one thread that ties together her myriad endeavors is her impulse to rebel against convention.

Many viewers see a method to her madness, as well as a message in what she says and does. Kring confirms that there is indeed a point to it all: "My overall message to people is to be yourself no matter what 'they' say. I hope my work enCOURAGEs people to follow their own heart and not feel they must follow someone else."

There's a preponderance of Shannon Kringen on the Web, including her Web site, some videos on YouTube, and her personal MySpace page (with over four hundred friends and counting). Please remember that some of her material is suitable for mature audiences only. If you're over eighteen and think you can take it, try experiencing some syn-Kring-nicity for yourself!

As Goddess Kring, Shannon offers viewers a largely experimental mix of freeform poetry, dance, video diary, show-and-tell, and editorializing.

Bobo: All Too Human

In the 1951 Ronald Reagan film *Bedtime for Bonzo,* the future president portrays a college professor who, in attempting to settle the "nature versus nurture" debate once and for all, decides to raise a chimpanzee as a human. Naturally, chaos ensues.

The movie might as well have focused on another conundrum: Does art imitate life, or does life imitate art? The question arises because a similar, real-life situation developed in Washington that very same year.

Bill Lowman, a divorced father of two who was living with his parents in Anacortes, shared his family's affinity for exotic animals. In 1951, Bill acquired a baby lowland gorilla, which had been taken from French Equatorial Africa at about two weeks of age. The story was that the baby gorilla was an orphan, which is a nicer story than the probable truth—that its mother was shot by some Great White Hunter, who probably wanted to sell the baby to a zoo. But never mind. Lowman was smitten by the hairy little tyke, and since he didn't currently have any gorillas of his own he bought it.

The Lowman family—Bill's parents Raymond and Jean, and daughters Sue and Claudia—had few reservations about taking in the orphaned ape. Jean was especially taken by bright-eyed little Bobo, as they named him—so much so that she began doting over him as though he were her own human child! Bobo was bottle-fed, diapered, and dressed in children's clothes. He was bathed regularly and slept in a crib with stuffed animals and his favorite rattle. In time, he began eating with the family at the dinner table. Reportedly, he was a lot less messy than a typical human toddler. Also, unlike human kids, when dinner was over he loved pitching in to help wash the dishes.

Treated like part of the family, Bobo developed a personality remarkably similar to that of a human child.

He loved toys and horseplay. In the 1995 documentary *Things That Aren't Here Anymore,* Bill Lowman recalled how the mischievous gorilla would tip over Raymond's rocking chair while he was sitting in it, running to hide behind Jean when his fuming foster-grandpa gave chase. He loved playing with the neighborhood kids, once even leading a little girl by the hand into the Lowmans' backyard to show her his toys.

Unfortunately, within two years Bobo's horseplay became a bit too wild and destructive. Dishes, records, and other household items were merely breakable playthings to him. Much of the Lowmans' furniture fell victim to Bobo's increasingly rambunctious behavior, and their friends stopped dropping by, intimidated by the growing gorilla's boundless energy. The Lowmans built an addition to their house, constructing an extra room for their beloved simian to live in, but the outgoing ape hated being so isolated. If he didn't simply refuse to go into the room, he would raise a ruckus while inside or find a way to break out. The Lowmans, short on money as well as any means to properly care for Bobo, had to bow to the inevitable: In 1953 they sold him to Seattle's Woodland Park Zoo.

It wasn't an easy separation for anyone involved; Bobo was more like a member of the family than a pet. Jean arranged to stay several weeks at the zoo, ostensibly to help acclimate Bobo to his new surroundings. In truth, her heart was breaking. She felt as if she were institutionalizing her own child and, arguably, she was. Raymond had a hard time coaxing her to come back home. Eventually, he and Bill had to literally drag her away as Bobo clung to her leg.

The Star Attraction

But things weren't all that bad for Bobo in his new digs. He was already well known to people in the Seattle area, and animal lovers flocked to see him at the zoo. By all accounts, he loved the attention. In time, he would grow to be six feet

allowed inside his enclosed room for some "family time." Though their visits grew less frequent over the years, Bobo never forgot them. During what would be Bill and Raymond's last visit, Bobo broke an apple in half, handing one of the pieces to Raymond over his shoulder, just as Raymond had regularly done for Bobo years before. The poignancy of the moment was compounded a few short weeks later by Bobo's untimely demise.

In late 1967 and early 1968, zoo staff noticed that Bobo had a slight limp and was intermittently breathing heavily and rubbing his throat. They also noticed that he'd recently lost sixty pounds! Though all this should've raised a red flag,

six and weigh 520 pounds. He would use his considerable bulk to ham it up for his audience, scaring kids with a "ferocious" act, only to display obvious amusement at their reactions. Eventually, Bobo's keepers decided to play matchmaker and introduced him to Fifi, the zoo's somewhat gruff-looking female gorilla. Though Fifi showed some amorous interest in him, Bobo was content to remain just friends. The pair got along fairly well but never mated, despite the zoo's hopes of producing some offspring. Though many theories were advanced as to why the two gorillas remained aloof, it wasn't understood at the time that gorillas are social animals that only thrive in groups.

The Lowmans visited Bobo on occasion and celebrated all his birthdays. Whenever they came around, they were

they didn't give it much thought. They said later that they thought he was getting better.

Unfortunately, he wasn't, and by the time zookeepers realized the gravity of the situation, it was too late. On February 22, 1968, Bobo was found dead at the tender age of sixteen. An autopsy revealed that his larynx was fractured and had been hemorrhaging. Bill Lowman suspected carelessness on the part of the zoo staff, speculating that Bobo had run into a sagging cable in his enclosure. Still, the family generally agreed that, based on what was known about gorillas at the time, he had received the best possible care.

The loss of Bobo was deeply felt around the Northwest, and folks yearned for something of him to be preserved for posterity. Perhaps taking this sentiment a bit too literally, zoo officials decided to have him stuffed! Seattle's Museum of History and Industry (MOHAI) unveiled the taxidermied version of Bobo later in 1968. Critics in the scientific community bemoaned some inconsistencies between the stuffed Bobo and standard gorilla anatomy; for instance, he was positioned upright, like a human, instead of hunched over on his knuckles. This, they complained, made him look more like Bigfoot than a gorilla. Defenders countered that, in life, Bobo had mostly walked upright anyway, and the taxidermied posture emphasized his half-human, half-ape personality. Controversy notwithstanding, for a while Bobo was as popular in death as he had been in life. He is still there today, in a new display called Gorilla in Our Midst. Here visitors can watch snippets of the Lowmans' home movies and see such Bobo memorabilia as his rattle and baby clothes.

With lessons learned through Bobo's care, the Woodland Park Zoo was better able to adapt its primate enclosures for the comfort and safety of the residents. The current outdoor gorilla pen is roomy and naturalistic, and its inhabitants quite content. This, then, is Bobo's legacy. Not a bad accomplishment for a local hero who grew up caught somewhere between person and primate.

The loss of Bobo was deeply felt around the Northwest, and folks yearned for something of him to be preserved for posterity. Perhaps taking this sentiment a bit too literally, zoo officials decided to have him stuffed!

The Honorable J. P. Patches, Mayor of the City Dump!

Mention the name J. P. Patches to Northwest natives age thirty and older and their faces light up like cathode ray tubes, as they fondly recall one of their favorite childhood icons. Long before *The Simpsons'* Krusty, whom he partially inspired, Seattle's famous clown pratfalled, slapsticked, and generally made merry for a generation of devoted television viewers.

Despite his association with Seattle, Julius Pierpont Patches first appeared in 1954 over sixteen hundred miles away. Daryl Laub originally portrayed the clown for a kids' show on Minneapolis TV station WTCN. When Laub was lured away to a competing local station, WTCN director Chris Wedes was asked to replace Laub as the frolicsome J. P.

A former disc jockey and dinner theater actor, Wedes was already hamming it up as several other characters at the station. Among them: Joe the Cook, a comical Greek chef; Chuckwagon Chuck, the frontiersman who presented screenings of western movies; and Captain Eleven, a sci-fi show host.

According to the official J. P. Patches Web site, when he was first asked to replace Laub as the clown, Wedes balked. He was hesitant to take on yet another role, especially one that required so much makeup. But, as a professional, he was well aware that the show must go on. So with big ears, patchwork coat, and an oversized tie, Wedes wrote some new comedy skits, which struck a chord even with adults. It didn't take long for J. P. Patches to become more popular than ever.

In 1958, Wedes was wooed by Seattle station KIRO to bring J. P. Patches to the Pacific Northwest. To the good fortune of thousands of fans, he accepted. At KIRO, he was set up in a cluttered shack as the "mayor of the city dump"—specifically Seattle's old Montlake Landfill 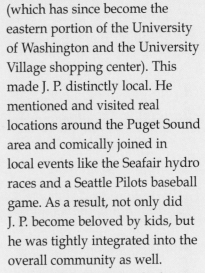 (which has since become the eastern portion of the University of Washington and the University Village shopping center). This made J. P. distinctly local. He mentioned and visited real locations around the Puget Sound area and comically joined in local events like the Seafair hydro races and a Seattle Pilots baseball game. As a result, not only did J. P. become beloved by kids, but he was tightly integrated into the overall community as well.

Like many children's shows, J. P. Patches encouraged some audience participation. One popular anecdote stands as a testament to the power of this kind of interactivity. In an episode where J. P. was searching for "Twinkle Dust" to give to the mystical Swami of Pastrami, he turned to the camera and asked if any viewers might have some at home. In short order, post office sorting machinery was being jammed by envelopes of sugar, salt, dirt, talcum, and other powdered or granulated substances mailed to KIRO by well-meaning kids.

The show lasted until 1981, when demographics and

the business of local television changed across the country. However, this didn't spell the end of J. P. Patches. Quite the contrary: Chris Wedes took his act on the road, making appearances all across the Northwest. Over the years, J. P. has cheered kids up at Children's Hospital and stopped a near riot at the Paramount Theater (both in Seattle) with his good-natured brand of wholesome humor. In these stints, he was often joined by Bob Newman, former floor director at the station, who played Gertrude, who fancied herself the love of J. P.'s life (a love, sadly, unrequited). For this role, Newman dressed in clown drag: a pink moplike wig, a flowery housedress, and face makeup with outsize lips. No effort was made to hide the brawny ex-marine's perpetual five o'clock shadow, hairy limbs, or combat boots. Wedes and Newman often reprised their roles on TV for anniversary specials and KIRO retrospectives.

Due to failing health, Bob Newman retired from portraying Gertrude in 2002. During a gathering at Seattle's Museum of History and Industry (where authentic J. P. Patches props and memorabilia adorn a corner of the gift shop), two hundred fans voted for antitax advocate Tim Eyman to replace him. (Prevailing sentiment held that this gig would keep him too busy to meddle in Washington's fiscal affairs.) So far, Eyman has shirked his duties as the new Gertrude.

As of this writing, plans are under way to erect a statue of J. P. Patches in 2008, to commemorate the fiftieth anniversary of the first airing of the Seattle show. To nobody's surprise, it will be located in Fremont, Seattle's most eccentric neighborhood. For Chris Wedes, it's the culmination of the role of a lifetime. For thousands of Patches Pals, it's a fitting tribute to their clown hero.

Whatever Happened to Blue Dog?

In the mid- to late 1990s, a panhandling pooch named Blue Dog marked Seattle's Pioneer Square as his territory. Wearing a cap, sunglasses, and vest, he would sit patiently with a paper cup in his mouth, giving puppy-dog eyes to passersby in hopes of getting some spare change, or at least a friendly pat on the head. He never lacked for either, as Pioneer Square regulars adored him. His best human pal, a friendly fellow transient, would usually be several feet away, keeping an eye on him.

Then, one day both Blue and his companion vanished. Repeated inquiries to locals over the years haven't yielded any clues as to their whereabouts. So now we're asking you, esteemed reader: Whatever happened to Blue Dog? If you know, please clue us in by e-mailing editor@weirdus.com.

Personalized Properties

When the concepts of ownership and freedom of expression converge, wonderful things can happen. When they converge among uncommon, free-spirited, or outspoken people, the results can be wonderfully WEIRD!

Submitted here as proof are examples of how some Washingtonians have gone beyond the pale in customizing two hallmarks of the American dream: real estate and vehicles.

These folks are as diverse a bunch as you're likely to find: artists, entrepreneurs, activists, retirees . . . and more. Yet they have one thing in common: Whatever their reasons, all have acted on the creative urge to distinguish their property from the ordinary.

In and of themselves, these homes, cars, restaurants, and monuments are just plain fun to look at. But a personalized property can also provide a fairly intimate insight about its owners: their likes and dislikes, opinions, obsessions, and so forth. And it can tap into our own creative sides, encouraging reflection on what our belongings, after a little decorative tweaking, might say about us.

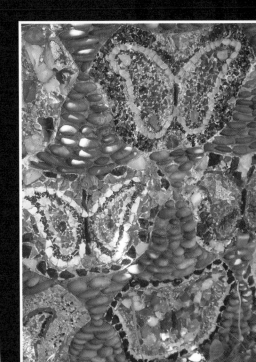

Home Sweet (Hubba Hubba) Home!

Iconic pinup queen Bettie Page is immortalized on the side of this house in Seattle, located just off I-5 North near the Sixty-fifth Street exit. The two-story mural was a thirtieth birthday present for homeowner Chris Brugos from his graphic designer friend John Green, who here describes its creation:

> I was going for a black-and-white comic book effect, as a homage to Bettie's resurgence in the early 80s. . . . I displayed the image against the wall using a big video projector, then masked it off in the dead of night, spraying paint during the day. The project took four or five days to complete as there was a lot of ladder work because it is about 17' tall. I'm mostly happy with it, but my friend is happy, and that's what counts most.

A Latter-day Saints church is located next door, with a back driveway that runs right past the mural. Church members generally seem to ignore Bettie, but someone eventually reported the image as "graffiti" to Seattle Public Utilities (the church denied any involvement with this complaint). Facing potential fines, Brugos successfully convinced SPU that the image was in fact not graffiti, but commissioned art.

Brugos and Green have vowed to fight any potential future attempts by the city to cover Ms. Page. Which is good, since Bettie has become a popular sight. The clever use of the eaves for a modicum of modesty is creatively admirable, if a bit disappointing to oglers stuck in rush hour traffic.

Johnny Appleseed of the Palms

Many people are surprised that palm trees can survive in Seattle, but the climate is surprisingly mild this far north. Warm currents off the Pacific Coast and pervasive cloud cover tend to make the local weather moderate: winter highs top out around 50°F and summer highs float between 75 and 85°F. This climate is perfect for the Windmill Palm.

Alain Lucier, a Canadian transplant now living in Seattle, loves palm trees so much he surrounded his home with hundreds of them. He ran out of room on his own property, and wanting to spread the tropical beauty through his neighborhood, planted trees on the boulevard in front of his home and then up and down the street in front of his neighbor's house. You know you're getting close to the Fremont neighborhood of this Johnny Appleseed of the palms—around the 4200 block of 3rd NW—when you start seeing the palm trees planted all around.—*Marlow Harris*

Rockin' Through the Walker Garden

Neighbors of the nosy variety must have had a field day with the Walkers. What WERE they doing in their backyard in a quiet West Seattle neighborhood?

The window curtains next door must have twitched when the Walkers began to bring home carload after carload of rocks—ten tons, in all, from an out-of-business Oregonian rock shop. Then the pile in the driveway began to swell with thunder eggs, agates, petrified wood, chunks of bright glass, and colorful river rock. Tongues must have wagged in the street's cozy homes as people speculated why

Milton Walker, after working a swing shift at nearby Boeing Company, chose to spend his "leisure" hours in manual labor.

Weighing in at one hundred thirty-five pounds and measuring five feet six inches in height, Milton was an unlikely candidate for a second shift as a stonemason. But what he lacked in bulk and experience he made up for in sheer perseverance and the pleasure of creation.

As wonderful as the rock creations are, they would be only half as marvelous if it hadn't been for Milton's wife, Florence, and her love of gardening. The exuberant ephemeral bloom of azaleas, rhododendrons, roses, iris, and even a topiary animal all thrived under the loving application of her green thumb and provided a lively counterpoint to her husband's solid arches and walls.

But as much as they loved working in their garden, the Walkers loved sharing it. They threw it open for Mother's Day and Father's Day every year, so all could enjoy the butterfly stepping stones, the bicentennial tower, and the grape arbor.

Maybe Milton Walker had a curious itch of his own to satisfy. "Mom said that Dad loved to dress up as a tourist and wander incognito among the visitors," says his daughter. When asked what he hoped to hear, she replied, "I don't think he ever heard anything bad. He always had a smile on his face at the end of the day."—*Peg Boettcher*

The Walker Rock Garden is open from June through Labor Day. The family happily continues the tradition of sharing the garden, but prefers that visitors phone for reservations. The number may be found under Walker Rock Garden in the residential listings of the Seattle phone book.

in the Lair of Leopard Bernstein

"I really don't have any particular affinity for leopards or big cats," claims West Seattle artist Kelly Lyles. Many folks might have trouble believing this. Since the mid-1990s, her favorite endeavor has been an ongoing work in progress that casts serious doubt on her purported neutrality toward felines. Kelly has decorated—*really* decorated—her 1989 Subaru station wagon with a bundle of big cats.

The car, named Leopard Bernstein after a stuffed animal from Kelly's childhood, is covered with leopard spots, sports a painting of a leopard's head on the hood, and even has leopard ears and a tail! Hundreds, perhaps thousands, of toy and figurine lions, tigers, panthers, and (of course) leopards are glued to the car's exterior and dashboard. The inside is filled with plush toy cats, while the ceiling is covered with notes and postcards left behind by admirers.

No "particular affinity" indeed!

Kelly is an enthusiastic participant in the national art car scene, and Leopard Bernstein—Bernie for short—has received *grrrreat* acclaim at art car events across the United States. It's been featured in books, documentaries, articles, and an untold number of anecdotes from surprised motorists who come across Bernie on the road.

Kelly's artistic spirit is displayed with equal fervor at her home. Hidden behind tall hedges, the front lawn is decorated with miscellaneous items such as carousel horses,

a reflective Easter Island head, a five-foot-tall inflatable cell phone, and a four-foot-tall paint tube, also inflatable. This is but a modest indication of the wonders on display indoors. Kelly counts artists from around the world among her friends and has adorned her home with an impressive collection of their artwork. Unusual paintings, a creepy customized baby doll, and a microwave converted into a "Love Tester"—to test your romantic potency—are only a few of the visual treasures on hand.

It's said that the bedroom is the part of a home that best reflects its occupants. This seems particularly true of Kelly's. Cheery and girlish, embellished with even more art, it hints at a forever-young *joie de vivre*. A closetful of eclectic, flamboyant clothing demonstrates her everyday mode of dress. Says Kelly, "My mom jokes that I've always dressed eccentrically: ballerina outfits in the winter, snowsuits in the summer. I remember getting into a big fight with her once when I wanted to wear pajamas to school!" There's a gem-covered telephone and a big fuzzy-dog chair to relax in while calling friends. On the veranda just outside the bedroom, a mounted rhinoceros head watches for eavesdroppers.

Besides collecting funky trappings and her work on Leopard Bernstein, Kelly is an accomplished traditional artist. Some of her oil paintings, particularly her evocative figure studies, belie her more prevalent offbeat streak. Still, she describes her art as "representative, with a sense of humor." Her dining room, where she displays a personal series of paintings—drunks adapted from donated photographic reference—underscores that attitude.

Her hubcap-covered garage-studio houses a gallery's worth of finished and in-progress art. This is also where she runs her commercial art business, Grrraphics, Inc. Leopard Bernstein bides his time one room over, always ready for a quick outing when Kelly needs a break.

Despite the years she's spent decorating and developing as an artist, her attitude toward her artwork, home, and car is relatively modest: "I don't think there's anything too deep about any of it. It's pretty blatant. I just like to laugh and have it hit you over the head!"

For those of you intimidated by art, we assure you she means that figuratively!

Kelly Lyles and Leopard Bernstein have their own little corner of cyberspace at www.kellyspot.com.

Gospodor's Monumental Controversy

What's a wealthy senior to do if he wants to contribute a little something extra to society? Start a charity? Sponsor a school? Fund a scholarship? Dominic Gospodor asked himself this question and came up with a unique plan. Gospodor, whose entrepreneurial spirit served him well in real estate and oil pipeline construction, decided to use his wealth to commemorate people and groups he felt were under-acknowledged.

The octogenarian's altruistic efforts are on display on a parcel of land he owns next to I-5 North between Toledo and Winlock. Towering over a field of perpetually overgrown grass are three copper-plated monuments honoring Mother Teresa, victims of the Holocaust, and American Indians. Planned in the late 1990s and erected in 2002, they are known as the Gospodor Monuments.

The central tower, honoring Mother Teresa, stands 108 feet high and is topped by two globes stacked one above the other, with a gold-painted wood carving of Jesus Christ at the very top. At the bottom of the monument, a similar wood carving of Mother Teresa is mounted on a cylindrical base.

The monument on the left, rising to 87 feet, honors Holocaust victims. At its top is an electric "eternal flame" about 10 feet high. Oddly, the flame is contained within a structure shaped somewhat like a lava lamp.

The monument on the right, honoring American

Indians (or all tribes, as it states on an explanatory roadside billboard), stands 100 feet high. It's a simple tower topped with a gold-painted carving of Chief Sealth, for whom the Seattle is named. All three towers are fitted with lights that are visible for miles at night.

The monuments have been fraught with controversy since the planning stages. Gospodor initially hoped to place them at the Sacred Heart Catholic Church near Seattle's Space Needle, but the Catholic Archdiocese of Seattle wasn't interested. Lewis County skeptically granted him permission to build, but required that each tower be shorter and thicker than originally devised, owing to engineering studies that indicated potential wind or earthquake damage. Gospodor agreed.

With a site and permission in place, Gospodor's dream finally began taking shape in late 2000. He had cameras installed on-site to watch the construction from his apartment in Seattle. The overall cost of construction was approximately $500,000.

Public reaction has been mixed: Many appreciate Gospodor's intent, but others just don't get it. Some have decried the monuments as eyesores and question the legitimacy of their status as memorials, because no government or civic organization sponsored them, an ironic criticism in conservative, pro–small government Lewis County. By far the biggest controversy is related to the monuments' location along I-5, where the speed limit is 70 mph. Many individuals and groups, including the Washington State Patrol, consider the structures dangerously distracting and blame them for sudden traffic slowdowns as motorists take them in.

Gospodor has argued against all the accusations, but the stigma—deserved or not—has stuck. In May 2003, he filed for permits to erect monuments honoring DUI accident victims and African American slaves. At a hearing, Lewis County rejected the permits under

advisement from the state department of transportation and the Washington State Patrol. In addition to traffic safety concerns, the county also mentioned that the site lacked both bathroom facilities and a parking lot from which to view the monuments.

The following month Gospodor filed a lawsuit against the county, the DOT, and the State Patrol, claiming that the decision was based on opinions and hearsay rather than fact. A few days later he announced that he hadn't decided whether to follow up on the suit (apparently, he still hasn't).

In 2005, Gospodor and his monuments were the subject of *What in God's Name?* a six-minute documentary by independent filmmaker Vance Malone.

What else is planned for Gospodor's Monument Park? Similar tributes to Susan B. Anthony, women's rights pioneer; Jonas Salk, polio vaccine developer; William Seward, who purchased Alaska from Russia in 1867; and Lewis and Clark. He would like to install explanatory plaques and is searching for an organization or government entity that would maintain the monuments after his passing, including paying the approximately $115-a-month electric bill.

Whatever they represent to people—decorations, eyesores, tributes, or distractions—they remain first and foremost monuments to one man's heartfelt admiration of others and his perseverance in seeing it expressed his own way.

For a more leisurely view of Gospodor's Monument Park, take I-5 exit 63 and head east. Make a right onto Camus Road and follow it south until you see the monuments on your right. Pulling over by the property's rear gate is much safer than pulling over to the shoulder of I-5. As with any private property, please refrain from trespassing.

Dick and Jane's Spot

Dick Elliott and Jane Orleman of Ellensburg don't just create art, they live in it! Their home—a fixer-upper with broken windows and no lawn when they bought it in 1978—has become an ever-changing folk-art fantasyland where the weird and the wonderful intermingle in decidedly dreamlike harmony.

At first, it didn't happen intentionally; it just sort of, well, happened. As they were repairing their new home, Dick and Jane sought a few unique items with which to decorate the property, to add just a little personal flair. One of the first pieces to go up was the giant hand above the front door. What the heck, they figured after acquiring a few more odds and ends, why not go a little further? Nearly thirty years and two art studio additions later, it's obvious a little further went a long, long way!

Dick and Jane are both artists who have embraced their calling in earnest, long ago realizing that their home had become their ultimate perpetual canvas. Every nook and cranny of the yard, as well as the outer walls of the house, are decorated with unique and diverse pieces of folk art. "We like to call it an aesthetic experience from the safety of your own car," explains Dick. About sixty to seventy percent of the *objets d'art* were created by Dick and Jane themselves, but many were contributed by other artists over the years or collected at art shows and other venues. Luckily, their home-based business (a cleaning service) afforded them enough time and income early on to pursue their whimsical art.

Observers will immediately note the abundance of reflectors used in decorating the property. This is Dick's trademark; a renowned reflector artist, he has created numerous public artworks at sites around the country. It's only natural that he'd apply his signature technique to his home. The fence is covered with reflectors, and there are colorful reflective mosaics of several sizes and patterns around the exterior of the house.

Impressive as all this is, it's only the tip of the iceberg! Among the too-numerous-to-count pieces at the Spot is a fence post painted to look like a giant Number 2 pencil; a twenty-foot-tall brick tower shaped somewhat like a melting glass bottle, with mannequins peering out

of the windows; and a sculpture of Beethoven attached to a wooden post, surrounded by large wood screws and bottle caps.

Credit Jane for creating the Spot's perhaps most iconic piece, Big Red: a wooden post in saucy seductress garb, complete with reflective cleavage, in a flower patch near the front gate. An accomplished painter whose work favors psychological imagery, Jane says many of the various objects in their yard are actually cast-off prep work made to aid in the creation of "finished" art. For example, artist Richard Beyer donated his original fiberboard guides for his famous sculpture in Fremont, *Waiting for the Interurban.*

Dick and Jane's property has garnered much media attention over the years. A lengthy list of publications, TV shows, and documentaries have profiled their efforts, and the city government of Ellensburg has certainly paid attention to it. Recognizing a good tourist draw, it donated an easement behind the house for a rear walkway so admirers can appreciate the artwork on all sides. The easement is contingent to the house's remaining a work of art.

Dick and Jane's Spot is visited and photographed off and on all day by people from all walks of life. A disclaimer for the curious, though: Dick and Jane's Spot is a home, not a business. As such, there are no hours of operation or admission fee. It is private property that Dick and Jane would prefer be admired solely from outside the fence. If you visit, take a minute to leave a friendly note in the guest book in the booth near the corner. Tell 'em *Weird Washington* sent you!

For more information on Dick and Jane's Spot and their individual artwork, visit their Web site at www. reflectorart.com.

Where Spirits of Iron Roam Free

Three miles east of Elbe on State Route 706, approaching the western entrance to Mount Rainier National Park, one man's sculpture garden celebrates not only his craftsmanship, but also that of the metalworkers and artisans who unknowingly produced the elements of his sculptures.

This is because Dan Klennert has an uncanny ability to sense aesthetic connections between entirely unrelated machine parts and hardware. Gears, auto parts, antique bathtub legs, piping, hooks, rebar, brackets, circular saw blades, horseshoes, and countless other parts gathered from local farmers' scrap piles or donated by neighbors and fans are the stuff from which Dan conjures up his creations. With the phoenix flame of his cutting torch and his four-hundred-amp stick welder, he resurrects the assorted scraps into a vast metal menagerie of animals, people, and objects that he calls his Recycled Spirits of Iron.

"When I handle an old piece of metal, it's like I can feel and see the spirit of the old-timer who used it in their everyday life," explains Dan. "As you view my work, you're also experiencing the many spirits of people from the past who are now on the 'other side.' In a way, I'm celebrating their life by recycling their spirits."

Each part is integral to the larger whole, implemented in a way that seems at once brilliant and amazingly natural. His medium of choice and all the work put into creating each spirit give Dan's work a distinct blue-collar vibe. The spirits roam here on Dan's property, which he's named Ex Nihilo, "From Nothing."

Originally from Minnesota, Dan's family moved to Seattle's Holly Park housing community in the mid-1950s. As a youngster, Dan was an independent, freewheeling kid "living the life of Huck Finn," as he puts it. At six, he fell in love with art. By his own account, "In school, I went to class mostly for art on Friday. It was great! I just loved it. I was the kid who refused to conform or be channeled in school."

His other love was scrounging through discarded junk to find items he likened to treasure. "It was like Christmas, finding cool stuff people threw out." He began creating his sculptures in his twenties, while working as a mechanic and construction worker. Not only did it provide a way to practice welding (which he needed to do at his day jobs), it also combined his loves of scrounging and art.

By 1998, after having lived in Renton, Kent, and Seattle's Ballard neighborhood, Dan was weary of a strictly urban lifestyle. He began to dream of having his own sculpture park and sharing his creativity with the rest of the world. Heading for open country, he found and purchased the unoccupied

property that was to become Ex Nihilo. "When I first viewed the property and heard the whistle from the little steam engine in Elbe," Dan fondly recalls, "I knew I was home!"

A giant smiley face at the entrance to Ex Nihilo invites visitors to PLEASE FEEL FREE TO COME ON IN. On top of the arched gate, another face, looking somewhat mischievous, welcomes you. The gate itself is adorned with three symbolic metal circles representing Dan and his parents.

The main attraction is the roadside corral next to the entrance, where much of Dan's best work is on display. For a $3 suggested donation, you can get up close and personal with a skeletal biker, a dog-size spider, horses (of the regular, rocking, and sea varieties), deer, dinosaurs, a stork, a guitarist, a life-size giraffe, and many other objects and animals. Walking through and viewing each impressive piece is a treat for the eyes. One quickly develops a distinct sense of wonder and appreciation for Dan's ingenuity. Perhaps, he hopes, we will leave with a realization that even the lowliest discarded item has value and can serve a purpose.

Though Dan has sold several sculptures, he creates his Spirits of Iron solely for the love of making them. He has resisted letting himself become motivated by money, even while knowing of the considerable profit made by artists of a similar persuasion. "I don't like prostituting my

soul," he says. Still, he makes a decent living, regularly selling or lending out his work.

Ex Nihilo does indeed celebrate the American can-do spirit. The sculptures emphasize people's freedom of expression, clever innovation, and a tangible demonstration of recycling, all wrapped within understated patriotism. Dan fondly remembers a tourist who, after spending some time with the many wonders of Ex Nihilo, apparently recognized this. "A guy was visiting here from Russia, and he came up to me and said, 'This is the real spirit of America. Not the technology, not the government.' And he got it. That's what I'm aiming for. And that's what I want the country to get back to!"

More about Dan's work and Ex Nihilo can be found at his Web site, www.danielklennert.com.

In the Labyrinth of Richart's Ruins

At Harrison Avenue East and M Street in Centralia, bizarre black-and-white spires rise from behind the fence of a peculiar corner lot. The structures are—to drastically understate it—quite distinctive in this modest working-class neighborhood. Are they a Martian city? A colossal Rube Goldberg contraption? Hell erupting through the earth?

In fact, they're the homespun handiwork of the property's owner, Richard Tracy, a self-styled art educator with plenty of time to spare and unconventional ideas about what constitutes art. Tracy converted his property into a personal folk-art paradise using a multitude of junk scraps that include glass, wire, bike parts, reflectors, and lots and lots of polystyrene (better known by its trademarked name of Styrofoam).

Tracy's property is called the Centralia Art Yard, or—more popularly—Richart's Ruins (Richart being an alternate spelling of his first name that Tracy adopted). This place is legendary among folk artists and oddity-seeking day trippers. It's even insured by Lloyd's of London; Tracy had to resort to the world-famous specialty insurer after several domestic insurance companies refused him coverage.

Not only insurers, but certain others look at Tracy with more confusion than appreciation. Many of his neighbors seem to harbor a cynical opinion of him. They see him as the local eccentric, the old man who began creating his "art" at age fifty during a stay in a psychiatric ward. Who, after his release,

spent the next twenty-plus years destroying his yard and imperiling neighborhood property values. In other words, they just don't get it! "In twenty years, the neighbors have never come over," Tracy laments with more than a hint of frustration.

But this shunning is made up for by the many out-of-towners who drop by to admire his work. On the purported last day of his loosely followed May-to-September "open yard" season, Tracy honored *Weird Washington* with a guided tour.

As we walked among polystyrene monoliths, makeshift scrap-metal frames, plywood art walls, and countless indescribable flights of fancy, Tracy's conversations were as erratic and meandering as the narrow, mazelike confines of his yard. As with his art, much of Tracy's gab has to be interpreted in a grand-scheme context, rather than trying to understand each seemingly random thought.

He mentioned his endeavors in art education here at his house, where on occasion he mentors up to five students for fifty-five minutes, for $5 each. We asked about his much reported obsession with the number five. As it turns out, it's not so much an obsession as a conscious ploy to reinforce his eccentric reputation. "I was selling some of my stuff in Portland [Oregon], and somebody asked about my work. I said that I never spend more than five hours on any project or sell anything for more than five dollars. And he said, 'Oh, that's interesting, this number five thing you have.' I hadn't noticed it before! If he

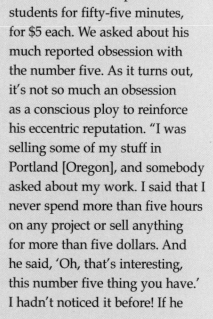

hadn't said that, I might've missed it!"

He guided us to some of his favorite art. He pointed out a display of several bicycle helmets, all adorned with various knickknacks. Crafting these became a tradition when participants in the annual Seattle-to-Portland bike race began stopping by en route. Tracy wears one for the day and then "retires" it (that is, puts it on display next to the others).

Then there's the piece with a World War II–era striker frame. At one time it was used to turn over injured soldiers while keeping them immobile. Now a mummylike mannequin lies within it, integrated aesthetically with a polystyrene-and-plywood backdrop. Perhaps his most prized possession is in the very back of the yard: a polystyrene sculpture that he keeps behind Plexiglas. A ten-year-old girl, a onetime student of his, created it.

Why all this polystyrene? It's the perfect medium for outdoor crafts. As frustrated environmentalists will attest, it takes forever to degrade. It blocks moisture, yet mildew can grow on it. Tracy loves the implied concept: man and nature collaborating to create art. In fact, he considers nature the ultimate art, as evidenced by his examination of a stray blade of grass at the base of one of his pieces. "Now THIS is real art!" he exclaimed enthusiastically, admiring its texture.

The more time we spent in Tracy's universe, considering his chaotic visions and listening to his unusual perspectives on art, life, and human nature, the more his eccentricities seemed to melt away into an appealing logic. Unlike his neighbors, we got it: At his core, the man is all about uncompromising full-steam-ahead self-expression. At the end of our visit, as we waved a sincerely appreciative good-bye, the world beyond Richart's Ruins seemed a bit drabber than we remembered.

Toilet Fence Trouble

A short list of things that annoy golfers: uneven greens, slow players, noise during a backswing, unrepaired divots, a red devil straining on a toilet.

Wait. . . . What?

It's true! At least, it was true in the town of Soap Lake between October 2006 and April 2007. That's when a dispute between Rick and Jody Froebe and their neighbors, the Lakeview Golf & Country Club, came to a head—to be more precise, even heads, two old tubs, six broken water heaters, and three dummies. Together, these elements formed the Froebes' infamous backyard Toilet Fence, an object of both scorn and delight.

It all started when Rick, who co-owns nearby Coulee Dam/Ephrata Plumbing with Jody's brother, Bob, learned of a clerical error with his recently paid-for club membership. Due to this oversight, his brother-in-law wasn't allowed to join him on the links. Rick cancelled the membership in protest, but the club refused to refund his dues. Furthermore, say the Froebes, golfers would wander onto part of their property assuming it belonged to the club. Consequently, their four dogs barked so much it resulted in neighbors complaining and the sheriff imposing fines. The Froebes decided to give a little back.

Decorating for Halloween, Rick gathered up some old plumbing implements and lined them up in the front yard. He and Jody improvised three dummies—including the aforementioned red devil—from old clothes and Halloween masks, and sat them on some of the toilets.

Staff and members of Lakeview no doubt assumed

Dummies and a devil take a seat on Soap Lake plumber Rick Froebe's creative fence.

David Cole/Columbia Basin Herald

Golfers teed off about toilets

BY DAVID COLE
Herald staff writer

SOAP LAKE — Rick Froebe erected a backyard "fence." It's not a white-picket fence. Instead, it's made of seven old toilets, a few used bathtubs and some broken down water heaters.

He said it's to "keep the golfers out" of his yard.

Froebe's home, 832 Canterbury Road, is nestled along Lakeview Golf & Country Club near Soap Lake. He watches closely from his back porch as golfers negotiate the green of the 354-yard, par-4 first hole.

"Choice real estate in Grant County," said Froebe, co-owner of Coulee Dam/Ephrata Plumbing.

On Monday, three scarecrow-like dummies sat on toilets and looked on as golfers finished their putts. The old commodes, bathtubs and water heaters first appeared on Halloween. The dummies came down for a few days, now they're back.

Froebe, who's owned the home for the previous 15 years, already had a backyard fence in place — the chain-link version. He claims it's not enough to keep golfers and neighborhood cats r... riled up.

barking as players drive their golf carts near the green, search for their balls, chat, chip and putt. Neighbors began complaining about the barking.

Gerald Coulter, representing the country club's nine-member board of directors, called the situation "completely ridiculous." That's the consensus of the board, Coulter said, following last week's meeting.

"I've had several people call that were upset with (the 'fence'). It's an eyesore," Coulter said. "I'm surprised the health department hasn't been out there because of the used toilets and water tanks. It's not a sanitary condition." Coulter, of Soap Lake, said Froebe is most likely trying to "alienate neighbors."

In the process, Froebe may also be attempting to upset members of the country club, he said.

A squabble Froebe had with course officials resulted in the 52-year-old plumber... membership in May. Froeb... plained that he h...

it was an eccentric Halloween decoration that would go away after October 31. It didn't: The toilets, dummies, and so on instead were moved to the rear of the house, facing the golf course's first hole. As the days wore on, Lakeview Club management began suspecting that they'd been treated to a trick! They complained about the distracting scene to Grant County, an act that not only flushed away hope of a prompt resolution to the dispute over the unrefunded dues but also attracted media attention.

During Thanksgiving week, the Froebes' "fence" leaked into newspapers nationwide. In various articles, Rick playfully boasted of his "plumber art" while Gerald Coulter, a member of the Lakeview Club's board of directors, bemoaned the "completely ridiculous" situation.

He called the display an eyesore and hinted, none too subtly, "I'm surprised the health department hasn't been out there because of the used toilets. . . . It's not a sanitary condition."

The Froebes insist that it bothered few people outside the club. "Everyone loved it," Jody told *Weird Washington*. "Besides," the newspapers quoted Rick as saying, "it's not like this is Pebble Beach. This is Lakeview!"

Grant County didn't see it that way. They took the club's side and threatened to fine the Froebes $950 each day the Toilet Fence remained in their yard after March 31. Incensed, Rick and Jody immediately painted the back of their house an obnoxious orange with green, yellow, and purple polka dots. The Froebes' attorney challenged the county's effort by asking them to cite an ordinance that prohibited the decorative outdoor display of plumbing fixtures. Although such a decoration is highly irregular, Grant County bowed to the Froebes' legal whiz and admitted there were no such laws on the books.

The Froebes had tried a few gestures of humorous goodwill to placate their critics: They planted shrubs in some of the toilet bowls and dressed the dummies for different holidays. There was an Easter theme going when Lakeview finally extended an olive branch: It would refund the club dues if, in return, the Froebes promised to remove the Toilet Fence for good.

Rick agreed to the deal. To the relief of golfers and the dismay of many amused fans, the commodes, tubs, and water heaters were removed in mid-April, 2007.

So was it worth all the trouble? "Yes, it was," says Rick. "We got our money back. It was the principle of the thing." Flushed with exhaustion from the whole ordeal, the Froebes were glad to return to less irritable day-to-day living.

Bandy's Troll Haven

Gardiner, on the Olympic Peninsula, is a low-key rural community some travelers might not notice, even as they pass through to more prominent nearby towns like Sequim and Port Townsend. This is a real shame, because all it takes is a turn from Highway 101 onto Gardiner Beach Road to find yourself in a curious place of fairy-tale wonderment.

A motley assortment of trolls, dragons, ogres, and other storybook denizens loiter in the surrounding woods, in front of homes, and along the sides of the road. A good many of them take the form of funny-faced fence posts. What are they doing here, of all places?

Their story is said to be carried in song by the north wind: A multitude of trolls and their cohorts sailed from Norway in great haste, seeking a new home. They braved many hardships, including the frigid cold of the Arctic Circle, before landing here on the quiet shore of Discovery Bay sometime in 1977.

The trolls settled on one hundred and fifty acres of farmland owned by Garrett Bandy, who

was very accommodating and duly named his property Bandy's Troll Haven. He had several large, ornately decorated houses built for his new friends. The buildings' architecture is modeled after that of the trolls' native Norway of ages past. The crown jewel of this effort is the Gatekeeper's House, an amazing castlelike estate that overlooks the surrounding pastures and lavender orchard.

Legend has it that the trolls are active only at night, and—according to the trollhaven.org Web site—are "often known to eat travelers foolish enough to stray into their domain after dark." The morning sun is said to turn the trolls back into stone for the day, allowing humans to visit safely. Suspiciously, these petrified trolls look more like carved wood. In fact, while in this state, a few of them double as decorative pillars for a small barn in one of the pastures.

Bandy's Troll Haven is not without its controversy. We heard through the grapevine that a few (human) locals haven't taken to Troll Haven too well. They complain about increased traffic in the area, and at least one neighbor raised a ruckus when a newly constructed troll building blocked his view of the bay. The irony of all this isn't lost on Troll Haven fans. After all, how many times have trolls been stereotyped as ill tempered?

The farmland, estate, and other nearby residences are private property and possibly occupied. Visits should be limited to admiring the site from the road unless you have permission to wander the grounds. Short- or long-term rental of Troll Haven buildings is possible, but pricey.

Roadside Oddities

f you're into sightseeing, you can't go wrong with a trip around
Washington. Such an excursion reveals an incredibly eclectic variety
of landscapes, including city skylines, evergreen forests, ocean beaches,
waterfalls, islands—all of which are covered in other books. Here we're focused
on the less expected scenery along Washington's highways and local byways:
eccentric establishments, wacky advertising, public art that defies
convention, and unusual displays intended to make a point . . . or no
point at all. For better, never for worse, what follows is just a taste of
Washington's many Roadside Oddities. Turn the page and enjoy, because
let's face it: Mount Rainier has NOTHING on a giant squirting razor clam!

Ye Olde Curiosity Shop: Cornucopia of Curios

"Are you through sorting the shrunken heads"?

Dialogue from a B horror film? Orders heard in hell? Nope, it's just business as usual at Ye Olde Curiosity Shop on Seattle's waterfront.

On a typical summer day, you'll hear the shop before you see it. Somebody's sure to have dropped a couple of quarters into the vintage Artizan military band organ just outside. The machine will be belting out "Falling in Love Again" loud enough to compete with the ferry horns from Colman Dock next door.

Inside, the player piano in back will be tinkling away, alternating overtures from obscure Italian operas (*Zampa,* anyone?) and hot jazz from the '20s. You'll hear the rattle of the penny-stretching machine, the clatter of lucky medallions dispensed by Black Bart, the one-armed bandit, and the giggling of yet another generation of schoolkids delighted to find that trinkets of goatskin

shrunken heads and plastic dog poop are well within their means.

Look up. There's Skinny Stubbs, shoplifting deterrent, all six skeletal feet of him hanging from a noose tied to the rafters. Feel as if you're being watched? You are . . . by a gigantic pair of bespectacled eyes that once advertised an English optometrist's practice. Examine the ancient and desiccated "devil fish" spread out like a cartwheel, the walrus skull with three tusks, the gleaming line of brass samovars from Mother Russia, the blue Chinese foo dog, the two-headed calf. . . . It's like your great-grandma's attic, if your great-grandma collected human skulls instead of old dress patterns.

It's taken the shop a long time to get this weird—over a hundred years, in fact. Ever since its birth as a trading post at the turn of the twentieth century, it's been packed to the gills with the exotic, the creepy, and the wonderful. Founder Joseph Edward Standley, fondly known as Daddy, had an appetite for oddities equal to his talent for promotion, and his tastes ran from the gargantuan—a whale's jawbones once framed the shop's entrance—to the minuscule (a grain of rice sporting a teeny painting of Mount Rushmore).

Over the years, the shop became a must-see destination for famous people who passed

YE OLDE CURIOSITY SHOP
MOST UNIQUE SHOP IN THE WORLD

1—Whale Jaw Bones, 1 ton each, 21½ feet, largest in U.S.
2—Skull of Alaska Buffalo, largest in the world.
3—Giant Clam Shell, weighs 161 pounds. From Bering.
4—Ivory Tusk of Alaska Elephant (mammoth).
5—Head of Arctic Walrus with ivory tusks
6—Shell, 815 pounds, fired from U. S. Fort Worden.
7—Navajo Rugs, from Navajo Indians.
8—Indian Totem Poles.
9—Jaw of a Saw Fish.
10—Indian Cooking Basket.
11—Old Ship Lanterns, brass.
12—Hat worn by Chief Seattle.
13—Alaska Snail, petrified, 67 pounds.
14—Chilcat Blanket from Alaska.

GROUND FLOOR AT COLMAN DOCK ENTRANCE, SEATTLE.

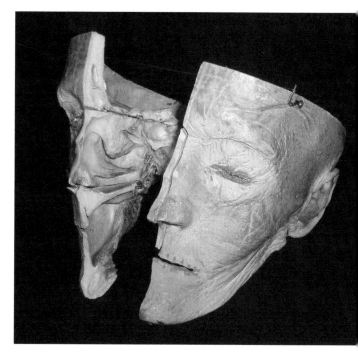

through the area, as well as for innumerable tourists. Among the illustrious could be counted Charlie Chaplin, Presidents Warren G. Harding and Theodore Roosevelt, J. Edgar Hoover, Katharine Hepburn, Sylvester Stallone—even Queen Marie of Rumania.

After Standley's death in 1940, the family continued to actively run the business, which expanded to another store nearby. On any given day, great-grandson Andy James can be found in the first shop fixing things up or chatting with one of the young Native American artists who come in to sell their carvings. "I buy from the great-grandkids of artists who sold to my great-granddad," says Andy. Wife Tammy takes charge of the second shop, where she can be found doing everything from stocking souvenir racks to building a "cave" to house Gloria, the child mummy.

Lest you think the store's attractions are a static bunch, acquired long ago and left to gather dust, you should know that the Jameses recently returned from a trip to Cornwall, England, where they attended an auction of the famous collection of Victorian taxidermist Walter Potter. They came away with a four-legged chicken, a two-headed bull calf, and a village made of cork, among other marvels.

There are a multitude of wonders to see, but the following curios win the popularity contest every time.

Sylvester the Desert Mummy

Of all the shop's attractions, Sylvester is definitely the star of the show. He's been drawing a crowd since shortly after his death late in the nineteenth century, fascinating audiences in the sideshows, carnivals, and World's Fairs of long ago with his near-perfect state of preservation.

Sylvester's existence as a de facto time capsule can be attributed to the fourteen

pounds of deadly arsenic used to preserve him. The technique, cutting-edge technology when it was developed during the Civil War (the body of Abraham Lincoln was prepared the same way), virtually halted the natural process of decay.

The Mermaid

With a fang-studded maw, nasty claws, and tufts of ratty hair covering its body, this monster couldn't tempt a sailor to save its life. Daddy Standley insisted he got it from a fisherman who shot it off the shores of Duckabush River in the '20s. The fisherman suffered terrible remorse after he got it back from the taxidermist's, and he couldn't wait to get rid of it. "He tells me it was years before he got over it," a local newspaper quoted Standley. "He never killed another." The shop's specimen is said to be the largest of its kind in the world.

Shrunken Heads

And the creep factor shoots off the scale! Daddy Standley agonized over the purchase of a collection of seven heads offered by George Gustav Heye, founder of the Museum of the American Indian. He made up his mind moments

before the door slammed shut on all international traffic in human heads, in the '30s. Tammy James attests to the shrunken head's extreme rarity. "Ripley's Museum would dearly love to get their hands on it," she says with pride.

Ye Olde Curiosity Shop and Ye Olde Curiosity Shop Too can be found side by side on Piers 54 and 55 on Seattle's waterfront. Learn more about the shop at www. yeoldecuriosityshop.com. *–Peg Boettcher*

Seattle Museum of the Mysteries

Seattle's Capitol Hill has a teeming community of neon lights and a funky good-time atmosphere—at the northern end of the main drag, a sitting, allegedly life-size model of Bigfoot rests at the bottom of a stairwell at 623 Broadway Avenue East. He's a mascot of sorts to the one and only Seattle Museum of the Mysteries.

The museum, a nonprofit organization started in 2003, exhibits some of the most baffling events in Washington State history, from the supernatural to UFOlogy. As per its literature, "The museum's mission is furthering education, research, and history of paranormal science, ancient civilizations, and alternate explanations of reality highlighting the Pacific Northwest."

Curators Philip Lipson and Charlette LeFevre enthusiastically guide visitors through several displays, starting with an overview of Bigfoot. The place is set up like a comfortable rec room, complete with tables, a couch, and video equipment. Along with key information on sightings, including maps and newspaper clippings, there are four plaster casts of the creatures' huge footprints, or at least Lipson and LeFevre think so. Other displays deal with Seattle ghosts, local crop circles, the Wellington avalanche of 1910 (the area is now considered haunted), and the 1947 Mount Rainier and Maury Island UFO incidents. The museum was funded by a grant from James Widener Ray, an altruist who passed away in 2005. Ray's bountiful book collection, housed in the museum, is a testament to the sense of wonder he held about the esoteric and unexplained.

Museum hours tend to vary due to its all-volunteer staff. More information can be found on the museum's Web site: www.seattlechatclub.org.

Codger Pole

There's plenty of Native American craftwork in the Pacific Northwest, and totem poles—a traditional art form often depicting great leaders, animals, and spirit guides—are among the most common. However, the town of Colfax, in eastern Washington, proudly claims quite an uncommon totem pole as its own. The story behind it is as wacky as the wizened faces it displays.

Dateline: November 1938. Two high school football teams, the Colfax Bulldogs and the St. John Eagles, engaged in a valiant gridiron battle on a snow-slushed field. Though the Bulldogs offered a worthy challenge, the Eagles soared to a 14–0 victory. This was a particularly stinging defeat for the Bulldogs, who strongly felt that dumb luck alone caused their loss. The game stuck in the players' collective craw and became the stuff of local legend, analyzed and debated for decades.

1988: As the fiftieth anniversary of the controversial game approached, local sports buffs suggested to some of the alumni Bulldogs, now all about seventy years old, that it was finally time to put up or shut up. And so one of the strangest football games of all time was organized: the Codger Bowl, a rematch for the ages! Members of both 1938 teams, their cheerleaders, and marching bands were tracked down and summoned for the sake of honor, sportsmanship, and—at long last, one way or the other—closure!

It was decided that this pivotal moment in sports history needed a proper commemorative landmark. Chain-saw artist Jonathan LaBenne came up with an ambitious idea: the Codger Bowl warranted a Codger Pole, with the likenesses of all fifty-two returning players! He fastened together five sixty-five-foot-tall cedar logs and got to work. Then, using the players or their photographs as reference, he carved and sanded caricatures of their faces into the wood. He gradually made them smaller as he got to the bottom so as to adjust for perspective when viewed from the base. (The topmost faces are about seven feet tall!) Standing atop the pole is a full-bodied pine carving of a football player. The final result is a funny masterwork that scored a touchdown with the masses.

As for the rematch, which was played as tag, not tackle, football: Following a pregame pep rally, bonfire, parade, and dance, satisfaction was attained as the Bulldogs vindicated themselves at last, winning 6–0. The Codger Pole remains Colfax's pride, a roadside reminder of second chances and glory. It's displayed prominently along U.S. 195 in the downtown area.

When it comes to peculiarity, the community of Long Beach is out to impress. The main drag, Pacific Avenue, offers one of the healthiest doses of weirdness in Washington! In some ways, this is born of necessity. The town climate for most of the year is notoriously cold and rainy, so the locals encourage summer tourism however they can. Their success is a testament to the appeal of roadside oddities. Consider the following.

Ugly Mermaid

It's pretty unanimous who Long Beach's homeliest girl is. How ugly is she? She's so ugly that she was banished from the town center! With her stocky frame, formidable bosom, and goofy grin, it's easy to see why. That she has the lower half of a fish and is carved from wood doesn't help matters either! The mermaid was carved by local chain-saw artist Fred Bero. She originally sat in the center of town, but her tenure there was cut short. The town was embarrassed by her looks and held a referendum to decide her fate. This resulted in her being moved farther north on Pacific Avenue, where she now serves 24-7 as the roadside mascot of the Mermaid Inn. Personality does get you places.

Praise the Lord and Fill 'er Up!

In the town of Long Beach, there is an old, abandoned gas station. The four holding tanks in back all have pictures painted on them, depicting four different times in Jesus Christ's life. There's an old gas pump that says JESUS IS LORD on top and CROSS WAY on the bottom. There is also a dedication plaque to THE GOOD CITIZENS OF THE LONG BEACH PENINSULA BY CROSS WAYS MINISTRIES AUGUST 22, 2001.–*Karen Connelly*

World's Largest Frying Pan

Razors, cockles, manilas, and macomas: Long Beach regulars will recognize these as being different varieties of clam. The Long Beach Peninsula has a much deserved reputation for "clam-centricity," due to the abundance of shellfish in the region. In fact, in decades past, Long Beach celebrated an annual Clam Festival. In 1941, the local chamber of commerce commissioned the creation of a gigantic metal frying pan to promote the event. It was made of steel plating by the able craftsmen of Northwest Copper and Sheet Metal Works in Portland, Oregon. Although they couldn't have known it at the time, they were creating one of Washington's best-known roadside oddities.

The gargantuan griddle, measuring 14.6 feet including the handle, wasn't just for show. That first year, local girls greased it up by skating inside on large slabs of butter; then celebrants used it to fry up the world's largest razor clam fritter! Presided over by Chef Wellington Marsh (of Marsh's Free Museum fame), this feat was accomplished with the aid of two garden hoes, four two-by-two-foot spatulas, and several able-bodied assistants.

Over the next few years, the clam fry became the festival's highlight. When the pan got too rusty and grease-caked from use, arrangements were made to scrap it. However, a retired local volunteered to restore it. After soaking it in acetone several times, he found that about three hundred people had etched their names into the metal over the years. He also discovered six bullet holes and spots where the steel was hopelessly disintegrated. The holes were filled in and repainted, so the whole thing was at least visually restored. However, the techniques required to repair it had taken their toll. The pan was no longer fit to fry a fritter. Still, this hasn't stopped it from being as popular as ever. Its retirement at the corner of Pacific and Fifth is marked by much admiration and an estimated three hundred photos taken per day in the summer.

A vestige of the original Clam Festival survives as Long Beach's annual Jazz and Oyster Festival.

Giant Squirting Razor Clam

Next to, and complementing, the World's Largest Frying Pan, stands its partner, the Giant Squirting Razor Clam. Measuring in at a height of ten feet, this mammoth mollusk is another Fred Bero masterpiece, carved from cedar wood in the late 1980s. Fitted with a water pump and electronic timer, it's supposed to launch a stream of water every hour on the hour. Unfortunately, the devices tend to be temperamental, so the clam doesn't always keep its commitment. Nonetheless, it's fun to look at for the shell of it.

Marsh's Free Museum

If the preceding items don't lend enough weird credibility to Long Beach, Marsh's Free Museum would do so by itself. In terms of both quantity and quality of weirdness, there's very little out there that can compare. A sort of unofficial sister establishment to Seattle's Olde Curiosity Shop, Marsh's Free Museum is a bizarre blend of old-time nickelodeon, dime museum, freak show, and souvenir shop. An informational sheet reprints an article by journalist Bart Ripp of the *Tacoma News Tribune*. In it, he refers to Marsh's as a "citadel of wholesome hokum." Wholesome is subjective, given the nature of some of the items on display, but there's certainly no doubt that among the T-shirts, mugs, seashells, and other tourist kitsch available for purchase are hundreds of the oddest curios you're apt to lay eyes on.

The museum is presided over by Marian Marsh and her son, David. He represents the third generation in charge of this legendary family business. The whole thing evolved from several different business ventures owned by David's grandfather—Marian's father-in-law—Wellington Marsh Sr.

In 1930, opportunity presented itself when the passenger liner *Admiral Benson* ran aground at Cape Disappointment, just south of Long Beach. While the thirty passengers and sixty-five crew members were eventually rescued, the captain stubbornly refused to disembark. He ultimately remained on board for nine days, symbolically "in command," before swallowing his pride and accepting assistance off the ship. Marsh senior observed the curious crowds that had gathered to observe the beached ship and its proud captain and sensed a business. He quickly set up a hamburger stand nearby and took in a healthy profit.

When Prohibition was repealed in 1933, Marsh opened a tavern in Grays River. Two years later he opened another in Long Beach. This second watering hole, Marsh's Tavern,

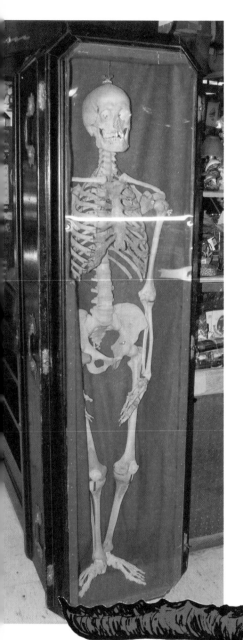

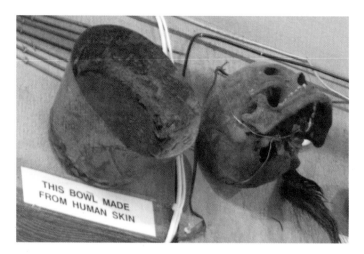

THIS BOWL MADE
FROM HUMAN SKIN

was where he began earnestly collecting odd items, often taken in barter from patrons who had little money to spare during the Great Depression.

During a 1944 vacation to Florida, Marsh senior noticed how local businesses were making a killing selling seashells and other knickknacks to tourists. Inspired, he gradually converted Marsh's Tavern from selling booze to selling baubles. In time, his collection of miscellaneous oddities was large enough to warrant a new designation for the business. Just after World War II, it officially became Marsh's Free Museum; it was moved to its present location in 1974.

Wellington Marsh Jr. grew up helping out at the museum and eventually became as passionate as his father about collecting. Marian and David, equally enthusiastic, inherited it from Marsh junior.

Absentmindedly handling a cane toad coin purse, David Marsh points out some of his favorite pieces with evident glee. There are taxidermal terrors like the two-headed piglet and two-headed calf (both authentic) and the head of a "giant barn owl" (actually a deer butt with glass eyes). Hanging from the ceiling is a Flathead Indian skull from Montana. Next to it is a bowl made from human skin. But the star attraction is a bizarre human-reptile hybrid named Jake the Alligator Man. This mummified whatsit is located in the back of the store inside a glass terrarium, its clawed hands digging into the fine gravel on the bottom. The aforementioned *News Tribune* article

MARSH'S LONG BEACH WASHINGTON JAKE the Alligator Man

contains several possible clues to the creature's origins:

> Some folks claim Jake the Alligator Man was a valet
> in a New Orleans whorehouse. Others say Jake . . .
> was a sideshow freak who smoked cigars and could
> nod yes or no to simple questions. A retired couple
> who drive from Kelso every summer to see Jake . . .
> claim they remember him, alive and nodding, in a
> Texas carnival.

Jake became not only the store's main draw, but also an unofficial mascot of sorts for Long Beach. His image is plastered on a Marsh's Free Museum billboard on the outskirts of town, offering tourists the first indication that Long Beach may not exactly subscribe to everyday convention.

Yet another fascinating, though somewhat underrated, denizen of the museum is Mary Lou. She's an authentic human skeleton residing in a coffin with a clear Plexiglas lid. Wellington Marsh Jr. bought her from an elderly widow who was selling off her late husband's estate. Mary Lou's history is unknown, but David Marsh speculates that she's someone who willed her body to medical science.

Other morbid trappings include Morris, a stray cat who wandered into the museum years ago, was taken in as a pet, and was freeze-dried and mounted after he died. There's a taxidermied jackalope—the half-jackrabbit–half-antelope creature of legend—and a one-eyed lamb head, gazing eternally through a diorama box hanging on the wall.

The customers love this stuff, and there's no shortage of them looking to make a buck with their own items of interest. As your *Weird Washington* representative was taking in the various wild game trophies near the museum office, a customer approached David Marsh. "Got a minute?" he asked. "I've got some skulls I'd like to sell."

But that guy was an amateur compared to the Marshes. "My father-in-law was a collector and so was my husband," Marian Marsh explains to a customer. "And my son is worse. He's got so much stuff, I don't know that he'll ever put all of it out!"

ONE-EYED LAMB
from the
BAILEY ESTATE
SUSSEX ENGLAND
OVER 40 YEARS OLD

In the realm of roadside architecture, there's a recurring theme of structures shaped like teakettles, coffeepots, or other containers of liquid refreshment. Washington is no exception to this phenomenon.

World Famous Bob's Java Jive

Bob's Java Jive in Tacoma is one of the roadside greats. It's quite a survivor—the last of a series of offbeat buildings to come and go along South Tacoma Way. Despite its appearance, it has never exclusively been a coffee shop, as many people sometimes assume.

The two-story, twenty-five-foot-high, thirty-foot-wide coffeepot was constructed in 1927 by local veterinarian Otis G. Button, after designs by artist and marketer Bert Smyser. It initially operated as the Coffee Pot Restaurant, later evolving into a speakeasy and then a food drive-in. In 1955, it was purchased by Bob and Lylabell Radonich, who changed its name to Bob's Java Jive and converted the interior to a Polynesian-themed nightclub. It was here that the rock and roll instrumentalists The Ventures got their start, working as the house band before their commercial success in the 1960s. They weren't the only music act to have worked there. Until the health department ousted them, two bona fide chimp drummers named Java and Jive once performed in the club's Jungle Room.

The Java Jive ventured into other kinds of entertainment over the years, including go-go dancing and karaoke. Perhaps it's this adaptability that's helped it stay in business through changing, and no doubt challenging, circumstances. Bob Radonich passed away in 2002, and his daughter Danette took over the business. The neighborhood has become more industrialized and bleak, and the Java Jive itself is now considered a dive bar. Still, it's these hardships that contribute to its current gruff-but-lovable character, intriguing many a bar-hopper and keeping Bob's Java Jive percolating.

Teapot Dome Gas Station

U.S. Secretary of the Interior Albert B. Fall probably never gave much thought to novelty buildings, but thanks to his malfeasance there's a classic example in the town of Zillah. In 1922, during the Harding administration, evidence surfaced that Fall had accepted bribes from a couple of oilmen in return for a no-bid tap into two federally owned oil fields. When word got out, the country was incensed, and the rest of the 1920s was marked by a long and complex tangle of politics, legal wrangling, and finally, in 1929, Fall's conviction on corruption charges. The whole big mess became known as the Teapot Dome Scandal, after Teapot Dome, Wyoming, one of the oil fields involved in Fall's shenanigans.

When the scandal initially broke in 1922, one Jack Ainsworth was boisterously discussing it while boozing it up with some buddies. Inspiration (or perhaps inebriation) struck, and the result was the Teapot Dome Gas Station, which he built shortly thereafter on what became Highway 12 in Zillah.

The fifteen-foot-tall landmark has changed ownership many times and has had a turbulent history in recent years. It's been relocated to its present spot to avoid the construction of Interstate 82 and nearly closed at least once because of vandalism. Keith Strader purchased it in 2001 and managed to hold out until 2004, when rising gas prices and few customers finally did in the business. The Teapot Dome is believed to have been the oldest operating gas station in the United States before its closure. It's now boarded up and unoccupied, but does have a spot on the National Register of Historic Places, which pretty much guarantees its preservation.

Milk Bottle Buildings

Like the Teapot Dome Gas Station, one of Spokane's milk bottle buildings—the one at 321 South Cedar Street—is on the National Register of Historic Places. A series of these structures, dating back to 1935, was commissioned by Paul E. Newport, owner of the prosperous Benewah Dairy Company, to serve as stores. At thirty-eight feet high and fifteen feet wide, the stuccoed structures were in large part intended to appeal to children. Today only two survive; the other is on the corner of Garland Avenue and Post Street.

Perky's Coffee

It's heartening to see a modern business promoted with new novelty architecture. Case in point, this coffeepot built a few years ago. Does the name refer to an owner named Perky, percolating coffee, or a caffeine perk? In any case, this eye-catching espresso stand is on A Street in Auburn, for those needing a break from the daily grind.

Footloose in Fremont

If local proclamation (and signage) is to be believed, the Center of the Universe is located just north of the Lake Washington ship canal, over a bright blue drawbridge. To the immediate east, the much larger and more sinister George Washington (a.k.a. Aurora) Bridge rises high above, spanning the water and continuing overhead, cloaking the road beneath in its shadow. This neighborhood is, of course, Seattle's famously weird Fremont.

By the late 1970s, decades of hard luck had transformed the traditionally blue-collar area into a low-rent district. This attracted a high concentration of artists, hippie holdovers, and eccentrics. In other words, a rich assortment of free spirits who were just off-kilter enough to tip the neighborhood's precariously balanced personality. The locals developed a tight community bond that not only inspired them to be good stewards of their home turf, but also reinforced their inherent weirdness.

This influence exists to this day, thanks to groups like the Fremont Arts Council. Fremont's official motto is "Delibertus quirkus"—allegedly Latin for "Freedom to be peculiar." An outing to see the area's roadside oddities—easily done on foot—verifies that this freedom is abundantly exercised on its colorful streets.

Fremont—the Center of the Universe

If, as the locals claim, Fremont is the Center of the Universe, the signpost at the intersection of Fremont Avenue and Fremont Place designates the EXACT center, for those who like to get specific about such things. For your convenience, it also points to several other destinations of interest. Among them: the Louvre (9757 km), Atlantis (663 fathoms), Wall Drug (1053 miles), and Noogie (top of head).

Fremont's Lenin

A bronze statue of a Soviet patriarch in modern-day America? It just goes to show that anything is possible in Fremont. Naturally, displaying such a relic has had a polarizing effect. Some folks, especially immigrants from former Iron Curtain countries, denounce the statue's presence as an outrage, a monument to totalitarian misery. Others claim that it's strictly a curio and the only statement being made is that art outlives politics.

Whatever your take, the facts are these: The statue, by sculptor Emil Venkov, spent five years in a Slovakian junkyard following the fall of communism in Czechoslovakia. In 1994, Lewis Carpenter, who was teaching there at the time, purchased and shipped the sculpture to his home in Issaquah as an investment in bronze. Tragically, he was killed in a car accident shortly thereafter. This left his family with a seven-plus-ton metal Bolshevik residing on their property.

Arrangements were made to temporarily display the statue in Fremont until a purchaser came forward. So far, no serious offers have been made, so Lenin remains at the corner of Evanston Avenue North and North Thirty-sixth Street, seemingly always about to jaywalk.

The Rocket

Leave it to Fremont to recycle a symbol of cold war anxiety into neon-accented, steam-spewing ornamentation! The Rocket is an authentic, circa-1950 Russian missile fuselage. In 1991, the fifty-three-foot-tall relic was salvaged from a defunct military surplus store. It spent some time in storage around Fremont, and in 1993, endured a failed attempt at assembly. A second go in 1994 finally yielded success, as the Rocket was secured to a retail building at North Thirty-fifth Street and Evanston Avenue. Now adorned with space-age fins, portholes, neon, graphics, and a steam-spraying mechanism to emulate liftoff, the space vessel remains the perfect complement to the Center of the Universe. The locals hope to eventually incorporate a transmitter in the top of the Rocket to broadcast neighborhood radio programming.

Troll Bridge

A favorite of many locals and tourists, the gigantic Fremont *Troll* continues to amuse at his hilltop haunt beneath the George Washington Bridge. The Fremont Arts Council, ever interested in fostering community identity through art, solicited proposals for something to occupy the bleak space beneath the bridge. The *Troll,* devised by a team of four local artists, was voted the winner, and the council sponsored his construction in 1990. Made of metal, wire mesh, and concrete, the *Troll* clutches a real Volkswagen Beetle and stares at admirers with a shiny hubcap eye. In 2005, Aurora Avenue North, spanning the underside of the bridge and leading right to the *Troll,* was renamed Troll Avenue in his honor.

Waiting for the Interurban

At first glance, there's nothing particularly weird about this whimsical sculpture by Richard Beyer. It's just a cast aluminum depiction of people waiting for a trolley (an anachronism, since trolley service in Fremont was discontinued in the 1940s). But take a look at the dog behind them, peeking out from the lower center. The bearded, human head closely resembles Armen Stepanian, recycling pioneer and onetime "honorary mayor" of Fremont. And that's no accident. The head grew out of a bitter dispute between Beyer and Stepanian over artistic sensibilities, among other things. Beyer later expressed regret that their disagreement ever got as bitter as it did. Neither of the men lives in Fremont anymore, but their dispute has become the stuff of legend.

Rootin' Tootin' Roadside

In the neighborhood known as Georgetown stands the last vestige of the golden age of roadside architecture in Seattle: the Hat 'n' Boots. Since December of 2003, the presence of the oversized structures in Oxbow Park has represented a victory for the residents of Georgetown, who fought for years to save them from neglect and potential demolition.

The Hat 'n' Boots were the brainchild of Buford Seals and Lewis Nasmyth. Seals was a local entrepreneur, and Nasmyth was a commercial cartoonist. In 1948, Seals embarked on an ambitious new venture: Frontier Village, a $2 million shopping center with space for 185 stores, a supermarket, and a gas station at the corner of Corson Avenue and East Marginal Way (Highway 99), which at the time was the main road linking Tacoma and Seattle.

Nasmyth was approached to design "really different" eye-catching structures for Frontier Village. The first portion scheduled for construction was the gas station, for which he presented concept drawings of a giant Stetson hat and a mismatched pair of cowboy boots (one male, one female). Needless to say, Seals and his associates were quite taken with the idea, and construction began.

Nasmyth was adamant about the Boots having wrinkles and bulges as in his sketches, but the builders were hesitant to include that extra detail in what was already a complicated project made of steel beams, chicken wire, and plaster. Nasmyth himself climbed the scaffolding to dent and bend the metal, shaping the Boots to his liking. In the end, the Hat 'n' Boots cost about $150,000 to construct, opening as the Premium Tex Service Station in 1954. The Hat served as the roof of the station kiosk, and the Boots contained men's and women's restrooms.

Because of sporadic funding, Frontier Village was never fully developed. Besides the Hat 'n' Boots, only a Thriftway supermarket was built, surviving for a relatively short time. But for a while, the station was immensely popular. It was THE place to fill up in the South Seattle area, surpassing gas sales records nationwide. Legend has it that even Elvis dropped by in 1963, while in town filming *It Happened at the World's Fair*.

Unfortunately, business on Highway 99 took a hit after I-5 was built. The station weathered its eroding profits through the years, undergoing occasional new paint jobs and changes in signage. The Hat 'n' Boots held their ground for over thirty years before the gas station finally closed in 1988. At this point, the property began its long period of neglect. Grass grew tall through cracks in the litter-strewn asphalt. The Hat's plaster surface was damaged when teenagers began climbing it to skateboard on the brim. Grafitti began appearing on the Boots.

For many residents this was unacceptable. Though the vibrancy of the buildings was diminished, the area's pride in its icons was as strong as ever. When the city of Seattle began the development of Oxbow Park, four blocks north of the Hat 'n' Boots, the Georgetown Community Council raised over $100,000 to relocate and restore the structures to the park. Their funds were matched by a Department of Neighborhoods grant. While the Boots have been repainted to their original bright color scheme (supervised by Lewis Nasmyth himself, now in his eighties), as of this writing the Hat still needs a much more drastic overhaul. It rests patiently in the park, surrounded by a protective chain-link fence, awaiting the final phases of restoration. Optimists believe that the Hat will be fully restored by 2008.

Dogs and Drollness

In Aberdeen, being in the Dog House is a good thing. The Dog House was opened in 1999 by Gene and Riche Sparks, and is located on the corner of Park and Market streets. The roof sports a giant fiberglass hot dog and a sculpture of a waitress, which can be seen from far up either street. The joint's Hot Dog Man mascot stands in front of its bright yellow-and-red sign, dabbing himself with ketchup.

High Up on the "Huh?" Factor

Nothing beats a non sequitur for promoting a business; just ask at any car dealership with a giant inflatable gorilla! Or better yet, ask Chinese Village, a restaurant on Highway 4 on the border of Longview and Kelso. What a vintage car on top of a sign frame has to do with Chinese food is anyone's guess, but there's no doubt it's attention-grabbing! Beyond that, it has become a cozy home for a flock of crows who've given it a rather spotty custom paint job!

Eyes on the Road

Feast your eyes on this propane-packed peeper. If you drive by on Meridian Avenue East in Puyallup and somehow don't notice it, don't worry—it will no doubt notice you. Much like a cat, this ocular oddity stares from both ends, keeping watch over the establishment it belongs to, South Hill Propane Connection. Just observe the NO SMOKING sign; fumes from traffic make this all-seeing propane tank bloodshot enough as it is!

Our Founding Noggin

Here's a photo of a giant wooden head of George Washington. I took the picture outside a real estate office in La Conner. I heard it was created to commemorate Washington's centennial in 1999.—*Submitted by Peg Boettcher*

Only Spiritual Relief at the Wayside Chapel

Life in the fast lane got you too busy to chat with your maker? If you commute along State Route 2 between Monroe and Sultan, pull over to "Pause, Rest and Worship" at the teeny tiny Wayside Chapel. Complete with steeple, pulpit, and seating for eight souls, the chapel was dedicated in 1960 and is supported solely by donations and volunteers. Record your prayers in the notebook provided, but expect nothing but spiritual relief . . . as the sign outside states plainly, NO FACILITIES.

The Wayside Chapel may be found along the Stevens Pass Highway, just east of Fern Bluff Road, in a small but well-lighted parking lot. Visit it 24-7 — "The door is always open; the light is always on." –*Peg Boettcher*

Stonehenge over the Columbia

State Route 14 extends about halfway across southern Washington, starting from Vancouver and continuing eastward along the scenic cliffs overlooking the Columbia River Gorge. At the other end, in the small town of Maryhill, just south of Goldendale, rests the nation's first World War I memorial, honoring men from Klickitat County who lost their lives in combat. Built between 1918 and 1930, its location on a bluff above the river can be awe-inspiring. However, its grand motif is based on incorrect information.

You may be asking yourself, "What in Sam Hill does that mean?" If you are, then you're on the right track!

Sam Hill (1857–1931), wealthy entrepreneur and the area's premier landowner (he named Maryhill after his wife and daughter), had been erroneously told that England's ancient stone calendar, Stonehenge, was used for human sacrifice. A pacifist Quaker, he extrapolated that false "fact" into a personal antiwar metaphor that is often repeated in articles about him today: "Humanity is still being sacrificed to the god of war." In other words, what could better serve as a memorial to lives lost in the Great War than a full-scale Stonehenge replica? It seemed like such a good idea that he had it built himself!

Sixteen hundred and fifty tons of concrete were poured into wrinkled metal molds that simulated the original Stonehenge pillars' texture. The insides of the molds were steel-reinforced, so as to strengthen the concrete as it dried. Thirty pillars, each eight feet high, were arranged as the inner circle, while another thirty pillars, these fifteen feet high, became the outer circle. There are five archways, eighteen and a half to twenty-four and a half feet high, in a horseshoe layout, containing fifteen more individual pillars. Eighty-two and a half feet from the circles is a fifteen-foot-high heel stone.

Unfortunately, Sam Hill died the year after the Stonehenge was completed. He was entombed nearby, intentionally on a hard-to-reach bluff.

The Maryhill Stonehenge is four miles east of the Maryhill Museum of Art, which was originally intended to be Hill's residence. A series of personal setbacks prevented this from ever happening, so friends encouraged him to convert the massive estate into the museum (which was finally completed in 1940, nine years after his death). It's worth visiting for its eclectic exhibits, as well as its other memorials to those lost in World War II, Korea, and Vietnam. Or go for the sheer surreality of being at a palatial, pseudo-European estate in such barren terrain.

Hooray for Hollywoodland

A note to eagle-eyed travelers on 167 South in Kent: Don't panic if you see white letters spelling "Hollywoodland." You didn't accidentally drive to California. A small replica of L.A.'s Hollywood sign (before "land" was removed in 1949) stands just off the highway, on a grassy mound, in a private storage yard. It's easiest to spot in winter, when foliage alongside the highway isn't obscuring the view. There are several other intriguing items farther back on the property, such as old train cars and a shed with a waterwheel.

A Sound Garden

Where's the sculpture? I scanned the grassy shores of Lake Washington and hunched my shoulders against the rain-laden gusts of November wind. More to the point, why had I picked this cold and blustery season to come looking for *A Sound Garden,* Douglas Hollis's intriguing sound-based work of art? In spring, the grounds of the National Oceanographic and Atmospheric Administration—the organization that commissioned the piece in 1983—would have been greener, the lake bluer, and the mood cheerier. Why hadn't I chosen a more reasonable season to troll for art?

I didn't recognize the real deal at first, convinced as I was by the romantic title that I should be looking for some kind of flower-and-wind–chime arrangement. I didn't connect the cluster of eleven tall and spindly metal towers with the idea of art. Must be some kind of weather-analyzing gear, I thought as I stood in the clearing, peering above at the long grey tubes attached to sheets of metal that shifted fitfully in the wind like weather vanes.

Then I heard it. A mournful cooing and hooting. A moaning and tootling that rose and fell like a choir of owls, a cote of mad pigeons. An underwater organist might make such music. Strong, dissonant chords randomly began and dropped away, note by note, and then built up again to wild and complicated harmonies. Edgar Allan Poe would have loved it. Members of a local music group liked it enough to name their successful band after it.

Now I know I picked the right season to visit after all. Some gardens aren't about daisies and robins. *A Sound Garden* provides the perfect background to a stormy day, against the hissing of the trees, the scuttling of dead leaves, and the wheeling of crows against the sky.

Remember patience is a virtue, because you will need it to visit this work of public art, quarantined due to security concerns. In Seattle, take the Forty-fifth Avenue exit from I-5 and go west, following the road as it turns into Sand Point Way and heads north. Just past Seventy-seventh Street on the right-hand side of the road you'll see the entrance to the grounds. Visiting times are Monday through Friday, 8–5. You'll need to stop at the guardhouse, produce identification, clip on a badge, display a marker on your dashboard, subject your vehicle to a possible search, and park exactly where you are told. The sculpture is visible from the day care center parking lot and can be reached on foot by a service road.—*Peg Boettcher*

Roads Less Traveled

A *road less traveled can be* a real place where few people dare to go, or it can be a state of mind. Some are both. One example of the latter is the lonely "last mile" a condemned prisoner walks before his execution in the state penitentiary at Walla Walla. Some roads less traveled are dark and frightening, like Maple Valley Highway, where a tearful ghostly girl may emerge, looking for a lost locket. Others are fun, like the Gravity Hill near Prosser, where a few explorers believe they have found a natural wonder, a road where a car will coast UPHILL.

Then there's the wonder of realizing that the ordinary road you drive down every day, like Vancouver's St. John's Road, may be thousands of years old and that you share it with the spirits of unknown numbers of travelers past. Whichever road you choose, one fact cannot be denied: There are many highways and byways in Washington that possess an indefinable but undeniable power.

Eastern Washington's Own Gravity Hill

"OH MY GOD!!! You will never believe it, but we visited Gravity Hill, and it worked. We stopped the car, which was facing uphill, and put it in neutral, then let off on the brake. AND WE WENT UPHILL!!! Before we did this, we put some talcum powder on the bumper of the car, and when we stopped and got out, we found a bunch of fingerprints from the ghosts pushing us uphill!!!"—*Steve*

It seems as if every state in the Union has a story of a road where cars seem to roll uphill. It does not take a long search on the Internet to find a post like the one above. Most of these are anonymous urban legends, and we were not too hopeful that we would find anything odd at Prosser's gravity hill. But we did. . . . "OH MY GOD!!!"

We will not say exactly where this gravity hill is located, except that it is within ten miles of downtown Prosser. It is not easy to find. The landscape around Prosser has lots of rolling hills, and the government put in many, many roads in a square gridwork, with a new road every mile. So one place looks a lot like the next. However, you will know when you have found the hill because someone spray-painted a line across the road, along with the helpful suggestion of "START." Even with good directions, it took us an hour to find it.

Once we got there, we drove to the start line and, facing uphill, put on the car's brake. In front of us, the road seemed to rise steadily to a small hillcrest about eight hundred feet away. We put the transmission in neutral and then let off on the brake. Slowly the car began to move forward without any power—uphill! We had a GPS unit along with us, and compared the elevation and speed it recorded with the car speedometer. According to both gauges, the car accelerated to a top speed of eleven miles per hour in about three hundred feet. It kept steady at that speed for about two hundred feet more, and then the road grade increased dramatically as we climbed the small hill.

We began to slow, but continued climbing up the hill for another three hundred or so feet. In the last forty feet, the ground rose sharply and the car slowed down even more. It may have been because of our sheer excitement, but it seemed like the car was inching its way uphill. The hill rose about five feet in height in the last thirty feet of road before it crested. The gauges now showed that we had slowed to about five miles an hour. It seemed like we were barely moving. We had to fight back the urge to jump out and push, but it was not necessary. We finally crested the hill and went down the other side as gravity increased our speed. Everyone in the car let out a yell, we were so excited.

We turned the car around to try again. As we drove back over the hill, we stopped the car on the steepest slope, just over the crest of the little hill. We were definitely on a downward angle. We put the transmission in neutral and let off the brake. We did not move. We did not roll downhill, but we did not roll uphill either. It was as if we were suspended. We waited for several seconds, then put the transmission back in gear and drove to the starting line. It worked the same way; stop, put the car in neutral, let off on the brake, and coast uphill.

Gravity hills like the one in Prosser have become urban legends. Perhaps the oldest story comes from a town in Texas, where a school bus was stuck on a railroad track. Before the children could get out of the bus, a train struck it, and all the children were killed. Supposedly, if someone stops their car on the tracks and puts the car in neutral, the children will push the car off the tracks and uphill for several yards. Some people have even put talcum powder on their car bumpers and claimed that they saw child-size fingerprints smudging the powder. At Prosser's hill, there were no train tracks or bus disaster. However, some Internet stories say that a woman drowned in a nearby irrigation ditch and that she pushes the car. We did not see any irrigation ditches.

The skeptics, of course, look for a scientific explanation

of how this could happen. There are a couple of theories about gravity hills. One idea is that in many places across the world, there are hills or mountains with lots of iron ore in them. This iron can become magnetized and will actually pull anything made out of metal uphill, to the center of the effect.

Another theory holds that it is all an optical illusion. Skeptics suggest that this kind of effect can happen when the surrounding landscape tilts in one direction and the road tilts in another. Because of the multiple angles, the human eye is fooled, and a road can look like it is going uphill, even though it is really going downhill. That may be true in a number of cases, but it seems unlikely in Prosser.

The GPS unit we brought along showed a steady increase in elevation as we traveled the road, which did undulate a bit, with small dips and rises. Could this have been enough to keep the car going? We honestly do not know. It will take a few more trips and some experiments to figure this one out.

For anyone who wants to try, there are not many clues of where to find Prosser's gravity hill. Some people just drive all the roads, looking for the start sign. It took a while before we found someone who knew and gave us directions. The price for the directions was that we do not repeat them here. After all, this chapter is "Roads Less Traveled," and we think we should keep it that way.

If you try to find Prosser's gravity hill, good luck. If you do find it, please remember some commonsense rules of courtesy. Even though it can be really spooky trying it at night, and it would be a great way to have a roadside party with friends, please don't. Some people drive too fast on these country roads, and accidents can happen. There are also many farmsteads along these routes. The people who live there go to bed early, and get up early too. Please be respectful of their privacy. After all, farmers carry guns to eliminate varmints.

Ghost Road

There is a road that lies in Kitsap County, between Bremerton and Silverdale, that is the site of many a local legend. It is officially known as Holland Road, but the local kids and even some adults know it as Ghost Road.

The history of the road differs depending on whom you ask, but the story of what happens when you get there remains the same. Legend has it that one night back in the 1950's a guy and his date were heading home from his Senior Prom and decided to take a quiet drive down Holland Road. The guy had been drinking and started to harass the girl. The car wasn't going very fast so the girl tried to open the door and jump out. Unfortunately while the guy and girl were fighting, they failed to see an older gentleman on his bike who couldn't move from in front of the car in time. The car crashed into the bike, killed the man instantly and threw the girl from the car. The driver, being unharmed, took off into the night.

The body of the older gentleman was never recovered and the girl herself laid in a ditch for three days before she finally died of internal bleeding. Her body was later found and buried in the pasture off to the side of the road. But both the girl and the bike rider are said to still haunt the road. Nowadays, brave high school students from all over the county come here on dark nights to try and steal a glimpse of the ghostly wanderers. The story goes that if you turn your headlights off and stop on a dark night, you can see one of two things. The first is a white mist that often appears drifting along the side of the road or walking down in the pasture that's off to the left. The second is that of a ghostly light that hovers several feet down the road before disappearing. This light is said to be the faint light of the bicycle man's light trying to complete his night ride to the end of the road.

Ghosts or not, the road is worth checking out. If you ever have nothing to do on a late night, gather some friends and head towards Holland Road. When you get there make sure the lights are off and the car is stopped, but look out for other vehicles using the road. Once parked, hop out and walk down the road a ways and I promise it will be a night you never forget.—*Cameron Schnell*

St. John's Road

There are roads in Washington that thousands of people walk or drive along each day, but few who travel along them realize their age and significance. One such road is St. John's, in southwest Washington, which runs for several miles from Vancouver, Washington, to Battle Ground. Although part of it runs in straight lines, east to west or north to south, St. John's Road has many twists and turns. It is an ancient road, predating the arrival of Europeans in North America, perhaps by thousands of years.

Native Americans' trails hardly ever traveled in straight lines unless they were moving across flat, wide plains. The native people blazed their trails following the contour of the land. They moved around high hills, rather than up through the middle, and paralleled rivers and streams until they could make a safe crossing. When the settlers came along, they usually followed these trails, widening them until they could support wagons. Sometimes the roads were realigned to follow modern property lines, but this was impossible along St. John's. The land that it runs through was full of small lakes, ponds, and bogs, which meant that much of the road had to follow the original Indian route. As time went by, the government paved over the wagon tracks and created the modern rural road.

The forest is gone now, but St. John's has avoided the urbanization that has come to characterize the Pacific Northwest. It travels through thousands of acres of open farmland, and an old Grange hall still remains on the road. Every day commuters make the trip back and forth from the country into Vancouver not realizing how old the road they travel really is. Would they care to know that they are part of a long tradition of travelers, some of whom may still be making their way down the old road, through time?

St. John's has a guardian spirit that may date from the days when the only people traveling it were the Indians. The road runs through an area still known as Minnehaha, which some pioneers called the Black Forest before they cut down the trees. These early pioneers told stories of a strange guardian: a dark figure who would appear in the woods, sometimes with a torch or other light, guiding a traveler through the trees. When the traveler left the woods, the figure vanished.

One night the doctor got an emergency message to visit one of his patients; he went out, in spite of a heavy rainstorm and the dangers of the dark.

In 1942, many families came to Vancouver to work in the Henry Kaiser Shipyards. Most of the workers settled in company houses close to the Columbia River. One contact of ours, Mike, preferred the quiet of Minnehaha and moved into a farmhouse near the junction of St. John's and Seventy-eighth Street. One dark, rainy night Mike looked out a side window and saw a light moving down the road. It stood out because there were no streetlights at the time, and it was a single light, not car headlights. Mike watched a small buggy, pulled by a single horse, travel north along the road. A man sat in the cart, guiding the horse through the rain by the light of a single kerosene lantern hanging from a pole tied to the buggy. Although this was unusual, Mike guessed that one of the older farmers preferred driving a horse rather than a car.

Mike saw him several more times, but only at night and in the rain. This was unusual, since most farmers were home and in bed before dark. A couple of times Mike tried flagging the man down; waving did not work, so Mike tried yelling, but the horse did not even slow down. A few minutes after the buggy passed, the light vanished. Mike walked down the road to the point where it vanished, but could not find the buggy, a house, or a turnoff. Finally Mike asked some of the old-timers who lived along the road about the strange apparition.

A few of them admitted that they too had seen the phantom buggy and driver. Some claimed they recognized the man driving it and told Mike that several decades earlier the man had been a doctor, with clients who lived along St. John's Road. One night the doctor got an emergency message to visit one of his patients; he went out, in spite of a heavy rainstorm and the dangers of the dark.

At that time, St. John's was dotted with many ponds and wetlands, so the farmers built wooden bridges crossing the worst places. The doctor missed one of the bridges and drove his buggy into a deep pond. The horse floundered as the doctor tried to get it to move, and they both drowned. Ever since, people have seen their ghosts hurrying to an appointment they already missed.

If you drive the roads of the Northwest today, the curved nature of some of them will clue you in to their real age. Even though this story highlights St. John's Road, there are dozens, if not hundreds of roads like it in Washington. Just look for the clues, and you may find yourself strolling or driving down the same road people have taken for thousands of years. Moreover, perhaps time is not such a great barrier to travelers meeting along the way.

Skid Row: A Seattle Original

Many young people know Skid Row only as the seminal heavy-metal band most famous for its 1989 hit *Youth Gone Wild*. They remain blissfully unaware that the term originally referred to the most down-and-out section of cities across America. Skid rows are known to be the home of the poor, the dangerous, the failed, and the hopeless—and the very first of these areas was found in Seattle.

The original skid row of Seattle was Yesler Way, which gained its curious nickname because Henry Yesler used the street to skid logs to his waterfront sawmill. This term was used in logging camps in the early 1800s, but its meaning changed when attached to this street in Seattle. An abundance of transient homeless people had come to settle there, and the label came to be more associated with them than it did with logs. During Prohibition, a popular clergyman named Mark Matthews began preaching against the dangers of such neighborhoods, and he is generally credited with spreading the definition of skid row to mean "bad neighborhood" as opposed to "logging route."

Over time, skid row came to refer not just to Yesler Way but also to the entire Pioneer Square area. For many decades, this vicinity was known as the stomping ground for Seattle's homeless population. With no laws against begging and a backed-up social welfare system that made fraud relatively easy, it was a lawless land where the tramp was king.

A 1986 *New York Times* article detailed what the author found upon visiting Seattle's skid row:

. . . men slumped on park benches, oblivious to the signs of the gathering storm that would drive them to shelter. When approached by a reporter, they mumbled requests for money.

A man who called himself Bill huddled, shaking with violent chills, his crutches beside him in a doorway where he begged for money for a pint of wine because "I can sleep in the parking garage if I have some wine to keep me warm."

Gentrification has turned modern-day Pioneer Square into an area full of Internet cafés, coffee shops, and art galleries. It's also officially a part of the Klondike Gold Rush National Historic Park.

Seattle's skid row has seen many changes since its days as a logging road. Today, it's a hip, trendy, revitalized area—but for the bulk of its existence, it set the standard for skid rows across the entire country.

Underground Beneath Seattle's Skid Row

Seattle's original grunge movement had nothing to do with music; it was all about living in the dark depths below what the eyes can see.

In 1889, the Great Seattle Fire spread through most of the city, destroying the bulk of its business district. While the devastation was severe, rebuilding presented a unique opportunity for improvement. Since the Pioneer Square area had been built upon tidelands, it often flooded, so city officials decided to rebuild it on a more elevated level than its previous incarnation. Unfortunately, restless business owners began rebuilding before the city had a chance to

speaks frankly about the subterranean area's use by drug and prostitution kingpins.

Penny Truitt, a tour guide of Seattle's underbelly, showed us around when we visited. She filled us in on the day-to-day routine of splitting time between the above- and belowground worlds.

"The city figured the solution was just to put a ladder at the corners, and that's how you would cross the street. Without dropping the kids, your packages. It was miserable," Penny told us. "And for men in Seattle, you know, these were loggers, and they're either chopping or partying." We asked her what the results were of having a heavily drinking portion of the population climbing up and down ladders all day. "Seventeen guys didn't make it," she said. "Seventeen men fell from the street to the sidewalk. They say the cause of death was involuntary suicide."

Penny also filled us in on some of the less legitimate activities that took place down in the deep. "Seattle is a Wild West town," she said with a hint of pride. "I mean, we're on the coast, how much more frontier can you get?" To serve certain segments of the population, Seattle had a large quantity of "sewing girls," as they called themselves. Or as Penny puts it, "We'll just say that's what the girls told the cops when they were arrested."

How large was the problem? "At one point, about ten percent of the population claimed to be working as, ah, seamstresses," Penny admitted. "Over two thousand seamstresses, all but six living in the same three-block area."

These days the underground version of Pioneer Square still stands, although public access is limited. Rumors swirl that it has become a de facto home for Seattle's homeless population, especially during bad weather. No word on whether the sewing girls are still stitching britches.

start its renovations, and the owners built at the old — lower — street level.

Nevertheless, it was decided to build the city up higher, but without shutting down what lay below. This meant that when the newer higher version of the neighborhood was completed, some sidewalks and storefronts were as deep as thirty-six feet beneath it. By building up brick and wooden walls to elevate the street level, Seattle had created a bona fide underground city. Visitors descended ladders to the lower-level streets and stores until a series of entrances was built to grant access to the subterranean section of town. Officials eventually condemned the underground city on the grounds that it was a breeding pit for any number of diseases, particularly bubonic plague. For decades, the underground sat unused, just beneath the surface of the very active Pioneer Square.

Starting in the 1960s, local entrepreneurs began running a tour of the netherworld city, appropriately named the Underground Tour, which has become a popular family activity. Recently tour organizers began offering the Underworld Tour, an adult version of the tour, which

Officer's Row

Some roads qualify as roads less traveled not because of their remote locations, but because of their otherworldly nature. Such is the case with Vancouver's Officer's Row, the former military housing that lines Vancouver's Evergreen Boulevard, which is filled to the gills with haunted buildings.

The buildings, the oldest of which date to the 1850s, are now owned by the city of Vancouver, and some are reputed to be haunted. For the last several years, the city has had Halloween "ghost walks" down Officer's Row. Key Property Services, which manages the buildings now, stressed their wish that we not contact their tenants directly. We are passing this request along to the reader. Please do not go knocking on peoples' doors looking for ghosts. You can walk down the street and admire the houses, but please respect the privacy of those who live there.

Gazebo

South of Evergreen Boulevard, in the Vancouver Barracks, there is a gazebo that was constructed about fifteen years ago and has been the site of many open-air concerts and public receptions. In the past, this open area between the Vancouver Barracks buildings and Officer's Row was used as a parade ground, on which a sentry post was once located. Many couples park near the gazebo and walk to the post at night to be alone in a romantic spot. At least one couple was confronted by the ghost of a past sentry, who threatened to fire and chased them off.

Ghostly Housewife

According to legend, in the nineteenth century Sarah, the pregnant wife of a soldier, fell down the stairs in one of the Officer's Row buildings and was killed. She has been seen off and on ever since. Sarah appears to women, especially when drinking is involved; on two separate occasions she warned two women against drinking too much.

Rose Lace Ghost

One female resident of Officer's Row seems to share her house with a ghost. In 1997, a woman saw a bluish gray figure, wearing a rose lace dress and with her hair parted in the middle, approach her in her home. The figure stared at her. It did not smile, it did not frown, it just stared at her. At that moment, the phone rang and the ghost vanished. In the woman's house, lights and clocks turned on and off of their own accord. The faint odor of perfume seemed to hang in the air.

Nanny of Windemere Realty

Windemere Realty has offices in two of the Officer's Row buildings, one of which is haunted by the ghost of a young nanny in the attic. In true Gothic tradition, the story goes, she fell in love with the head of the household and became pregnant by him. In a fit of depression, she hanged herself in the attic.

One person told us he was outside the empty building one night and watched the lights go on from room to room in sequence. It looked to him as if someone walked into a room, turned on a light, then went into the next room and turned on its lights. This happened all the way up to the attic. The staff at Windemere have reported their own experiences. Sometimes all the telephone lines on the building's switchboard will light up. Bells have rung, papers are ruffled, and footsteps are heard where no human is walking. Like the Officer's Row buildings, Windemere does not offer ghost tours, so please don't ask to see their ghosts.

Blue Walking

Fall City's Carnation Back Road is home to the ghost not of a man, but of perhaps his best friend. Travelers on the road often report sighting the specter of a white dog that appears at multiple points on the road—even though that would necessitate traveling faster than their car. Many believe that this ghost may be that of Blue, a dog that counselors at a nearby camp say died and is looking for its master. The ghostly canine is even memorialized in a song, "Blue Walking."

Faces of Cherry Hill

The Cherry Hill section of Granger is supposedly terrorized by the ghost of a woman who died alongside her young son on the treacherous road. Ever since she plunged off a cliff along the road into the Yakima River, people have seen images of her face appear on trees along the dangerous street.

Pilchuk Road

Residents of the Marysville area have long talked about Pilchuk Road, where drivers have reported being chased by a man on foot who can somehow keep up with their car. Many think this is the spirit of a Native American who lived on this land centuries ago.

Purdy Bridge

Purdy residents often report being distracted by the image of a young boy running across the Purdy Bridge. He is believed to have been killed while playing there, and to this day, he is still dangerously playing on the bridge.

Maple Valley Highway

This dark road in Renton is the home of many legends. Chief among them are stories of a teenage girl who stands alongside the road and cries. Those who stop to help her are told a story of a lost locket; before any can offer help, she disappears. She is believed to be the source of the strange fog that often hangs low above the road.

Five Mile Road

Tacoma's Five Mile Road is said to have been the site of the brutal killing of a young girl who was riding a bicycle. Today many who visit the road report hearing the sounds of a bicycle being ridden, although they see nothing of the sort.

Haunted Trails

The construction of Mayfield Dam in the 1960s created Lake Mayfield, which would flood the traditional lands and dwelling areas of the Cowlitz Indians. However, before the dam was finished, several Cowlitz graves were moved, some to Lake Mayfield State Park. In 1971, the park was renamed Ike Kinswa State Park in memory of the Cowlitz tribal spokesman and leader.

A few years ago several Cowlitz Indians, including the descendants of Ike Kinswa, visited the park and walked along one of the trails, which led to the cemetery where their ancestors were reburied. They had brought a camera and took several photographs, including one of a tree standing in an empty field. When their film was developed, all but one of the negatives were black. The only good exposure was of the tree, which had a wispy figure standing in front of it.

Haunted Places

Do you believe in ghosts? Many people are skeptical about the idea of spooky things that go bump in the night. These doubters contend that reports of such phenomena are just the product of overactive imaginations, maybe even outright fraud.

But other people aren't so sure. They've heard too many stories of strange happenings that can't be explained by anything in this realm. These people believe it is possible that some souls linger here on earth, even after death, because of some unresolved issues surrounding their demise. Or perhaps they just like it here! A fair number of those souls seem

on, and we think you'll agree that Washington is a spirited place indeed.

Some of the stories in this chapter include the experiences of paranormal investigative groups, which have recorded Electronic Voice Phenomena (EVPs) at many of the locations written about here. EVPs are thought to be the voices or other sounds of ghosts; interestingly, they usually are not heard during the recording process, just in the playback later on. To many investigators, EVPs are paranormal gold, and *Weird Washington*'s readers are invited to google the respective Web sites of these groups to hear the evidence for themselves.

The Tacoma Sunday Ledger.

VOL. XXIX. NO. 291—40 PAGES—1 TO 12. TACOMA, WASHINGTON, SUNDAY, JANUARY 21, 1912. MEMBER ASSOCIATED PRESS

PICTURES SISTER'S SLOW STARVAT

Burns at Work in Lorimer Case

DEATH SCENE IS DESCRIBED

English Heiress Tells Graphically How Claire Williamson's Life Ebbed Away.

COURT SCENE IS TENSE

Principal Witness in Trial of Dr. Hazzard Recounts Life at Starvation Heights

RINGS WERE TAKEN

Money Transactions Are Set Before Jury—Diet of Asparagus Broth Said to Be All Patients Were Allowed

Woman of Alleged Mental "Control"

RECALL HAWKER CHANTS 4 HOURS

Dissertates Learnedly Between Intonations Seeking to Beguile Less Knowing Voters.

GETS BELLA JOHNSTON

H. L. McMillan, Ex-Cigarmaker, Also Tells Some Confidential Things About the "Old Man."

Bridegroom, Harnessed To Cart, Forced to Haul Wife Through Streets

DETECTIVE DEALS BLOW TO DEFENSE

Reports That He Has Secured Confession of Witness That He Was Bribed.

WORKED THREE MONTH

Was Employed at First by Senate Committee and Later by Interests Fighting to Un seat Senator.

Index of Today's Issue

Ghosts of Thornewood Castle

Chester Thorne formed the National Bank of Tacoma, founded the Port of Tacoma, and eventually became one of the richest men in the Puget Sound. In 1908, he bought a hundred acres along American Lake and spent over $1 million to build his dream home, Thornewood Castle, a 24,000-square-foot Gothic Tudor mansion, completed in 1911. Thorne's daughter Anita and her family also lived at Thornewood, and though one of Anita's three children drowned tragically in an ornamental pond on the property, the family lived there until Chester Thorne died in October 1927. The family owned the house for years afterward, but sold it in 1959. Deanna Robinson, who now owns Thornewood with her husband, Wayne, kindly spoke with us about a number of ghostly occurrences at their bewitching bed-and-breakfast.

Great Hall Ghosts

One late afternoon, shortly after moving in, Deanna was reading alone in the Great Hall. Suddenly the hall was filled with the sounds of a noisy cocktail party. She heard people walking and dancing across the floor, the clinking of glasses, and the mutter of conversation. It sounded as if a hundred invisible people had suddenly appeared in the house.

Deanna felt like an intruder. It was their house, and their party. She believed that they somehow felt her presence, and it bothered them. It was as if they were real and she were the ghost. It frightened her, and she said, "Okay, you guys, have fun. I'm going away now!" Then she slipped out of the room.

Deanna has seen what she described as a vortex in the Great Hall. It appeared one night on the grand staircase. This stairway, like most fixtures at Thornewood Castle, is hundreds of years old. She saw several spirits come out of the vortex, but having previously had a near-death experience of her own, she did not investigate this unusual occurrence, for fear of being pulled to the other side.

Other people have seen a man and a lady appear together on the grand staircase. The man is dressed in a leather outfit, and some people have reported smelling a hint of old leather. Some described the gown the

woman is wearing as an Empire-style dress, with a very high waist. She also wears a garland in her hair.

A Thorne-y Light Issue

The ghosts at Thornewood Castle seem to prefer dim lighting. Most of the illumination comes from small, candle-shaped lamps, mounted high on the walls. After the Robinsons moved in, Deanna noticed that every so often a random lightbulb in the Smoking Room would become unscrewed. She would screw it back in, only to return a few minutes later and find a different lightbulb unscrewed.

Another time, a guest watched the arms on a lamp swing so hard on their own that the light globes on either arm collided and broke. Strangely, when the globes shattered, the shards of glass did not fly around

as they should have, according to the laws of physics. Instead, they fell straight down to the ground, forming a pile under the lamp.

When *Weird Washington* visited Deanna at Thornewood Castle, we talked in a side parlor. In the middle of our interview, we noticed that one of the light fixtures was not working. Sure enough, the light bulb was unscrewed just enough so it wouldn't light up. Deanna believes that this is Mr. Thorne's way of getting people's attention. He certainly got ours.

Deanna Robinson shares Thornewood Castle with people as much as she can. It is located within a gated community, so you must schedule an appointment to view the castle. For more information and the history of Thornewood Castle, visit www.thornewoodcastle.com.

Hungry Ghosts of Starvation Heights

The community of Olalla is just across the Puget Sound from Seattle. Olalla means "berry" in the local tribal language, and the area is well known for its strawberries, which are celebrated in festivals during which people overindulge in berry-laden cuisine. Strangely, this same community was also once the place where people came to starve their way to health—and sometimes to death. All with the help of a self-proclaimed doctor named Linda Burfield Hazzard, whose starvation cure may have been most effective in producing a ghost or two.

Hazzard turned her Olalla cottage into the Wilderness Heights Sanitarium, and from the 1890s until 1912 she rented the attic to patients who had come to experience her cure. She was not a medical doctor, but practiced a form of homeopathy. She wrote a book, titled *Fasting for the Cure of Disease*, in which she declared that her treatment could cure everything from cancer to constipation. The treatment? Patients ate one small bowl of tomato or asparagus soup daily, for over forty days. Long walks, enemas, and vigorous massages were also required one or more times a day.

Following this regimen, patients inevitably grew thinner and weaker. They were free to leave Wilderness Heights if they wanted to, but Hazzard and her fasting cure exerted a strange power over them. Local farmers watched as the patients took daily walks from the cottage to the store and back. These walks soon became daily "crawls" as the patients' energy dissipated and they slowly faded away.

There were patients who survived and left Olalla, but many died. How many is not known: Estimates range from two dozen to over forty, possibly higher. Hazzard seldom filed death certificates with the authorities, and had a special arrangement with a discreet funeral home in Seattle for burials. Conveniently for Hazzard, most of the patients who died left all their property to her. Few knew that her husband Sam had been kicked out of the U.S. Army for forgery and embezzlement.

In 1911, British heiresses Claire and Dora Williamson came to Wilderness Heights to take the cure. Both lost more than fifty percent of their body weight and while Dora survived, just barely, Claire died. Someone had also embezzled money from the sisters' bank accounts. The British Consulate went after Hazzard, filing criminal charges against her, and she was found guilty of manslaughter. She spent less than two years in prison, lived briefly in New Zealand, then returned to Olalla in 1920, where she built a larger sanitarium and nursing home. This time, however, local authorities made sure that none of her patients experienced the same fate as the Williamsons.

It's hard to tell whether Linda

Hazzard set out to murder her patients. When rich people (with no relatives) began to sicken from the treatment, Sam and Linda may have decided it was best for business to take over their dying patients' estates. She may not have understood the consequences of her actions. She firmly believed in her fasting cure, and that people died only because they were beyond help. The proof? Hazzard became ill in the 1940s and died while taking her own "cure."

The cottage, also known as "Starvation Heights," where Hazzard established her sanitarium changed very little over the years, and the family living there before it was torn down experienced some ghostly phenomena. On one occasion, the woman of the house was in the kitchen cooking dinner. She was facing the stove, which was against one wall, and the bathroom door was behind her. She moved back and forth between a counter on her left and the stove for several minutes. When she turned around, she saw that every chair in the kitchen, and a few from the room next door, had been piled up against the bathroom door.

The woman had been alone in the house at the time, and it's doubtful that someone else would have taken the time to sneak in and silently pile all the chairs up against the door while she was making dinner.

In the attic of the cottage, where most of her patients were treated, were several low "ledges" where the family stored small items. A psychic once said that she saw the spirits of many of Hazzard's victims sitting on the ledges, too afraid to move, even in death. The psychic burst into tears several times over the anguish she felt saturating the walls of the little house.

Three times during 2005–2006, Washington State Paranormal Investigations and Research (WSPIR) visited Starvation Heights and *Weird Washington* spoke to its president, Darren Thompson, about some of the group's experiences there.

The first time they broke into three teams, each of which included a psychic. To keep the destination a secret, they blindfolded the psychics and put them into separate cars. During the drive, technicians sat next to the psychics and recorded with a video camera every action and statement made along the way. En route, two psychics felt as if they would be going to a large institution having something to do with medicine. When they arrived at the cottage, the teams removed the blindfolds from the psychics and kept them from communicating with each other. Each psychic was to go through the house alone.

One team recorded a video that starts inside their car, then pans outside, where the microphone recorded a muffled statement made by a team member. The video then pans back inside the car, where the microphone picked up a strange, breathy voice, saying, "Help me!" The voice could only have come from inside the car and was not made by team members either inside or outside the car.

Another WSPIR team recorded pictures and audio outside the house while walking toward a ravine where Hazzard may have hidden victims' bodies. Their audio recorder picked up a voice that said, "Are you talking about me now?" The team members did not hear the voice at the time and continued their conversation. Another voice seemed to be saying, "Take us up" or "Dig us up."

During the second investigation, WSPIR learned that the cottage would be torn down once the owners put a new house up on a different part of the property. They quickly organized a third investigation, during which several members spent the night there.

One man tried relaxing in the Hazzards' former bedroom the room in which Linda had died. The man never had any psychic experiences before, but he felt as if something spiritual were in touch with him. He went into a trance and answered simple questions with rumbles of "yes" or "no" from deep within his chest. It seemed as if he were communicating with Linda Hazzard, who was still in the house. She refused to leave and was refusing to let anyone demolish the dwelling. Her spirit was wrong, however. The family living in the cottage did indeed move, and the cottage was leveled. Was this last communication the result of investigators' prodigious imaginations or a final attempt by the former owner to interact with the world of the living?

The cottage that was once Starvation Heights is now gone, but it isn't known if the spirits detected there—whether they were those of Hazzard or her unlucky patients—left with its demolition. It seems that we'll just have to remain hungry for an answer.

Ghostly Displays at Fort Lewis?

Some people believe that not only can buildings be haunted, but objects, such as clothing, furniture, and weapons, can be haunted as well. This might be the case at the Fort Lewis Military Museum, outside Seattle, where there are rumors that certain objects on display are infused with some of the violence of the wars in which they were used.

Museum burglar alarms have been tripped both day and night, even though no one has been inside the building. People have reported seeing other people looking out the third-floor windows when the museum was empty.

Employees point out that the museum is an old building that sometimes creaks and settles, which may set off burglar alarms. They also store display mannequins on the third floor, which could be mistaken for a ghost in a window. However, employees admit that at least one person died there in the past, when the museum was a hotel. And once an exorcism was held to put suspected spirits to rest.

The museum has military displays from the earliest days of settlement in Washington, as well as from units that were based at Fort Lewis. It's also got the Jeep of General H. "Stormin" Norman Schwarzkopf Jr., a Vietnam and Gulf War hero. We don't know which items trigger ghostly activity, but if you want to try to figure out which ones are the culprits, you can stop by the museum from Wednesday through Sunday, when it is open.

This Old Soldier Won't Fade Away

The United States Army built the Vancouver Barracks in 1849, and it is one of the oldest U.S. Army posts on the West Coast. One of the oldest surviving buildings there is the Grant House, which started as a combination headquarters building, officers club, and residence for its post commander.

Ulysses S. Grant was a lieutenant who served as quartermaster at the Vancouver Barracks in 1852. It's strange that the building was named for him, since he never lived there and only visited it to be reprimanded by the post commander, who was never pleased with his performance. The building should have been named for Lieutenant Colonel Alfred Sully, a onetime post commander and possible ghost candidate.

Sully was born in 1821, the son of portrait artist Thomas Sully, and graduated from West Point in 1841.

Lieutenant Colonel Alfred Sully

During his military career, he fought in the Seminole War, was involved in campaigns against various Native American tribes, and fought in the Civil War, where he rose to the rank of brigadier general and commander of the 1st Minnesota Volunteers. After the war, he was demoted to lieutenant colonel and served in many locations, the last of which was as post commander at the Vancouver Barracks in 1874. He'd remain there until he died in 1879.

According to some, Sully had rheumatism, which caused muscle stiffness and severe stomach cramps. He was in constant pain and developed a reputation for being short-tempered. Based on descriptions of his illness, it's likely he suffered a long and painful death from stomach cancer. Today, the city of Vancouver owns the Grant House and leases it to restauranteurs, who operate it as the Restaurant at the Historic Reserves. The restaurant owners report many strange occurrences there.

Alfred Sully's private quarters were on the second floor of the building, but he seldom slept the entire night through. Because of chronic pain, he spent hours pacing the floor, rather than lying in bed. A restaurant manager used to hear someone pacing outside of Sully's old room. Once, she left her office to investigate, and as she stood in the center of the hallway, the disembodied footsteps did not pause, but literally walked right through her, pacing back and forth down the hallway.

Some years ago, the restaurant needed to have a new phone system installed. A technician arrived early and was let in by a tall man with a beard, who was wearing a long, old-fashioned coat. The man took the technician to the basement and left him there to finish his work. The owner arrived later and was surprised to find the technician inside, because the owner was the only one with keys to the building. He searched, but the building was empty except for the technician.

In the summer of 2006, the restaurant's executive chef invited his family to the restaurant for a private dinner on the veranda. His sister went inside to use the restroom and saw a tall, thin, bearded man in a long coat. He was staring out the window at her table and ignored her presence. When she came back, the man was still standing by the window.

"Is there anything I can do for you?" she asked.

He replied, "No. I lived here before, and I am just looking around."

She said to herself, "All right" and went back outside, where she told everyone about the odd exchange. The building was supposed to be empty, so the rest of the family went inside to look for the tall man. As in the earlier sighting, the place was empty.

Recent laws made smoking in public places in Washington illegal, and from time to time in the early mornings, people have stopped in to complain about a tall man they see smoking a pipe on the upper veranda. When the employees go upstairs, nobody is there, though they sometimes smell tobacco and, strangely, rose water, a gentle reminder perhaps of a distant past and a soldier still at his post.

Vancouver Barracks Hospital

It's been a long time since the Vancouver Barracks Hospital has seen any patients. It was originally two separate hospital buildings, constructed at different times—the south half in the 1880s, and the north half just before World War I. When Interstate 5 was built in the 1970s, the older building was moved to its present location. The first and second floors of the buildings were used as wards, offices, and operating rooms. Both buildings operated as a hospital until the end of World War II.

When the older part of the hospital was built, surgeons had been washing their hands before operating for only a few decades, and deadly postoperative infections were still common. Open fractures were still treated by amputating the limb above the break. In all, hospital treatment was a frightening, painful, and traumatic experience, and death was a very real possibility for the soldiers who were brought here. It's not hard to imagine that many dark spirits could remain here from this time.

As in many older hospitals, the operating room floors in the Barracks Hospital were sloped toward a corner, or the center of the room, to help drain blood and other fluids from an operation conducted there. In some hospitals, the blood drained into rain gutters and down into the ground, but here "blood pipes" were used. The pipes ran into the basement, where the blood was collected in large containers that were later loaded onto wagons, taken to the Columbia River, and dumped. Try doing that today!

According to one employee, the basement seemed to be the focus of many of the eerie happenings. In March of 1996, my wife Janine, our friend Brian, and I decided to investigate the old Barracks Hospital for ourselves. We arrived around 6:45 p.m., intending to stay overnight,

and brought sleeping bags, food, and a camcorder. Brian said he was hoping for some "big action" from the resident spirits.

We looked around the entire building before moving down to the basement at around 10:30 p.m. We observed what we thought were the blood pipes from the operating rooms. A few of the offices had tile walls and medicine cabinets, and a friend with medical experience later suggested that these were autopsy rooms.

At 11:30 p.m., we decided to lay out our sleeping bags. Brian set his sleeping bag up on a table. All was quiet until a little after 2:00 a.m., when a squeaking noise woke me up. The room was not completely dark, and I looked around to see what was causing the commotion, but I couldn't pinpoint the source of the noise.

I could see that Brian was awake, though, and that his eyes were opened wide. He whispered, "The table's shaking!" He spread out his arms on the table and lay very still.

He was right. The table was shaking and making the squeaking noise. Brian whispered louder, "It's not me!"

I whispered the first thing that came to my mind, "Well, get off!"

Brian rolled off the table like a karate master and faced the table with his hands open, ready to fight off an opponent. But the shaking then ceased.

Was the table vibrating from cars on the nearby freeway? Or was the motion caused by a playful ghost? We were near a room that had once been a morgue. Could it have been the spiritual remains of someone else who had been laid out on a cold table in years past?

At 3:00 a.m. Brian felt compelled to go home. My wife and I decided to go home as well. It was not that any of us were afraid to stay the rest of the night . . . honest.—*Jefferson Davis*

Point Wilson Lighthouse

There has been a lighthouse at Point Wilson, on the northern tip of Fort Worden, since 1879. The first lighthouse was built of wood, and replaced by a rock-and-concrete tower in 1914. The new lighthouse used the original lighthouse lens, which can be seen over thirteen miles out at sea.

In April 1921, the passenger liner S.S. *Governor,* traveling with 240 passengers and crew, collided with the freighter S.S. *West Hartland.* The *Hartland* sank in ten minutes, with a loss of eight people. Most of the survivors were taken to Seattle, but some people believe that one lifeboat landed at the Point Wilson Lighthouse.

Years later at least one person reported seeing the ghost of a woman walking around the lighthouse, which was automated and kept locked after 1979. More than one night watchman told stories of seeing the glowing specter of a woman wearing a long dress. They usually saw her wandering between the lighthouse and the outbuildings. She would then open the door to the lighthouse and walk inside. When they investigated, the watchmen found that the door was still locked. They believe that this ghostly woman died in the collision and is still looking for her daughter, lost at sea.

The Coast Guard still owns the lighthouse and its outbuildings. In 1999, the crew of the cutter *Osprey* and their families moved into the old lighthousekeeper's residences. There were two buildings, one of which was divided into two apartments. One day a Coast Guard wife was in the kitchen, and saw something out of the corner of her eye. A few minutes later she heard the sound of someone walking around on the second floor, and sounds like someone rummaging through boxes or closets. She yelled that she had a gun, and the noises ceased.

On another occasion, one of the families had a guest who slept on a couch on the first floor. He woke up in a panic after dreaming that someone was choking him. As he bolted upright, he saw some motion and what he believed was a woman walking from the living room to the kitchen. He quickly followed, but didn't see anyone in the kitchen. There was no way out other than the front door, which he would have heard open and close.

Walking with Ghosts in Seattle

As Washington's largest city, Seattle has many neighborhoods with their own paranormal heritage, and the group Advanced Ghost Hunters of Seattle-Tacoma (or AGHOST) leads excellent ghost walks through two of them. One is the prestigious Capitol Hill neighborhood, and the other is Seattle's seamier piers and docks.

AGHOST gives these tours for many reasons: to raise funds for equipment, to increase the group's visibility, and to educate the public about the paranormal. Local businesses help sponsor these tours by selling tickets and acting as starting points, but AGHOST members volunteer as researchers and tour guides. Before volunteers can guide a tour, however, they have to pass an examination during which they must demonstrate their knowledge of local history and ghost hunting.

The Pier Walk is the most popular tour, perhaps because Seattle's seamier stories are more appealing. It's a two-hour walk with over twenty stops, and covers both haunts and unusual historic places in Seattle's history.

One of the more interesting haunts on the tour is Kells Irish Pub, formerly the bottom floor of the Butterworth Funeral Home. Yes, the pub where people currently enjoy pints and lively conversation used to be the place from which the dead would be transported to their final resting places. (E. R. Butterworth was supposedly the inventor of the terms "mortuary" and "mortician.")

Before the bottom floor was converted into Kells, a plumber lifted up the floorboards to repair some pipes and found little piles of ashes and dirt underneath. Was it regular ash and dirt, or perhaps residue left by some clumsy morticians from the past?

Ross Allison

Sloppy morticians don't seem to anger the spirit haunting Kells, which is more mischievous than frightening. Candles sometimes burst into flame on their own, customers find drink stirrers in their hair, and locked doors are sometimes found open. According to Ross Allison, founder of AGHOST, some customers have reported seeing the spirit of a little boy. Others have heard the sound of a child's laughter after some of these spirited pranks.

A Kells manager told Ross about an experience he had with a writer who was interviewing him. The writer brought her daughter along, and as the adults talked, the child wandered away. The two of them eventually went searching for the girl and found her in a back room, holding a conversation with an imaginary friend. The mother grabbed her child and left, never finishing the interview.

One evening Ross told this story to his tour group, and pointed to the back room. The door opened a crack, just wide enough to admit a child, and then closed. Ross looked at tour group, saying, "I had nothing to do with that." They continued with the tour, and just before they left, they heard a child's laugh.

The Capitol Hill tour starts at the Harvard Exit Theater. It was built in 1924 as the home of the Women's Century Club, which was founded by Bertha Knight Landes, Seattle's first and so far only woman mayor. She was elected in 1926 on an anticrime platform, and despite her success in cleaning up corruption in Seattle (or perhaps

One time, she found coals and a partially burned log in the fireplace, indicating that a fire had been burning there overnight.

because of it) she wasn't reelected. She championed both women's and social issues throughout her life, and after her death in 1945 her organization launched many programs that helped shape Seattle.

In 1969, the Women's Century Club sold the building, which was converted into the Harvard Exit Theater. As part of the sales agreement, the lobby was to stay the same as when the Women's Century Club sold it. The club still meets there twice a month, and in the winter, they arrange their chairs in front of the large fireplace.

The woman who worked as the theater manager during the '70s was usually the last person to leave the theater at night, and always made sure there was no fire burning in the fireplace and that the chairs were returned to their proper place. But the next morning she'd often open the theater to find that the chairs in the lobby had

been arranged around the fireplace as if an intimate meeting had been held there. One time, she found coals and a partially burned log in the fireplace, indicating that a fire had been burning there overnight.

While many people dismiss these incidents as the products of lively imaginations, there have been witnesses to these occurrences from the news media. One AGHOST tour guide, Danny, gave a tour and interview for a local television station around Halloween. While she told stories of the Harvard Exit Theater and Bertha Landes, a window behind her started to shake. The television camera captured this. There was no earthquake, and even stranger, only one window was shaking. An earthquake or another natural cause would have made all the windows shake, but a ghost might content itself with shaking just one!

Beverly Says BOO!

The cutoff from Highway 101 to Lake Quinault Lodge is relatively easy to find, provided it's not raining—and Lake Quinault averages 146 inches of rain a year. Despite this, the lodge, which is located in Olympic National Park, has many loyal guests and employees who appreciate the green beauty the rain brings. Some guests, like Beverly, never leave.

The Quinault Lodge was built in the late 1800s and did a brisk business among travelers who wanted to rest by or fish in the lake. The hotel burned down in August 1924, but a bigger, grander hotel was constructed in its place, opening in August 1926.

Had the builders thought things through, they might have chosen another site on which to build the new lodge, since a ghostly presence still lingers here from the original building, a former front desk employee named Beverly. Stories vary, but Beverly was apparently very

sick the day of the fire. She insisted on coming to work, however, and fell asleep at her post. The fire spread so quickly that she couldn't make it out and died at the front desk. Sadly, Beverly roomed in the boathouse, which did not burn in the fire and is still on-site today. Had she stayed in bed and rested, instead of going to work, she would have lived.

In many cases, ghosts are confined to their original surroundings or to the place where they died. This is not so with Beverly; she has been seen and felt everywhere in the lodge. She is friendly, though she does like to play pranks on people. According to hotel manager Heidi, guests report strange incidents about once a month or so. Some could be traced to natural causes, like wind or small animals in the attic. But others are harder to explain away.

Like the piano in the lobby playing late at night, when nobody is up. Several guests have reported hearing the piano in the wee hours, though most don't bother to investigate further. One guest was curious—and probably angry—enough to find out who the culprit was. He walked downstairs, but as soon as he got to the lobby, the playing stopped. He watched in surprise as a female figure in a wispy gown fled across the lobby and into a back hallway. It could have been a lonely guest in her negligee, but he decided not to pursue her.

Carl worked at Lake Quinault for over twenty years. He remembers two mature women guests visiting their daughters, who lived nearby. The older women stayed in the lodge to see what it was like, after hearing stories about Beverly. The women asked Carl if he had seen the ghost. He replied that he had never seen her, but added, "If you're open to it, you'll see Beverly."

The third night, Carl served one of the women at dinner and knew she had not ordered any liquor. He did not think that she had any in her room, either. The next morning she came down to the dining room, looking ashen and in a state of mild shock. She said that she had awakened in the middle of the night and had seen an apparition of a woman enter her hotel room. Further, the air became cold and clammy while the apparition was in

her room. She was still shaky the next morning when Carl spoke with her.

Beverly also has an interest in the housekeeping and security staff and their activities. She turned the radio on in the night watchman's office several times one night. Staff members have also reported that glasses sometimes fall off the shelves in the dining room, and that glasses sitting on a table have shattered when no one was standing nearby. Is Beverly just conveniently blamed whenever one of the kitchen staff breaks something, or is she a ghost with a glass-shattering temper?

Shadows at Southhill

Since the early twentieth century, many of Spokane's wealthiest citizens have lived in its South Hill neighborhood. Among them was a quack doctor named Rudolph Hahn, who arrived in Spokane in 1899 and opened an office as a physician, despite never having gone to medical school. He pedaled quack medical treatments and quickly built up a clientele of wealthy locals who probably needed attention more than they needed true medical care.

In 1924, he bought a twenty-six-room, Craftsman-style home in South Hill that is known today as Southhill Mansion. The same year, the fifty-nine-year-old Hahn married twenty-seven-year-old Sylvia. Theirs was a stormy relationship, and during the course of it, the couple divorced, remarried, broke up, then reconciled. In May 1940, police found Sylvia's body in her bedroom, shot in the head. The door lock had been shot off, and the bedroom walls and bedstead had bullet holes in them. But Hahn said Sylvia had committed suicide. The other bullet holes were from another time, he said, when he took a little target practice in the house. With the help of money and a few important clients, Sylvia's death was ruled a suicide by the local coroner.

Why would Hahn's clients rush to defend the "suicide" story? Perhaps because, when Hahn moved into Southhill, he added a secret operating room, designed for an occasional, discreet abortion. It's documented that he performed the then illegal operation, because in 1945, he

was charged with manslaughter when a woman died after he botched one. He was acquitted, but convicted on two counts of performing illegal abortions. Hahn, who was eighty years old at the time, still didn't go to prison. He was fined $1,000 and put on probation.

Deep in debt, Hahn eventually sold Southhill and moved into an apartment in the New Madison Hotel. There were stories that he had a large cache of money and other valuables there, and a hearing aid salesman who tried to rob him ended up stabbing the phony doctor in the chest with an antique bayonet, killing him. Hahn's ghost does not haunt the place where he was murdered, however. It seems he'd rather be at Southhill Mansion.

In the 1990s, new owners renovated and restored parts of the mansion. During the renovation, workers found the hidden "abortion" room. Caretakers and workers complained of noises like knocks and footsteps, which could not be blamed on the new construction or the house settling. Some reported seeing human shadows moving across a wall, even when the room was empty except for the witness. One former owner admitted that he had seen a shadowy figure standing at the top of the mansion staircase as he stood at the bottom.

The figure could have been Hahn or Sylvia or some unfortunate patient on whom Hahn operated. We don't know for sure, and following the remodeling, many of the manifestations ceased. The new owners zealously guard their privacy and are not talking, so it's not worth asking.

Kelso Theater Pub

Since 1997, the Kelso Theater Pub, in Kelso of all places, offered its patrons the opportunity to enjoy first-run movies in an atmosphere that goes beyond the usual multiplex. In addition to regular seating, there are several couches in the balcony and tables everywhere. Beer is available to those of age, and everyone can order food from the snack bar. It's not your usual movie theater experience, but then, the Kelso Theater Pub is not your usual movie theater.

It was built in 1937, possibly on the site of a former funeral parlor (or another theater that burned down—take your pick). According to the owners, the back room had been used by undertakers at some point. The Southwest Washington Paranormal Researchers (SWPR) did some research into the history of the building, finding out that some time in the late 1950s or 1960s, a man was fatally shot in front of the theater.

SWPR has conducted several investigations there since 2005. The first time, the group experimented by playing music from various eras, to see if there were some way to get the spirits to interact with them. When they started playing 1930s music, they could hear and see someone walking around in the balcony. The group immediately started up the stairs to confront the figure, which, despite the dim lighting, some thought was a man. It moved back into the shadows, as if to run away from them. When the group reached the top of the stairs, they were alone on the balcony. They had a recorder going while this was happening, and when they listened to the audio playback, they heard a man's voice say, "I'm sure I am dead."

Customers have seen a woman in the upper floor of the theater and immediately know something isn't quite right, because she is transparent. She may also haunt the women's bathroom, where strange noises (not of a bodily nature, mind you) have been reported, as well as stall doors moving on their own.

SWPR put alarms on the bathroom door so anyone touching the doorknob would set the alarm off. They also placed an audio recorder in the bathroom. The alarm went off once, and on playing the recorder back, the team heard the sound of the bathroom door opening and then a stall door slamming open and closed. No other sounds were recorded until the SWPR team arrived, and there was nobody in the bathroom when they investigated. So how did the intruder get out without opening the bathroom door again?

When SWPR member Kim Travis returned to her previous location, she picked up her recorder, which she had left on, and listened to the playback. A few seconds after she left, a voice said, "I'm cold," into the microphone. One researcher believed that they recorded another playful ghost, saying, "Spank him."

Then there is the mysteriously appearing money, which makes this a very welcome haunting to the few people who have reported money appearing in their pockets. One day a woman named Anna visited the theater. She was short on money, as evidenced by her empty pockets. Shortly after entering the Kelso Theater Pub, she put her hand in her pocket and found a $20 bill. A generous ghost!

Snohomish's Oxford Saloon

The gem of historic Snohomish is the Oxford Saloon. It was built in 1900 and for a decade was known as Blackman's Dry Goods store. It then became a saloon, and, over the years, has changed owners and uses, but each owner incorporated Oxford into its name.

When it was remodeled as a saloon again (one of as many as forty-five saloons in Snohomish at the time),

the owners added a vestibule to the entrance, with a stairway leading to several rooms on the second floor. These were supposed to be boardinghouse rooms, but there are rumors that a prominent local businesswoman named Kathleen (or Katherine) rented them out for use as a high-class bordello. She herself did not go into the saloon, but kept an office at the local Eagle's Lodge, where she made reservations for her tony clientele.

Over the years, the Oxford Saloon was often the scene of violence, especially around the basement, a men's card room, and the bar. One well-documented killing was that of a policeman named Henry. He was a regular at the Oxford and may have moonlighted as a bouncer. One night there was a fight, and when Henry attempted to break it up, he was knifed to death in the melee.

Henry seems to have stuck around and actually enjoys certain aspects of his ghosthood. He hangs out around the stairs leading to the basement and has been seen many times in the ladies' restroom. Seen and felt, as many women report being pinched by him. However, Henry always disappears when confronted.

Beginning in 2005, the Washington State Ghost Society (WSGS) performed several investigations at the Oxford Saloon. *Weird Washington* spoke with two people, Russ and Sandy, who were members of WSGS at the time.

Sandy and Russ investigated the second floor first, turning on their tape recorder and starting up the stairs. At the time, Sandy said, "Russ, take some pictures."

One of the pictures shows what looks like a man standing in front of the camera, looking up the stairs. Another shows the man turning toward the camera.

10/23/2005

When the tape was played back later on, they heard a male voice echo hers. A few seconds later they heard a child's voice laughing or crying in the background.

The manager gave them keys to all the offices on the top floor. They tried several times to open the rooms, only to have the key fall out of the lock, as if some unseen hand were pulling it out before Sandy could turn it. Eventually, they managed to open some of the rooms. While this was going on, on the playback, they heard a voice say, "I dropped the keys to my room." It was as if they were being mocked.

In room 4 they turned on their recorders and tried talking to any spirits who might be there. They later found that they had received a response: a strong male voice that spoke directly into the microphone and said, "I am the one." As they left the second floor, they were followed by a voice that gave them a not-so-fond farewell, saying, "You'll die."

Russ and Sandy met two other investigators down-stairs, and after some conversation they went down to the lower bar and then to the basement. At the bottom of the basement stairs, Russ took ten pictures of the stairs with his digital camera. One of the pictures shows what looks like a man standing in front of the camera, looking up the stairs. Another shows the man turning toward the camera. Because the photos were digital, a professional photographer analyzed them and determined that it was unlikely for the picture to have been altered after it was taken.

At the end of the investigation, one group member used the bathroom. As he was relieving himself, he heard a man's voice whisper in his ear, "Get out!" Remembering to zip up his pants, the man did as he was commanded. In the future, he always made sure to go before he arrived at the Oxford Saloon.

After we die—and the people who remember us die—often all that's left of us for future generations to ponder is our gravestones: what they look like, where they are located, what's written on them. These final markings tell the world who we were and what people thought of us while we were on this earth. This can be said about graves anywhere, but examples abound in Washington State.

There are graves of the famous—Bruce and Brandon Lee, or Jimi Hendrix, for example—that receive thousands of visitors every year. But there are other graves in the Evergreen State with stories to tell. Some of the tales, like the deceased themselves, have been buried by time: the grave of prisoner 21520 in Walla Walla state pen, for example. You'll need some Weird help to find out who he was or why he was there. Other graves we may never find, like that of convicted killer Henry Timmerman, who cursed the town of Goldendale for hanging him, a curse that came true (at least in part)!

But many other interesting graves are right out there, easy for the curious to investigate. Just be careful not to disturb the spirits who lie below. They have been known to be very

Cemetery Safari

COMET
LODGE
CEMETERY

Est. 1895

FOREVER IN OUR HEARTS
JAMES M.
"JIMI" HENDRIX
1942 — 1970

Visiting the Lees in Lake View

In Seattle's Lake View Cemetery, two of the most famous residents are Bruce Lee and his son, Brandon, both of whom died early deaths. Every year thousands of people from all over the world come to visit their final resting place. Visitors are so common that when we recently went into the cemetery office to ask about another matter, the receptionist did not even look up from what she was doing. She pointed to a little box beside the entryway and, in a tone that suggested she repeated the same thing several times a day, said, "There are maps to the Lee graves in the box beside you."

After Chairman Mao, Bruce Lee is probably the most recognized Asian in the world. He was one of the greatest martial artists in history, creating the discipline of Jeet Kune Do, or The Way of the Intercepting Fist. He was also a star of film and television. As a child, Lee starred in several movies made in Asia. In the 1960s, he was the crime fighter Kato on television's *Green Hornet*. Bruce Lee taught Kung Fu to actors like Steve McQueen and James Coburn. Because of his talent and hard work, he managed to break Hollywood's racial barrier and became internationally famous as a leading man.

Like many well-known people, Bruce Lee had his enemies and critics. When he died in 1973 at the age of thirty-two, there were rumors that he was killed for revealing Asian fighting secrets to Westerners. An autopsy surgeon told a skeptical public that Lee probably died of an allergic reaction to a prescription drug.

Brandon Lee died in 1993 at the age of twenty-eight, while filming the movie *The Crow*. He was killed by an improperly loaded stunt gun. In the case of both father and son, their final movies were released posthumously to rave reviews.

Many believe the Lees were like stars that shined too brightly and burned out before their time. They are buried side by side; local fans and some of Bruce Lee's former students take care of the grave sites. It is not difficult to find them, even without a map. There is usually a car or two parked nearby and a small crowd gathered around the father and son. The Lee family had a bench erected at the foot of the graves, on which fans may sit. Many people leave symbolic offerings, like flowers, coins, letters, toy weapons, and food.

When we visited the Lees, there was a couple from Washington, D.C., there who had brought a friend from Poland. He talked about how he idolized Bruce Lee and how seeing his movies as a child (not an easy feat in a country that was Communist at the time and considered Lee's movies to be Western decadence) influenced his study of the martial arts. He eventually earned a fourth-degree black belt in his discipline and considered his visit the smallest respect he could pay to Bruce Lee.

Some people believe that the spirits of the departed may come to the grave site when friends and family gather there. Many people say they have somehow touched the spirits of Bruce and Brandon at their graves, and at least one person may have evidence of that in a photograph. In 2004, T. C. O'Reilly sent us an e-mail along with a curious photograph:

I recently visited Bruce Lee's grave in Seattle and took some pictures and found something very interesting in one of them. My girlfriend and I were the only people there that day and she was standing in front of the tombstone when it was taken, yet there's still a reflection of what looks like a small Asian man [in it]. Take a look and tell me what you think, especially look in the reflection on the tombstone.

BRUCE LEE

李振藩

NOV. 27, 1940 — JULY 20, 1973

FOUNDER OF JEET KUNE DO

BRANDON
BRUCE LEE

李國豪

FEB. 1. 1965
MAR. 31, 1993

YOUR INSPIRATION
CONTINUES TO
GUIDE US TOWARD
OUR PERSONAL
LIBERATION

...CAUSE WE DONT KNOW WHEN WE
...WE GET TO THINK OF LIFE AS AN
...EXHAUSTIBLE WELL. YET EVERYTHI
...HAPPENS A CERTAIN NUMBER OF TIM
...AND A VERY SMALL NUMBER, REALL
...HOW MANY MORE TIMES WILL YOU
...REMEMBER A CERTAIN AFTERNOON OF YO
...CHILDHOOD, SOME AFTERNOON THAT'S
...DEEPLY A PART OF YOUR BEING THAT YOU
...CAN'T EVEN CONCEIVE OF YOUR LIFE
...WITHOUT IT? PERHAPS FOUR OR FIVE TIMES
...MORE. PERHAPS NOT EVEN THAT. HOW
...MANY MORE TIMES WILL YOU WATCH THE
...FULL MOON RISE? PERHAPS TWENTY. AND
...YET IT ALL SEEMS LIMITLESS...

For Brandon and Eliza
...In True Love's Beauty

Electric Graveland

'Scuse me while I kiss the sky.

So goes one of Jimi Hendrix's most famous lyrics, and kiss the sky he did, much too early by any standard. The Seattle-born rock musician, known for his overdriven guitar riffs and flamboyant attire, was only twenty-six when he died in a London hotel from asphyxiation caused by vomiting. September 18, 1970, marked the tragic end of a major talent who, in all likelihood, had not yet reached his full potential.

Jimi reportedly told friends he wished to be buried in England. However, his father, James "Al" Hendrix, had him returned to the Seattle area and interred in a family plot at Greenwood Memorial Park in Renton. His grave was marked by a simple headstone with an etching of a Fender Stratocaster guitar, his instrument of choice (though the guitar pictured is right-handed, and Jimi adapted his to play left-handed). At the time, this basic grave was all Al Hendrix could afford.

After his death, Hendrix's popularity grew. In the 1990s, a generation of young Seattle grunge musicians was inspired by his musical technique. Jimi's legacy instilled local pride, and fans regularly made pilgrimages to his grave site. The cemetery's management began worrying about damage to nearby graves from all the foot traffic.

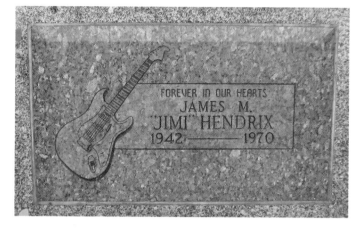

To ease concerns and to vastly expand the family's burial space (since the extended Hendrix family had significantly grown beyond the original plot's five graves), Al Hendrix announced plans for a new memorial to his son, bigger and more fitting to his iconic status. Al envisioned such a memorial for a long time, but didn't gain the financial means to build it until the mid-1990s after acquiring the rights to Jimi's music.

Designed by architect Mark Barthelemy, the memorial was constructed over the next few years by Cold Spring Granite of Minnesota. It was dedicated, still unfinished, in June 2002. Sadly, Al Hendrix had died two months earlier.

The memorial consists of a circular plot of land with a granite dome supported by three columns. The slightly raised structure is accessible by steps and a ramp. The outer base is circled with headstones for Hendrix family members; there's space for fifty-four graves, with Al Hendrix and a few other relatives currently occupying some.

Hendrix is interred in the ground beneath the gazebo, with his original gravestone embedded on a pedestal that is intended to support a much-delayed brass statue. Fans presently use it as an altar for paying their respects: They tape guitar picks to it and drop offerings to Jimi's memory into a hole where a peg on the statue's base will one day be inserted.

Disputes over the remainder of Jimi's multimillion-dollar estate have divided the surviving members of the extended Hendrix family. It's speculated that this is why the statue, supposedly being sculpted in Italy at the time of the 2002 dedication, has not been mounted in the memorial. Instead, fans can admire the statue of Jimi in Seattle's Capitol Hill, on Broadway just north of East Pine Street.

Hendrix biographers have noted an odd situation involving the family and Greenwood Memorial Park. Jimi's mother, Lucille, who died in 1958 when he was just fifteen, lies elsewhere in an unmarked pauper's grave. Why was she buried this way? Why didn't Jimi buy her a gravestone after achieving rock stardom, especially given his well-known devotion to her? Why hasn't she been moved to one of the plots at the memorial? The answers may point to more family discord.

Greenwood Memorial Park is located at 350 Monroe Avenue NE in Renton. The Jimi Hendrix memorial is easily visible on the west side of the cemetery.

Garden of Eternal Peace

Adjacent to the Jimi Hendrix memorial is a rather elegant section of Greenwood Cemetery called the Garden of Eternal Peace. Based on traditional Asian design, the garden features a central shelter surrounded by a shallow manmade moat. Its water is pumped around boulders and over small waterfalls, providing a calming ambient sound to break the cemetery's mournful silence. On either side of the shelter are rows of gravestones with the tops shaped to resemble curved Asian roofs. The back of the garden is partitioned into gated brick enclosures for private family plots.

The garden was dedicated in April 2006 for the memorial park's first commemoration of the Ching Ming Festival (the traditional Asian holiday dedicated to grave tending and honoring one's ancestors); the vast majority of graves are still unused, the gravestones blank. The Garden of Eternal Peace is a culturally significant accommodation for the large Asian community in the area; but more than that, as the blank gravestones are gradually carved with occupants' names, it can serve as a profound reminder of the passage of time toward our shared fate.

Henry Timmerman's Curse

Reality and fiction are both full of tales of innocent men and women sentenced to death for crimes they did not commit. Before they are put to death, many of the condemned make final statements proclaiming their innocence. Some even put curses on the heads of their oppressors, and these curses usually come true . . . in fiction. But in the real-life case of Henry Timmerman, the first half of his curse did come true, leading many to take drastic action to prevent the second half from doing the same.

In 1888, Henry Timmerman stood trial for the murder of a former friend. No one saw him kill the man or even placed Timmerman at the scene, but he was the only candidate for the crime. He was caught after a monthlong manhunt, and the location of his trial had to be changed three times due to threats by vigilantes. Despite his pleas of innocence, he was found guilty and sentenced to hang. His case was appealed at the Territorial Supreme Court, and the German government became involved because Timmerman was a German citizen. Despite these efforts, all appeals were denied, and Timmerman was scheduled to hang in Goldendale on April 6, 1888.

The people of Goldendale built a special gallows on a hill overlooking town. (A gallows with a view!) Timmerman rode up to the site in the back of a wagon, sitting on top of his coffin. As his final request, he asked for a cigar and a bottle of whiskey, and all the way up the road, he puffed his cigar, drank the whiskey, and jeered at the hostile crowd.

No one knows who actually did it: the lying witnesses, the real murderers, or even the sheriff, but somebody sneaked into the graveyard and dug up Timmerman's grave, thus fulfilling part of the curse themselves. After making sure he was still dead, they threw his body into a nearby stream.

Timmerman did have some supporters, and when they heard about the desecration, they found his body and reburied it in a hidden grave. Perhaps this broke the curse, because none of the people involved in Timmerman's trial died mysteriously—or maybe Timmerman's spirit was satisfied after making the people of Goldendale sweat it a little bit.

In our research, we often find that legends like this are too good to be true. But the Klickitat County Historical Society in Goldendale verifies this tale, at least the parts about the trial, the hanging, and the great fire. The town has even celebrated Henry Timmerman Day on special occasions over the years. Records of Timmerman's burial, though, are less clear. The historical society directed us to Mountain View Cemetery, north of Goldendale. There we looked at a detailed map with the locations of all the graves in the cemetery, but found no mention of Timmerman. A caretaker we spoke to confirmed the legend, but said that there was no gravestone or marker.

Just in case, we wandered the cemetery, hoping to find Timmerman's grave. We didn't, but this isn't proof the grave was never there. Several headstones were so worn that their inscriptions were illegible. Regardless, neither vandals nor time have erased the memory of Henry Timmerman. This might be fitting justice in an imperfect world.

When the wagon arrived at the gallows, the crowd paused, waiting to see Timmerman dragged from the wagon to his death.

Instead of cowering in fear, Timmerman jumped down from the wagon and walked up the thirteen steps of the scaffold. With clear contempt for his audience, Timmerman threw his cigar into the waiting crowd and watched them tear it apart, fighting for scraps. He proclaimed his innocence one last time and then cursed the group, saying that if they hanged him, within three months the town of Goldendale would burn to the ground. Not only that, the men involved in his conviction would die. He also said that he would rise from the grave.

Timmerman waited quietly while they fitted a noose around his neck, and a few minutes later, he was dead. The crowd dispersed, probably disappointed in the show and trying to forget Timmerman's curse. But a month later their memories were no doubt refreshed when the town caught fire. The blaze started in the business district; then it swept through the streets, burning the city hall and jail. Remembering the rest of Timmerman's curse, many of the townspeople were frightened. Would it also come true?

Separated Together: Roslyn Historical Cemeteries

It's not really Cicely, Alaska; it just played it on TV. The town of Roslyn, in Kittitas County, is perhaps best known as its quirky alter ego in the 1990s television program *Northern Exposure.* In real life, it's a quiet small town in the Cascade Mountains. Downtown buildings still evoke the nineteenth century, while some area homes are pure Norman Rockwell, complete with white picket fences. The population has remained steady, in the nine hundreds, for years.

In fact, here the dead outnumber the living 5 to 1.

This is because the town, founded in 1886, has kept generations of its deceased close to home. Specifically, they're in the forested hills along Pennsylvania Avenue, on a fifteen-acre expanse comprising twenty-six separate but contiguous cemeteries. Collectively, they're referred to as the Roslyn Historical Cemeteries.

By walking the grounds, there are two things you quickly realize about Roslyn's past. First, its coal-mining industry attracted a multinational, multiethnic mix of workers. Poles, Italians, Slovakians, and other nationalities were well represented, as were African Americans—all sharing the town in relative peace. Secondly, folks here loved organizing themselves into fraternal organizations: Along with the Masons, Odd Fellows, Moose, and Eagles, lesser known societies like the Red Men and Sokol had lodges in Roslyn.

These groups and nationalities all have dedicated cemetery space. Veterans have a place of honor right in front, in what resembles a mini-Arlington. Then there are general-purpose burial grounds like the Old and New City cemeteries. The Old City Cemetery is the most antique, with its family plots fenced in to keep out foraging animals.

Roslyn suffered its greatest disaster on May 10, 1892, when a mine explosion killed forty-five workers.

The memory of this tragedy is literally etched in stone throughout the cemeteries on the grave markers of some of those killed.

Though the grounds are mostly well kept, many of the graves, particularly those corresponding to defunct lodges, are showing their age. This contributes to the "long ago and far away" aura permeating Roslyn in general and the cemeteries in particular.

Prisoner 21520: The Grave You Can't Visit

The cemetery at the Walla Walla penitentiary is a place of true anonymity. It's off-limits to the general public, and when a prisoner passes away, a simple brick marks his grave with his inmate number, like that of prisoner 21520: Jake Bird.

"Jake who?" you might ask. Therein lies the point of this tale.

Even though serial killers do their business anonymously, many crave fame and notoriety. They write letters and give clues to the press and police that can eventually lead to their capture. Once caught, serial killers tend to take on a celebrity status that follows them even after they die. Perhaps the single greatest fear of this kind of monster is to be forgotten, which is exactly what happened to Jake Bird.

As an African American, Jake Bird doesn't fit the profile of the usual group of serial killers. And he wasn't tripped up by writing letters or leaving cryptic clues behind; rather, he was caught as a result of a robbery gone wrong.

On October 30, 1947, he broke into a Tacoma home, carrying an axe. He'd later tell police he just intended to rob the house, but its owner, fifty-three-year-old Bertha Kludt, surprised him. So he killed her with the axe. In the middle of this, Bertha's daughter Beverly June arrived and tried to stop Bird, so he killed her too. The police heard the screams of the two women, and they captured Bird as he fled the area.

Bird pleaded innocent and said he wanted to represent himself in court, but a lawyer was appointed for him. The trial lasted two days, and the jury deliberated for only a half hour before declaring Jake Bird guilty of the premeditated murder of Beverly Kludt. Before sentencing, Bird's attorney told the judge that Bird deserved the death penalty.

When Bird was asked for comment, he spoke for twenty minutes. Noting that his defense team was against him and his request for self-representation was denied, he declared that all the men involved in his case and conviction would die before he did. The judge, unimpressed, sentenced him to be executed at the state penitentiary in Walla Walla on December 7, 1947.

Jake Bird changed strategies at the penitentiary. He filed a series of motions to set aside his murder conviction on technicalities, and argued his own case at the Washington State Supreme Court. Strangely, even though he continued to plead innocent to the Kludts' murders, Jake Bird admitted to killing another forty-four people across the United States.

Like many other serial killers, Bird knew that information could buy him time. He told authorities he had traveled the United States for nearly thirty years, working mostly on the railroads. He claimed to have killed people—mostly women—in twelve states, including South Dakota, Florida, and Oklahoma. He received several stays of execution as he met with law-enforcement officials from across the country. Many thought it was a stunt to delay the inevitable, but Bird gave enough details to make officials think that he committed at least eleven murders.

Reporters visiting Bird in prison noted that he seemed to be in charge, sitting back in a chair and smoking cigars while the guards acted more like his assistants.

He especially got a thrill when one of his "oppressors" died, which they did with regularity. Between the day of Bird's conviction and his execution early on July 15, 1949, five men involved in his case died: the trial judge, three policemen, and Bird's defense attorney. With each death, Jake Bird misquoted the Bible, suggesting his curse was divine justice.

It's likely that the serial killer in Bird hoped there would be a parade of visitors to his grave site in the years to come. It would not have mattered to him if they were fans or enemies, so long as they remembered him as one of America's most prolific serial killers. In reality, his ending was justifiably pathetic. Since the general public can't get access to the cemetery, parades of gawkers never materialized at his grave. Even a request by *Weird Washington* failed to gain entry into the penitentiary or cemetery. Perhaps the greatest blow to Jake Bird's ego would be that penitentiary officials were too busy to take pictures of his grave site for this book. But it's probably for the best, so Bird can sink back into the obscurity he justly deserves.

Cemetery Beneath Seattle's Suburbia?

In the movie Poltergeist, a real estate developer built houses on top of an old cemetery. While the tombstones had been removed, the bodies remained buried, causing suddenly restless spirits to throw a temper tantrum of Hollywood proportions.

Some believe a similar scenario is taking place in real life on Seattle's Beacon Hill.

Comet Lodge Cemetery is located on South Graham Street between Twenty-second and Twenty-third avenues South. The vibrant grass of the 2.5-acre memorial park is a surreal contrast to the weathered old grave markers dispersed throughout the grounds. It's a marked improvement from the bramble jungle it had been for decades, but given its history, any perceived serenity in this final resting place is fleeting at best.

Bereavement, Bureaucracy, and Breakdown

First known as the Old Burial Grounds, this is where the Duwamish Indians laid their loved ones to rest. The Mapel family, among Seattle's first settlers, bought the original five acres of property as part of their estate. They began interring their own here in 1880. In 1895, they officially established the land as Comet Lodge Cemetery for an Independent Order of Odd Fellows lodge of which a Mapel family member was president. The cemetery was used until 1936.

Two years later Seattle and King County foreclosed on the property, citing failure to pay back taxes. Some considered this a blatant land grab, since cemeteries are legally exempt from foreclosure. Regardless, it set the stage for decades of controversy. The cemetery was caught in a bureaucratic limbo as confusion reigned over its rightful ownership. The only certainty was that the more time passed, the more the cemetery succumbed to neglect and vandalism. In a 1948 letter to the Seattle City Council,

city treasurer Herbert Collier described the cemetery as being "in a deplorable condition. Graves were sunken, tombstones were scattered here and there, and the brush has overgrown everything with the exception of a few foot paths. It would be almost impossible to estimate the number of graves, but a rough guess would be . . . considerably more than one hundred."

One way or another, Collier was drastically underestimating. King County records indicate 494 burials at Comet Lodge Cemetery. Others report as many as 1,000. Why such a great disparity? The extra 500 could represent estimated burials by the Duwamish Nation. Or, as some believe, it accounts for burials in the northern 2.5 acres, where eleven homes were eventually built atop possibly unexhumed graves. Some of these are said to be part of the cemetery's Babyland, a section for common burial of children prior to the purchase of a family plot.

John Dickinson, a local activist who has ancestors buried in the cemetery, has gathered about one thousand pages of evidence that he contends demonstrate several unethical and (potentially illegal) indignities committed against Comet Lodge Cemetery by Seattle and King County. His research shows that in addition to houses, both a portion of Twenty-second Avenue South and the western half of Twenty-third Avenue South are also built on grave sites.

As suburban homes expanded onto Beacon Hill, residents launched occasional cleanup efforts at the graveyard, which for various reasons never reached fruition. Meanwhile, vagrants camped in it, trash was dumped in the wild brush, and gravestones were damaged or stolen.

In 1987, local resident Don Kipper obtained permission to clean up the site. By the time officials realized he was an unabashed eccentric who wanted to build a dream home on the cemetery, he'd already bulldozed about two hundred

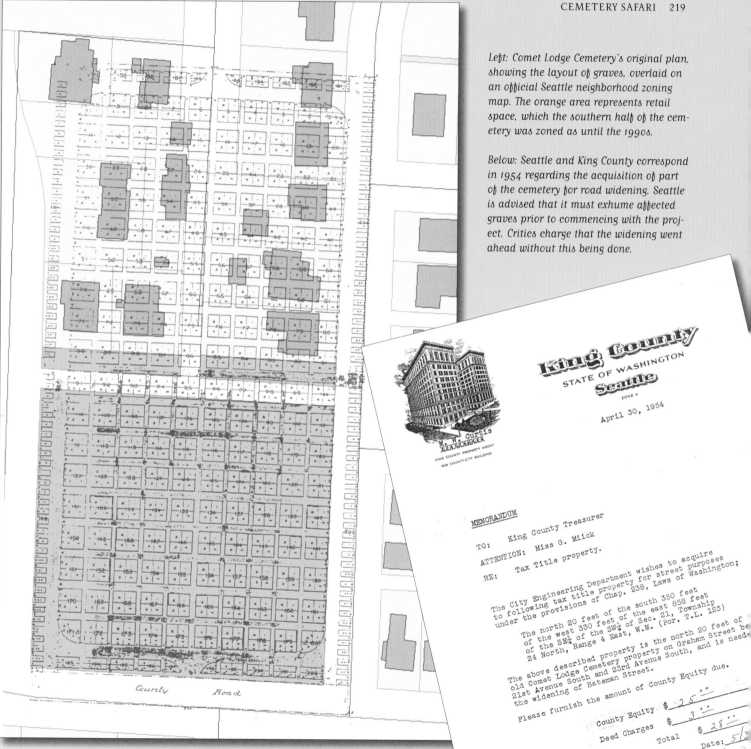

Left: Comet Lodge Cemetery's original plan, showing the layout of graves, overlaid on an official Seattle neighborhood zoning map. The orange area represents retail space, which the southern half of the cemetery was zoned as until the 1990s.

Below: Seattle and King County correspond in 1954 regarding the acquisition of part of the cemetery for road widening. Seattle is advised that it must exhume affected graves prior to commencing with the project. Critics charge that the widening went ahead without this being done.

King County

STATE OF WASHINGTON

Seattle

ZONE 4

April 30, 1954

M. W. Curtis

KING COUNTY PROPERTY AGENT

608 COUNTY-CITY BUILDING

MEMORANDUM

TO: King County Treasurer

ATTENTION: Miss G. Miick

RE: Tax Title property.

The City Engineering Department wishes to acquire the following tax title property for street purposes under the provisions of Chap. 238, Laws of Washington;

The north 20 feet of the south 350 feet of the west 330 feet of the east 858 feet of the SE¼ of the SW¼ of Sec. 21, Township 24 North, Range 4 East, W.M. (Por. T.L. 123)

The above described property is the north 20 feet of old Comet Lodge Cemetery property on Graham Street between 21st Avenue South and 23rd Avenue South, and is needed for the widening of Bateman Street.

Please furnish the amount of County Equity due.

County Equity $ 25.00

Deed Charges $ 3.00

Total $ 28.00   Date: 5/

grave markers. Eyewitnesses still mention the startling sight of broken gravestones in a pile, and visitors who helped themselves to these "mementos." Although Seattle city leaders were supposedly incensed by Kipper's actions, more graves were later bulldozed (ironically on All Souls' Day) to install a new sewer line.

In the 1990s, John Dickinson organized a volunteer group and obtained a permit to attempt his own restoration, but efforts were impeded, he said, by claims that the work was destroying trees "where falcons were nesting." He pointed out it was in the middle of winter and that no nests were in the trees.

Eventually, King County executive Ron Sims proposed clearing out the remaining gravestones and turning the property into an off-leash dog park. Activists balked; they would accept no less than a dignified restoration of the cemetery. So the county finally took up the effort, grooming it into its current well-kept state. However, controversy remains.

Of the 494 graves on official record, only thirty-one grave markers have been salvaged or retrieved. Eighteen of these remained on (or were matched to) their corresponding graves. The remaining thirteen were dispersed "aesthetically" around the grounds, but their intended grave sites are unknown. A pile of broken grave markers still lies beneath a tree on the property. A promised fence was never installed, and dogs run leash-free there.

The Dead Weigh In

How might the dead in Comet Lodge Cemetery feel about all the decades of neglect and disturbance? Film fantasies like *Poltergeist* are hardly required to answer this question. According to local legend, deceased residents make themselves known from time to time.

gained some fame by sharing her supernatural experiences with the local media. She claimed to have peacefully shared her home with some ghostly Comet Lodge inhabitants. A spectral woman and a little boy (perhaps the same one who walks around the grounds) would sit at the foot of her granddaughter's bed. She described flickering lights and a cloudlike transparent figure swooping from room to room. When some of her yard was dug up in 1987 for the sewer line, her phantom housemates panicked. Suddenly more aggressive, they engaged in threatening and destructive behavior until the construction ended. Similar activity was reported in other nearby homes.

If these incidents are meant to express dissatisfaction with the cemetery's current state of affairs, the ghosts certainly have living allies. John Dickinson, for one, continues to promote the cause whenever possible. As he puts it: "There is no statute of limitations excusing ongoing desecration of a federally protected, Native American, designated Historic Cemetery."

Clearly, this elysian field has a long way to go before it's truly at rest.

There are recurring accounts of the spirit of a little boy walking around the grounds and of the distant sound of children laughing. It's said that stepping over certain unmarked graves might yield a sudden, mild feeling of distress. Or you might hear sticks breaking underfoot, even if you're alone and didn't step on any. Floating orbs of light are occasionally spotted at night.

Beverly Washington, who lived in one of the houses on the northern half of the cemetery,

Afterglow Vista

Most people think family cemeteries, particularly ones in the western United States, consist of a couple of tumbledown marble or wooden headstones surrounded by a rotting picket fence. Sad to say, this is mostly true, but there are exceptions. Take, for example, the family plot of the McMillins in Roche Harbor.

John McMillin owned the local lime works and was active in local and state politics. He believed he owed much of his success to his religion, personal philosophy, and family, and he wanted to express this through the construction of a family tomb that was full of symbols that would be rich

to him and to others. The meaning of many of the tomb's symbols has faded, but visitors can find several places in Roche Harbor that have maps to the tomb and pamphlets explaining the design and purpose of the magnificent structure.

The mausoleum is located near Roche Harbor and can be found by following a trail in the local cemetery leading through a green, overgrown wood; a sign reading AFTERGLOW VISTA marks the entrance.

After going through the gates, visitors must walk up three flights of stairs. The steps symbolize many things, especially to Freemasons. The first flight has three steps, which represent the three ages of man. The second has five steps, which represent both the five orders of classic architecture and the five senses. The last flight of seven steps represents the seven liberal arts and sciences and also symbolizes the seven days of the week.

Once up the stairs, visitors reach a raised platform on which several pillars support a domeless roof. In ancient times, pillars lined the western entrance to any house of worship. At Afterglow, one of the western pillars was installed broken to symbolize the way death breaks the column of any man's life.

Perhaps the most striking feature of Afterglow is the large limestone table on the platform, which symbolizes the entire McMillin family meeting in unity over dinner. Around the table are chairs for each family member, with the corresponding names written on the chair backs. A hollow niche inside each seat serves as the place in which the family member's cremated ashes rest.

Besides the family, one other person is buried here: Ada Beane. She was McMillin's governess and more like family than an employee. After she died, she was cremated, and the family kept her ashes, which were later interred in the family crypt.

Unfortunately, vandals turn up even in remote places like Roche Harbor. A few years ago they attacked the McMillin crypt, damaging one chair back and removing another completely. Even so, the place still has a peaceful aura. As the sun goes down on summer evenings, the light shines through the trees on the tomb. Some people believe that when it does, the shadows somehow change, and the McMillin family meets again to have a ghostly dinner together in the afterglow.

Maltby's Cemetery of Mystique

A hilltop on the outskirts of Woodinville is where the Doolittle family and their descendants have interred their dearly departed since the early 1900s. This family plot, known as Maltby Cemetery, currently contains about forty graves along an elevated forest trail that extends into the backyard of a suburban home.

Given its somewhat isolated location and unusual configuration, it's no surprise that the small graveyard became big in supernatural folklore. Generations of thrill seekers have contemplated it with curiosity and imagination. In fact, it seems as if most locals have ignored the prominent NO TRESPASSING signs at least once to see for themselves what all the fuss is about.

Among the cemetery's rumored elements and tales:

The Gates (or Pillars) of Hell

Really neither gates nor pillars, these two four- or five-foot-tall concrete obelisks reportedly once supported a gate from the yard into the cemetery. These days they represent an ominous point of no return, a landmark suggesting, "Abandon all hope, ye who enter here!"

Ghosts and Apparitions

The apparition of a woman is sometimes seen wandering the grounds alone, searching for her child through eternity. Alternately, another—or perhaps the same—ghost is seen with a child, both wearing old, ragged clothing. These are just two of many ghostly tales ascribed to the cemetery. Others include an eerie whispering in the air as the wind blows through surrounding trees, ghosts shoving or hitting trespassers, and, of course, floating orbs of light.

The Changing Gravestone

One legend concerns a particular gravestone that changes its appearance from a fairly small, generic marker to a larger, ornate monument. To observe this phenomenon, one has to walk past all the graves, then turn around, walk back, and look at the spot where the original marker stood. According to one account, "It's not something you actually see happen; it's more like you notice it afterwards."

The Pentagram Gravestone

Many people mention a gravestone with a satanic pentagram design. Far be it from *Weird Washington* to burst any bubbles, but we have it on good authority that the "pentagram" is actually a square-and-compasses symbol, identifying the grave of a Mason.

The Den

Details are vague on what or where exactly the Den is supposed to be. Some say it's the ground between the Gates of Hell and the graves beyond it. Others specify a clearing nearby in the woods. Either way, legend has it that its entrance is protected by some kind of spiritual force and that anyone who manages to breach it will go irreversibly insane.

The Thirteen Steps to Hell

This is the most-often cited Maltby Cemetery legend, though accounts of the steps' location are inconsistent. Some believe they're hidden somewhere on the forest trail; others say they lie beneath a fallen slab in the cemetery itself. In any case, watch that last step. It's a doozy! Rumor has it that many a young person has emerged catatonic from the Thirteen Steps after catching a horrifying glimpse of the infernal netherworld. Or maybe it was the tequila they sneaked from Dad's liquor cabinet.

Mystery Guards

Like the stories of men in black who frequent areas with

UFO activity, tales of mysterious uniformed guards at Maltby Cemetery briefly cropped up a few years ago. Though they were doubtless flesh and blood, a few accounts classified them as supernatural.

There's a logical reason for their presence: vandalism. The owners and caretakers of Maltby Cemetery have had to deal with the destructiveness of a few inconsiderate jerks for the past few years. Take our word for it that their patience has worn very thin and the cemetery is strictly off-limits. In addition, the neighbors keep an eye out for trespassers at all hours. Be warned: You risk very real arrest by going there without permission. We strongly suggest you bask in the Maltby Cemetery mystique solely from the pages of this book.

Pickled Willie's Grave

The oldest grave in a private little hilltop cemetery that lies between Raymond and Menlo belongs to nineteen-year-old Willie Keil. Willie actually died over a thousand miles from Washington State, but his untimely death may have given his family safe passage as they traveled across North America to the West Coast.

Willie was the son of William Keil, who was a member of a Christian religious order known as the Bethelites. Seeking religious freedom, William Keil and several followers emigrated from Prussia to the United States in the 1830s. They settled in several places, including New York and Pittsburgh, before reaching Missouri in 1844. They remained there for several years, and the community grew.

In 1855, Keil decided that God wanted him to set up a colony in the Pacific Northwest, so they prepared to head out. His son Willie asked permission to ride in the lead wagon, but a few days before they planned to leave, Willie died.

The elder Keil kept his promise. He lined Willie's coffin with lead and filled it with whiskey. He draped a wagon with black cloth and bells, and put the coffin in the front. This wagon took the lead as they set out along the Oregon Trail.

Along the trail, the Keil party heard tales of wagon trains being wiped out by hostile Native Americans. Many tribes approached them, including the Sioux, Cayuse, and Yakima. Most Native American tribes had a long tradition of respecting burial grounds and parties escorting the dead to them. Each time the Indians arrived, William Keil took the lid off the coffin and showed them his son's body floating in the whiskey. The rest of the party, dressed in black, gathered around and sang dirges and other mourning songs in German. Doing this enabled the Keils to pass safely all the way to western Washington.

They settled near the Washington coast, along the Willapa River, and buried Willie on a hilltop. In the next year, however, the entire colony relocated to Oregon's Willamette Valley, where they founded Aurora. Perhaps they left Washington because of the weather or because William Keil received new guidance from the Lord. The only thing they left in Washington was Willie's grave.

The grave is locally famous and marked by a Washington State historic landmark sign. To find it, from Highway 101 turn south on SR 6 and head south. You will see the marker and vehicle turnout just west of Menlo. It is recommended that visitors not try to visit the grave itself. The hilltop cemetery is still in use by local families and is located on private property behind a gate that is usually locked to keep in cattle.

MOTOR FERRY "KALAKALA", WORLD'S FIRST STREAMLINED VESSEL

IN SERVICE BETWEEN SEATTLE AND BREMERTON, WASH. ON PUGET SOUND

Washington Lost and Found

Many things lie moldering and all but forgotten in the vastness of Washington State. These relics of the past have become obsolete in many different ways: some due to changing needs or values, some due to some stark tragedy that can't be forgotten, and sometimes a combination of both.

Regardless of the cause of their present desolation, these abandoned places raise questions in the minds of more thoughtful passersby, those not focused only on the next shiny, new thing. Who once lived here? Why did they leave, and most intriguing—what evidence of themselves did they leave behind? These are the questions we ask ourselves as we walk through the rotting wood, crumbling furniture, and broken glass of these once proud structures. We may not always find the answers, but piecing together the puzzles of their former lives can take one down some very weird memory lanes.

Odd Leavings by the Odd Fellows

The Odd Fellows is a fraternal organization that traces its lineage back to seventeenth-century England. Like similar organizations, it is full of symbols and rituals with meanings known only to the members. The Odd Fellows has a history of taking care of members who might be experiencing tough times, including providing inexpensive funeral services. Because of this, it has an interesting initiation ritual. New members are shown a coffin, inside of which is a skeleton that represents death. Usually the coffin and skeleton were fake, but sometimes they weren't. In small towns, the Odd Fellows Lodge was usually located in the shop or warehouse of a local member, with the skeleton and coffin hidden in a storeroom somewhere. Some larger Odd Fellows Lodges were ornate buildings, and a real skeleton was kept in a hidden room.

At one time, the Odd Fellows had many members in lodges across the country, including Washington State, but by the end of the twentieth century, their numbers dwindled as older members died and weren't replaced. Some lodges sold their buildings, leaving all their ritual materials behind, including the coffins with fake or real skeletons. What do you do with a bunch of old bones, anyway? Leave them for the new owners to find!

An Odd Fellows Lodge in Ridgefield was sold in the 1990s to a nonmember. When the new owner toured his property, he could not find a key to a back room. He broke the lock and opened the door to find a small, badly lit room. As his eyes adjusted to the light, he saw an open coffin lying on a table. With understandable hesitation, he walked up to the foot of the coffin. It was

several more seconds before he stepped close enough to look inside. When he did, his heart seemed to stop, until he realized that the bony figure inside was only a mannequin.

Spokane's Odd Fellows Lodge

In 1998, the Spokane Odd Fellows moved out of their lodge on West First Avenue and put it up for sale. It was a while before anyone bought it, but eventually two businesswomen turned the large brick building into the Cameo Catering and Event Center. After months of renovation, the new owners found several robes, uniforms, books, and other ritual-related regalia the Odd Fellows had left behind. But the group might have left something else that the new owners have yet to discover.

Weird Washington visited the

old building a few years ago and was impressed with the restoration work. The main entrance featured an Eye of Horus mosaic—an important symbol to the Odd Fellows—that seemed to wink at visitors as they entered. The wooden floors were beautifully restored, and the dark paneling in the grand ballroom gleamed in the soft light.

The owners showed us into the billiard room, where the Odd Fellows used to meet, talk, and smoke cigars. They told us they had cleaned every room in the building and never found a hidden room, with or without the requisite coffin or skeleton. We kept this in mind as we walked through the rest of the building, looking for signs of a hidden room they might have missed.

When we returned to the ballroom, something looked a little bit odd. The room had high ceilings, and the builders had tried to create a theatrical look by constructing a set of ornamental balconies over the front entrance. These balconies were very small, about four feet wide, and only two or three feet deep, but each had a set of French windows, as if they opened into other rooms. When asked where the stairs leading to the balconies were located, the owners said that the balconies were purely ornamental and that the doors did not open into another room.

We weren't so sure, and paced off the ballroom, comparing distances to the floor above, where the balconies were. We suspect there might have been a small room on the other side of one of the balconies, but could not figure out how to get there. We weren't willing to scale the wall, so the mystery remains. How many other Odd Fellows Lodges in Washington hold a secret or two that their present owners do not suspect?

Cameo Appearance

Along with their ritual gear and paperwork, the Odd Fellows left some spiritual remnants behind at the Cameo. Employees have told the managers that they sometimes feel someone following them around the building. A few thought they heard someone calling their names or heard echoing footsteps when the building was empty. Is this the overactive imagination of people alone in an old building?

In one case, it's especially hard to pass off the phenomenon as purely imaginary. When employees— particularly female employees—work in the billiard room, they report a strong odor. They describe it as a sweaty male-type smell. Once in a while, this smell follows them from the billiard room throughout the building before fading away.

Wellington Train Wreck

Wellington, once a thriving railroad town in the Washington Cascades, was abandoned long ago for a tragic reason: It was the site of what may have been America's worst avalanche-railroad disaster of the twentieth century, a disaster the town could not survive.

The Great Northern Railway built the 2.6-mile-long Cascade Tunnel as part of a network of tunnels and rail lines through Stevens Pass in 1893. The town of Wellington was located in a valley at the west end of the tunnel, along the Tye River. About a mile to the west, the railroad built a second tunnel, which opened into western Washington.

The trains that passed through the Cascades were serviced in Wellington, and the town was also a stop for passengers if the train was delayed due to heavy snow in the passes. It had a small hotel, a general store, and a restaurant.

At the end of February 1910, a nine-day blizzard hit the Cascade Mountains. Eleven feet of snow fell on the last day alone. Two trains from Spokane were delayed in Wellington, waiting for the snows to clear before they could head to Seattle.

When the storm broke on February 28, passengers and crew boarded their trains and waited for snowplows to clear the tracks. The trains stood under some of the wood-roofed sheds just outside the western tunnel. As the day wore on, the weather warmed up, and it began to rain. The passengers sat in the trains all day and into the night. They were still there, waiting under the sheds at around one a.m. on March 1, when the rain turned into a thunderstorm. High above the trains, a slab of snow broke loose, starting an avalanche ten feet high and a quarter mile long. The avalanche missed Wellington, but it swept the trains 150 feet to the bottom of the valley.

Officially, ninety-six people died, but there were rumors that the death count was higher and that the railroad and newspapers lied about the numbers. It might have been an honest mistake, however, since all the bodies were not recovered until the end of July. It was considered a miracle that twenty-three people survived.

The town and the railroad quickly received a bad-luck reputation. In October 1910, the railroad renamed the town Tye, after the river valley. It also built a concrete snow shed, so the disaster could not repeat itself. Even so, people were still uncomfortable stopping there. When the railroad built a new depot farther west, in Skykomish, the little community of Tye faded away.

Some believe the spirits of the dead from the 1910 avalanche still relive the trauma of the crash. Those

100 DEAD IN AVALANCHE.

Thirty-five Bodies Recovered from Train Wreck in Washington.

EVERETT, Wash., March 3.—Railroad men who have been at the scene of the Wellington avalanche said to-day that the chance of rescuing any of the persons reported missing was small, and that all are almost certainly dead.

Thirty-five bodies have been recovered. Sixty are missing whose names are known, besides a number of laborers. It was estimated late to-day that probably more than 100 persons were killed.

The report that another slide had descended upon the workers is discredited here. The snow is melting, and the mountains are in tumult, with snow, rocks, trees, and earth rolling and plunging down the steep places.

No attempt will be made at present to bring the bodies of the dead down the mountainside. It is not unlikely that traffic will be opened from the eastern side first, in which case the dead and the wounded will be taken to Spokane.

The cars of the wrecked train are not in sight; they are under forty or fifty feet of snow and trees. The few men who are working in the snow cannot accomplish much, and it would take them months to dig out the cars.

SPOKANE, Wash., March 3.—The Oriental limited train eastbound, on the

who visit the Wellington town site in the winter claim that in addition to the wind, they can hear the sound of a ghostly avalanche, the crash of the train as it falls down the mountainside, and the screams of injured people. Others claim they have heard the sound of train whistles as they walked through the tunnel.

Mystery of the Cascade Tunnel

In 1929, the Great Northern Railroad built a second Cascade Tunnel near the first. At 7.8 miles in length, it is the longest railroad tunnel in the United States. Once this tunnel was finished, the railroad abandoned the Wellington tunnels and rail lines.

In the 1990s, the U.S. government built the Iron Goat Trail, which begins at Martin Creek, near milepost 55 on Highway 2, and runs through Stevens Pass to the Wellington ghost town. From the trail, visitors can see the remains of the old rail lines, supporting structures, and a train crash at the bottom of the canyon.

Some friends and I walked through one of the tunnels. There was no electricity, so we relied on headlamps and flashlights. Near the tunnel entrance and just off the tracks we found a built-in room, which was probably created for railroad employees. We could see someone had been holding parties there: They left behind beer cans, dirty blankets, and other things.

We continued walking through the tunnel for what seemed like an hour. It was cold and damp, and at one point, we encountered a fog bank. After a while, we came to a strange modification to the tunnel. It had been blocked by a partition made of wood and covered with corrugated metal. There was a small door in the wall. "Wait till you see what's on the other side," my friend Ross said.

We walked through the open door and came to the rotting remains of a wooden platform and the walls of a small shack. There was lots of fiberglass insulation, and oddly, someone had strung lines of high voltage conduit along the walls of the tunnel. From what I know about wiring and construction, I guessed this all was set up in the late 1960s or 1970s.

We walked for as much as another half mile before coming out of the tunnel. The wiring, insulators, and conduit ran along its remaining length, and along the way, we also found two or three concrete pads that had been poured directly on top of the train tracks.

So, what was it all for? I have never been a conspiracy theorist, but I was thinking that something like this would have taken a lot of money and authority. Had the tunnel been used as some kind of storage facility—possibly for hidden missiles? I suggested this to someone, and he laughed, saying that there had been an earthquake monitoring station in the tunnels several years ago. There went the conspiracy theory—unless of course that was the cover story.—*Jefferson Davis*

SAD Story of the Cascade Tunnel

This is the end of the old Cascade Tunnel at Wellington. Wellington was the site of a large avalanche in 1910 that killed many people. The tunnel was still in operation until the late 1930's when it was replaced by another tunnel through the Cascade Mountains. The irony is that the only letters left on the CASCADE sign are s, a, d.—*Choi Halladay*

Bad Luck of the *Kalakala*

One of the wonderful sights in the Puget Sound in the early twentieth century was the art deco sculpturelike passenger ferry the *Kalakala*, which sailed the waters of the sound between Bremerton and Seattle from the 1930s to the 1960s. She left the sound, supposedly forever, in the 1960s, only to return like a ghost in the 1990s.

The *Kalakala* began her existence in 1927 in San Francisco as the *Peralta:* a passenger and auto drive-on, drive-off ferry. It was open at both ends, and cars drove on board, headed to the far end of the ship, and parked. When the ship docked, the cars simply drove off the front of the ferry, rather than backing off. To prevent sinking as the weight shifted with the cars, the *Peralta* had a series of trim tanks at either end that acted as ballast. When the cars unloaded at one end, the tank at the other end filled with water, keeping the ferry on an even keel.

Some suspected from the beginning that the ship was bad luck. During her launch, the *Peralta* got stuck in the launching ramp. To old salts, this was a sign that the ship

was jinxed. The bad luck was still hanging over the ship on February 14, 1928, when the ferry crew filled the wrong trim tank. As the passengers unloaded, the docking end of the *Peralta* sank. Waves swept over the landing ramp, and many passengers went overboard. Five people drowned.

Another disaster struck on the night of May 6, 1933. The *Peralta* was docked at the Oakland ferry terminal, which caught fire. The fire spread to the ferry, and by morning the upper decks were burned and twisted. Only the hull beneath the waterline remained intact.

The Puget Sound Navigation Company bought the remains of the ferry for $10 and towed her to the Lake Washington shipyards, where they rebuilt the superstructure. And rather than just rebuild a functional ferry, they decided to incorporate art deco features and aerodynamic stylings into its design. A Boeing employee carved a wooden model that the shipwrights used as a template. They welded aluminum and steel plates together on the new superstructure and painted it silver. The end result looked like an airplane without wings (or a giant floating toaster). Even the new name fit the design: *Kalakala* is from the Chinook language and means "fast flying bird."

The *Kalakala* certainly seemed to fly. She was the fastest ferry in the Puget Sound, making eight round trips between Bremerton and Seattle every day at a brisk eighteen knots an hour. There was room for 110 autos on her car deck. The remaining decks would hold two thousand passengers. There were shower facilities for shipyard workers returning home, a lunch counter, three observation rooms, a sun deck, and a ladies-lounge. The *Kalakala* became a hot nightspot. The lunch counter catered parties, and an observation deck became a ballroom.

Despite the ferry's rebirth, bad karma seemed to dog her new incarnation. The ship's distinctive design had serious drawbacks. The crew in the pilothouse had a hard time seeing where she was going, and she ran into other ships and the ferry docks several times over the years. Sadly, at least one woman committed suicide in the ladies' lounge.

Despite this, the *Kalakala* was a Seattle icon for decades, until she was simply too old to serve. Her engines needed an expensive overhaul, and by 1967, the increasing size of automobiles made it impossible to fit more than sixty cars on the car deck. The *Kalakala*'s owners decided to sell her that year, and a fishing company bought her and towed her to Alaska, where she spent over thirty years as a floating fish processor and cannery.

In 1998, Seattle sculptor Peter Bevis and the Kalakala Alliance Foundation purchased the ferry and towed her back to the Puget Sound. They had plans to restore her, but the *Kalakala*'s notorious bad luck seemed to follow, as the foundation went bankrupt in 2003. Even after a private buyer purchased her rusting bulk in 2004 she continued to be unlucky. She was towed to Neah Bay, where the Makah Indians had donated moorage, but she damaged one of their docks and they sued (but later dropped the suit). Another buyer purchased her, and she's been moored in Tacoma since October 2004.

Today the Kalakala Alliance Foundation has plans to fully restore the ship. They've obtained state and national historic registrations and created a new master plan that places her in a park, called Columbia Gardens, located in Tacoma. Perhaps the fast flying bird has really come home to roost this time.

Kalakala Ghosts

In 2001, Ross Allison, president of the Advanced Ghost Hunters of Seattle, Tacoma (AGHOST,) noticed the *Kalakala* and contacted Peter Bevis. He asked if the ferry was haunted, and Bevis had a few tales to share with Allison, including a story from when the ferry was towed back to the Puget Sound in 1998.

The trip back took several days, during which Bevis and several workmen stayed on board. Bevis slept near the ladies' lounge and several times heard women talking and laughing, which at first he attributed to a nearby cannery. One night he heard what sounded like three women talking as they walked along the companionway outside his quarters.

Bevis put on his shoes, grabbed a flashlight, and followed the sounds of the conversation. He trailed the sounds down the next two decks, catching up at the foot of a spiral staircase, where he could hear women giggling but could not see anyone. Then the sounds stopped abruptly.

Bevis thought this ghostly manifestation might have had something to do with a passenger from 1940 named Adelaide Bebb. She had recently lost her father and sister in a car crash, and was not married (practically a tragedy itself in those days). Unable to cope, she shot herself in the ladies' lounge.

In 2002, AGHOST and the Washington State Ghost Society toured the *Kalakala* with Bevis. Some of the sensitives in the group felt drawn to the ladies' lounge, and a female psychic detected the spirit of a woman who did not like men. Other investigators brought devices that measured electromagnetic energy, which detected energy readings in the ladies' lounge. The investigators set up motion detection sensors and energy detectors connected to a computer that recorded all the readings at the same time.

They left the lounge and investigated other locations on the ferry, where they got more energy readings that coincided with the presence of the sad female spirit. When the psychic detected the spirit, the meters around her went off. As the technicians moved forward, the energy went down. The psychic moved, following the spirit, and the energy readings rose. The psychic suggested that the spirit moved away because the technicians were men and she did not want them nearby.

When the group returned to the lounge, they had surprising results. The motion detectors worked by emitting low-level noises that bounced off the walls. If someone stepped in front of the emitter, the signal bounced back, telling the computer something had stepped inside the room. The motion detectors had spiked several times while the investigators were away. Oddly, the computer indicated one of the sounds took too long to bounce back from the wall. The only way this could have happened was if the walls of the *Kalakala* had moved farther away from the sensor.

Ross Allison speculated that the sound emitted by the sensor may have traveled out to the wall and back, but passed through something that was not solid; something that slowed down the sound waves long enough to trip the sensors. Unfortunately, they were not able to return for more investigations.

A Bughouse in Bug Town

Some people think the derogatory name Bughouse came from Northern State Hospital in Sedro-Woolley. The town was, after all, originally named Bug by its first settler, Mortimer Cook, thanks to the copious amounts of mosquitoes in the area. But it just isn't so: The term was used in the 1800s, before Northern State Hospital was built.

In 1909, Washington had two overcrowded asylums: Western State Hospital in Steilacoom and Eastern State Hospital in Medical Lake, near Spokane. Rather than enlarging these asylums, the state decided to build a third. Several towns submitted proposals, seeing an asylum as a new source of jobs. Sedro-Woolley won the bid, and the first patients arrived at the new hospital in December 1912. At its height, the facility housed over two thousand patients and employed one thousand people.

It was amazing what kind of "illness" could land someone in Northern State. Men committed their postmenopausal wives when the women became "too excitable." At least one man was committed because he had what was called "religious mania." There were cases of orphaned children being sent to the facility for what today would likely be diagnosed as attention deficit disorder. Many more were committed due to "imbecility" or other learning disabilities. Perhaps a third of the inmates had diseases like senile dementia, manic depression, schizophrenia, and other mental illnesses.

Northern State Hospital treated its patients with occupational therapy, hoping that physical labor, like farming and felling timber, would aid in patients' recovery; many of them learned a trade for the day when they would be released. But the doctors also used other techniques popular in the twentieth century to help cure mental illness, including electroshock therapy and lobotomy. Many patients were also sterilized, following

While some of the deceased may be at peace, there have been reports of unquiet dead who walk the crumbling halls of the old buildings.

She's Got (Ghostly) Legs

In 2006, a paranormal investigation group received permission to visit the old hospital, and one person, Vanessa Rent, took pictures in the basement using infrared film. She didn't see much when she was taking the photographs, but the following describes what happened when she developed her film:

It was at the end of the night and I was getting lazy about documenting how I took each photo. Plus running around that big place with all that equipment was cumbersome, anyway. I didn't think anyone was wearing shorts that night, so I double-checked at the [after ghost hunt] meeting. No one remembers anyone in shorts. It is clearly bare legs in what may either be a patient's gown or nurse's uniform.

Also, someone in the group helped validate it a little more, since I had my shutter open more than 10 seconds. It couldn't be a real person or else it would be lots more blurry. And I'm 95% sure I took that pic without anyone there 'cuz it looked creepy as a long, lonely hallway, I probably wouldn't have taken it if someone was standing there already!

the belief of the times that it was for their own good as well as society's.

The hospital closed in 1973, and Washington converted part of the complex into a Job Corps facility and drug treatment center. Although some of the buildings are still in use, some have been torn down, and others are empty and deteriorating. In 2006, local citizens erected a monument to the forgotten dead in the hospital's graveyard. While some of the deceased may be at peace, there have been reports of unquiet dead who walk the crumbling halls of the old buildings. Several people have said they saw a little girl darting around, sometimes playing with a red ball. A man who never seems to find her follows. Other people claim to have seen a nurse in a certain building, pushing a man in a wheelchair.

Remember, some of the buildings at Northern State are condemned, and for good reason. Most of them are filled with debris and asbestos, and it can be dangerous to walk through them without an employee as a guide.

Roche Harbor: Company Town

With trees being plentiful in the Pacific Northwest, it's easy to see why most houses built there in the nineteenth century were made of wood. But there are drawbacks to relying on wood for construction: Buildings could be only as high as four stories, and there was always the danger of fire. Several cities that relied heavily on wood alone—including Seattle—would burn down, sometimes more than once.

The alternative construction materials were stone and brick. Stone was easy to find and quarry, and there was plenty of clay to make bricks. But until the late 1800s, the mortar necessary to hold them together had to be imported. Mortar was made from quicklime, created by burning limestone in a very hot furnace. There were many limestone deposits in Washington, but only the purest limestone would do, and that was hard to find.

Prospectors found small but pure limestone deposits in 1881, and in 1886 John McMillin formed the Tacoma and Roche Harbor Lime Company on vast limestone deposits found at Roche Harbor. A company town grew up around the lime plant; it had its own school, stores, housing, and utilities. Like most company towns, it paid its workers in scrip instead of money, but unlike in other company towns, the company kept prices in its stores down by buying in bulk and passing the savings on to the workers. Company housing was also a step above what other workers could afford in Seattle.

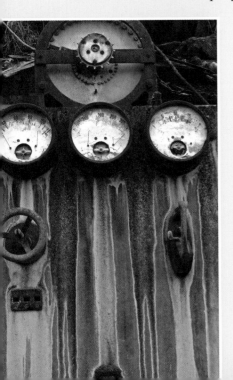

When the lime deposits ran out, the Tacoma and Roche Harbor Lime Company ceased operation and the main reason for Roche Harbor's existence went away too. Underbrush and trees grew over the remains of the warehouses, and the docks were torn down or left to rot. All that was left was several kilns, loading docks, and the rotting Roche Harbor wharves.

In 1957, the Tarte family bought the property, rebuilt some of the wharves, and reopened the place as the Roche Harbor Boatel & Resort. In the last decade, Roche Harbor has undergone many changes, becoming a stopover for yacht owners and summer tourists. In 2007, the Roche Harbor Resort continues to make improvements around the remnants of the old lime works. Today you can get a map of the historic village at the front desk of the Hotel de Haro and conduct your own walking tour of the area.

Putting the "Wash" in Washington: Soap Lake

Among the local American Indian tribes there is a legend about an old woman who died near Soap Lake. Her people had to leave before the snows fell, and they did not have time to bury her. So they threw her body into the lake and continued on their journey. A few days later the old woman caught up with them. The lake water had brought her back to life.

Since prehistoric times, people have sought healing from the waters of hot springs across the world. Washington State has several, which is not remarkable, but what about an entire lake saturated with minerals like sodium, silicon, chloride, various sulphates, aluminum, potassium, and magnesium? That place is Soap Lake, in the northeast of the state.

The American Indians of eastern Washington recognized the healing powers of the lake when they drank its waters. In the summer and fall, members of many tribes gathered there, calling it Skokiam, which meant something like "strong" or "healing" waters. They camped there for days or weeks, gathering roots, racing horses, and socializing with their friends and relatives.

American settlers moved into the area in the mid-1800s. They found that when they swam in the lake, they floated more easily in its mineral-rich waters than they did in normal water or even in the ocean. And they were amazed to find that when they washed their clothes, they did not need soap. The water formed suds and lathered when they rubbed their clothes against the rocks—and so they named the place Soap Lake.

Many settlers also noticed that although the lake was cold, they felt better after a plunge in its waters. They promoted the lake water as a cure for rheumatism, arthritis, lumbago, and skin diseases such as eczema. In the early 1900s, several businessmen opened spa resorts in the area and piped in water from the lake for bathing as well as for patrons to drink. Some people gathered mud

from the east end to coat the bodies of people suffering from joint pain. It may have also cured a condition known as Berger's Disease, a cardiovascular ailment caused by exposure to mustard gas in World War I.

Soap Lake is not easy to get to, and over time the inconvenience made it less appealing. Today many people stop at Soap Lake only because they are on the highway headed to other places, like the Grand Coulee Dam. Consequently, the town now has a somewhat forlorn look. The buildings are in good repair, but many display FOR SALE signs. Although some of the original resorts have been torn down, there are still plenty of other places to stay: motels along the lake and several campgrounds and RV parks that hug its south and east sides.

In a bid to regain some of its former glory, Soap Lake took ownership of a fifty-foot-tall lava lamp and hopes to install it downtown. However, it is not easy for the town of about a thousand people to come up with the several thousand dollars needed to set it up.

Not a Washout

Soap Lake was formed over a period of several thousand years by a dramatic geologic process involving an ice dam that blocked the Columbia River, causing it to cut a channel through what is now the lake. The dam burst at the end of the Ice Age, allowing the Columbia River to flow in its present-day channel. Water still flowed into Soap Lake, however, through layers of basalts, granites, and other stone, carrying many minerals with it.

Over the last twelve hundred years, hot, dry weather evaporated much of the lake water, concentrating the minerals. These minerals divided into two distinct layers: The bottom of the lake is ten times saltier than the Pacific Ocean and cooler than the water on the lake's surface, making it too heavy to rise and mix with the warmer upper layer, which has a high alkali content. The healing mud at the bottom of the lake also seals the lake bottom, stopping minerals from leaching back into the bedrock.

Larger aquatic animals cannot survive in the lake due to its heavy mineral content. It is home instead to algae, bacteria, and small crustaceans, which may be the key to some of its healing powers. It also contains a substance called ichthyols, created when the crustaceans in the lake die and decompose. Ichthyol oil is used in Europe as a salve for cuts, burns, and minor injuries.

In the 1950s, several engineering projects increased the amount of water flowing into Soap Lake, diluting its mineral content. The citizens of Soap Lake appealed to the federal government to have a pump and well system set up to drain off the fresh water before it flowed into the lake, hopefully preserving its benefits for future generations of bathers.

Aberdeen

The city of Aberdeen is the center of several smaller towns that follow the shoreline of Grays Harbor, in the middle of the Washington coast. Aberdeen is the birthplace of grunge: It's where the band Nirvana first started out. The band's trademark flannel shirts might have been a holdover from loggers a few decades earlier, when the town was known as the gateway to the Olympic Peninsula.

Aberdeen was founded in 1884, a few years after the nearby towns of Cosmopolis and Hoquiam. It was originally named Wishkah, after the river that ran through it; the town changed names when the Aberdeen Cannery was built on its wharves.

Aberdeen competed for years with the towns of Cosmopolis and Hoquiam in the timber, fishing, and canning industries. More importantly, each wanted to

become the main line for the Northern Pacific Railroad. It was a big shock to all when the railroad located the line in the town of Ocosta. Instead of admitting defeat, in 1895, Aberdeen's and Hoquiam's citizens built their own rail line, which connected to the Northern Pacific rails. This brought about economic prosperity for Grays Harbor for several decades. By 1900, Aberdeen was one of the fastest growing towns in Washington. In addition to factories, lumber mills, and stores, it was filled with saloons, brothels, and gambling dens, all serving the sailors and lumbermen who came to town looking to spend their pay.

Many deepwater ships sailed from Aberdeen to Asia, making it somewhat of a gateway to the Pacific, but sailors didn't see it that way. They'd often refer to Aberdeen as the "hellhole" of the Pacific. Considering the fact that one of its citizens was the sailor-robbing and murdering Billy Gohl, that's not surprising. (See "Local Heroes and Villains.")

Aberdeen weathered the Great Depression and grew again during World War II. However, by the 1950s, many of the lumber mills had shut down because most of the old-growth timber was gone. The local fishermen complained that the runs were declining, and they moved to other locations. The canneries followed the fishing

fleet to Alaska. In the 1990s, the spotted owl went on the endangered species list, and more lumber jobs went away. Although Aberdeen is still a collection and shipping point for raw logs, there are few sawmills left in Grays Harbor County. In the 2000 census, the population of Aberdeen was 16,461, down from 26,073 in 1930.

Today the private railroad grade is still there, but most of the wharves along the Wishkah River and Grays Harbor itself have rotted away. Many of the old buildings near the harbor survive, but most are empty shells and the haunt of vagrants, who will chase you away with shouts and thrown beer cans if you venture near. Nature is taking back part of this abandoned area. On a recent visit, we saw a sea lion trying to eat a fish while seagulls dive-bombed it. Just twenty years ago there would have been too much water traffic and pollution to attract that much wildlife.

Despite these challenges, the people in Aberdeen and the surrounding area are trying to reinvent themselves and their city. It's the home port to the *Lady Washington:* a reproduction of a tall sailing ship used by Captain Robert Gray as he explored the Pacific Northwest. A few new businesses have opened up in the surviving buildings on the waterfront. Local business owners also hope a biodiesel plant will bring more industry to their town. Timber harvests have increased, as more trees have grown and the lumber mill technology adapts to cut them. But even if the changes happen, Aberdeen will never again be the town it once was.

INDEX

Page numbers in **bold** refer to photos and illustrations.

PICTURE CREDITS

All photos by the authors or public domain except as listed below:

Page 2 background, **3** © Ryan Doan; **4–5** © Hulton-Deutsch Collection/CORBIS; **7** © George Sozio; **9** Self portrait by the authors; **10** bottom right **13, 15** © Ryan Doan; **17** © Gary Braasch/CORBIS; **18** © Morhiggan; **19** © Cody Cobb; **20** © gettyimages/John Kobal Foundation; **22** © iStockphoto.com/Gregg Nicholas; **30** © Bettmann/CORBIS; **31** ©Ryan Doan; **34, 35** © Chip Clark/Smithsonian; **36** courtesy Cheryl Mack, U.S. Forestry Service; **38** © creativephoto; **39** © HO/Reuters/CORBIS; **42** © Jack Olsen; **45** © Edmond Meany 1905/Courtesy University of Washington Library; **46** bottom, Library of Congress; **49** left, Mark Frey and Michael Lamont © Michael Lamont Photography, background © Ryan Doan; **51** © iStockphoto. com/Matthias Nordmeyer; **54** Mark Frey and Michael Lamont © Michael Lamont Photography; **56–57** © oksanaphoto; **59** © Ryan Doan; **62** Library of Congress, Prints and Photographs Division; **63, 64** © Bettmann/CORBIS; **66, 67** © Ryan Doan; **68** © iStockphoto.com/Graffisimo; **69, 73, 74, 77, 78, 81** © Ryan Doan; **82** top © iStockphoto.com/andipantz; **84, 85, 86–87, 88** © Ryan Doan; **92** © Bettmann/CORBIS; **95, 96** © Ryan Doan, **97** background © Mark Jensen; **99, 100, 101** © Ryan Doan; **102** bottom right courtesy Shannon Kringen;**103** top left, courtesy Photo Collection, Washington State Archives, top center courtesy Florida Photographic Collection, bottom left courtesy J.P. Patches, bottom right © Post-Intelligencer Collection, Museum of History & Industry; **104** courtesy Joe Mabel/Wikepedia; **107** photo collage © Mark Moran; **109** courtesy Florida Photographic Collection; **110** © Bettmann/CORBIS; **111–112** courtesy Photo Collection, Washington State Archives; **115** courtesy Shannon Kringen; **117** © Post-Intelligencer Collection, Museum of History & Industry; **119–120** courtesy J.P. Patches; **141** courtesy of Rick and Jody Froebe; **169** © Danita Delimont/Alamy; **167** top right © Peg Boettcher; **172** top © Mark Moran; **178** © Ryan Doan; **181** © Kelly-Mooney Photography/CORBIS; **184** © Wayne Robinson; **185** top right courtesy Sandy Wells/ FOG Paranormal; **186–187** © Wayne Robinson; **193** © Danita Delimont/Alamy; **195** Design Pics Inc./Alamy; **198** courtesy Lake Quinault Lodge; **199** bottom © Itani/Alamy; **202** Courtesy Southwest Washington Paranormal Research; **202** © Tony Rodgers; **203** courtesy Sandy Wells/ FOG Paranormal; **216** top courtesy Washington State Archives; **225** ©James W. Spencer; **228** top right courtesy AGHOST; **229** top © Doug Murray, bottom right © Vanessa Rentschler; **230** top © Hulton-Deutsch Collection/CORBIS; **232** top, **233** insets © Washington State Historical Society, background courtesy AGHOST; **234** © Doug Stepphens; **235, 236** © Washington State Historical Society; **237** © iStockphoto.com/Mark Jensen; **240** © Brett C. Sandstrom; **241** © Vanessa Rentschler; **242** lower left, **243** lower left © Eddie McHugh; **247** top left © Andrew Filer, top and bottom right © Doug Murray.

WEIRD WASHINGTON

By

JEFF DAVIS and AL EUFRASIO

Executive Editors
Mark Sceurman and Mark Moran

ACKNOWLEDGMENTS

JEFF DAVIS

There are so many people to thank; this book was such a collaborative effort. Perhaps because they are the saviors of our society, I should thank all the librarians who have helped me. Thanks to Joanne Porter, Jody Grip, Judy Liddle, and Rayette Sterling. Archivists at a wide variety of Washington State organizations were invaluable for photos, including Mary Hammer, Elaine Miller, Greg Griffith, Benjamin Helle, and Michael Houser. I had several Weird contributors, including Richard Walker, Phillip Lipson and Charlette LeFevre at the Museum of Mysteries, Lilith St. Crow, Eric Booth, Mary Branson, Grady Caulk, Cheryl Mack, Deanna Robinson, Ryan Durocher, Sheila Boudreau, T. C. O'Reilly, Suzy Taylor, Amanda Walker, Gregg Olsen, Tonya Gould, the supervisor at the Walla Walla State Penitentiary, and Joe Follansbee.

In a separate category are Bigfoot researchers Cliff Crook, Andrew Peterson, anonymous members of BRFO, and ghost hunters Ross Allison, Henry Bailey, Jeffrey Marks, Shannon Steadman, Jill and Darren Thompson, Kim Travis, Vanessa Rentschler, and Sandy and Russ Wells. I am sure I missed many of you. Please forgive my lapse; it has been a long book and a long year.

AL EUFRASIO

Projects of this kind always become a group effort to some degree. It's as natural as it is advantageous to the material we cover. With that in mind, I offer my sincere thanks to the following people and organizations who pitched in, shared stories, provided leads, and/or offered encouragement: my navigator, photography assistant, and infinitely patient wife, Tammy; Peg Boettcher, who began as a contact at Ye Olde Curiosity Shop and ended up an enthusiastic contributing author and friend; Andy and Tammy James and company at the Curiosity Shop; Marlow Harris, Dick Elliot, Jane Orleman, Steve Bard, Kelly Lyles, Dan Klennert, Sandy Adams, Richard Tracy, and Rick and Jody Froebe--a fine bunch whose helpful hospitality made the "Personalized Properties" chapter a blast to write; Danette and Junior from Bob's Java Jive; Chris Wedes; John Dickinson; Shannon Kringen; the Porter family; the Workinger family (good friends and Weird U.S. enthusiasts who personally know Virginia's evil Bunnyman); the staffs of the King County Library System and the Tacoma Library; the people of Long Beach, especially the staffs of the Super 8 Motel, Marsh's Free Museum, Mary Lou's Tavern, and the Visitor's Center; the Museum of History and Industry, Seattle; History House of Greater Seattle; Washington State History Museum, Tacoma; all the good Internet folk who were kind enough to grant permission to use their photography (whether we used it or not); and, lest I forget, my canine "nutty buddy," Cooper, who kept me company into the wee hours as I researched and wrote.

Dedicated to the memory of my mother, Maria da Luz Eufrasio, who was astute enough to raise a couple of weird kids.

SHOW US YOUR WEIRD!

Do you know of a weird site found somewhere in the United States, or can you tell us about a strange experience you've had? If so, we'd like to hear about it! We believe that every town has at least one great tale to tell, and we're listening. It could be a cursed road, haunted abandoned site, odd local character, or bizarre historic event. In most cases these tales are told only in the towns in which they originated. But why keep them to yourself when you could share them with all of America? So come on and fill us in on all the weirdness that's lurking in your backyard!

You can e-mail us at: Editor@WeirdUS.com,

or write to us at:

Weird U.S., P.O. Box 1346, Bloomfield, NJ 07003.

www.weirdus.com